MAKING A DIFFERENCE

The Peace Corps at Twenty-Five

Edited by MILTON VIORST

*with a Foreword
by President Ronald Reagan*

Copyright © 1986 by Peace Corps Twenty-Fifth Anniversary Foundation, Inc.

All rights reserved. No reproduction of this book in whole or in part or in any form may be made without written authorization of the copyright owner.

Published by Weidenfeld & Nicolson, New York
A Division of Wheatland Corporation
10 East 53rd Street
New York, NY 10022

Library of Congress Cataloging-in-Publication Data

Making a difference.

1. Peace Corps (U.S.)   I. Viorst, Milton.
HC60.5.M26   1986   361.2'6'06073   86-9055
ISBN 1-55584-010-8

Manufactured in the United States of America

Designed by Irving Perkins Associates, Inc.

First Edition

10 9 8 7 6 5 4 3 2 1

To Arlene —
You made it happen —
With affection,
Timothy

MAKING A
DIFFERENCE

Also by Milton Viorst
Hostile Allies: FDR & Charles de Gaulle
The Great Documents of Western Civilization
Fall from Grace: The Republican Party and the Puritan Ethic
Hustlers and Heroes: An American Political Panorama
Fire in the Streets: America in the 1960s

Contents

Acknowledgment *by Loret Miller Ruppe*	9
Foreword *by President Ronald Reagan*	11

THE IDEAL — 13

The Vision *by Sargent Shriver*	15
Passing the Torch *by Alan Guskin*	25
LBJ and the Bureaucrats *by Bill Moyers*	30
The Mystique *by Harris Wofford*	33
An Exchange Between President Kennedy and Tom Scanlon	42

THE PEOPLE — 45

The Volunteer *by Jody Olsen*	47
Letter from India (1962)	56
Letter from Iran to the Peace Corps Director (1965)	58
Letter from Mauritania (1985)	60
Reports and Letters on Life, Work, and Love in the Peace Corps	62
The Benefits *by Warren W. Wiggins*	71
Reminiscence: The Dominican Republic *by Christopher J. Dodd*	78
Reminiscence: Malawi *by Paul Theroux*	81
The Veterans *by Roger Landrum*	87

THE JOB — 97

As a Development Agency *by M. Peter McPherson*	99
The Experience: Africa *by C. Payne Lucas and Kevin Lowther*	108

From a Talk with Dr. Siaka Stevens	116
Letter from Kenya (1965)	117
Report from Niger (1965)	119
The Experience: The Pacific *by Russell G. Davis*	121
Remarks on the Decision to Withdraw from Indonesia (1965) *by Alex Shakow*	127
The Experience: South and West Asia *by John Chromy*	130
Letter from India (1964)	135
Letter from Iran (1965)	137
Letter from East Pakistan (1963)	138
The Experience: Latin America *by Frank Mankiewicz*	139
Peace Corps Bulletin #5, Guatemala (1965)	148
Letter from Bolivia (1965)	150
The Vocation *by Francis A. Luzzatto*	153
Reminiscence: The Philippines and Mali *by Parker W. Borg*	167
Reminiscence: Thailand *by Judith Guskin*	173
In the Developing World *by Abdou Diouf*	178
Excerpts from Interviews with Foreign Leaders (1981)	182
In a Changing World *by John W. Sewell*	185

THE PLACE   **191**

In a Changing America *by Loret Miller Ruppe*	193
A Conservative Institution *by James A. McClure*	201
A Liberal Institution *by Hubert H. Humphrey III*	205
The Future *by John R. Dellenback*	209
Afterword *by Milton Viorst*	217

And so, my fellow Americans, ask not what your country can do for you; ask what you can do for your country.

My fellow citizens of the world, ask not what America can do for you, but together what we can do for the freedom of man.

John F. Kennedy
Inaugural Address, January 20, 1961

Acknowledgment

The Peace Corps' twenty-fifth anniversary year has provided the opportunity to increase American understanding of the developing world and the unique partnership that has resulted from people taking time to help one another. As the Peace Corps looks to the next twenty-five years, it is fitting that a book should be published about the Peace Corps' past, present, and potential for the future.

In all matters of substance, someone works behind the scenes with a creative spirit that gives birth to an idea. Ailene Goodman is the person who in this instance provided the inspiration for what you are about to read. We are thankful for her pioneer efforts, which are reflected in the pages that follow.

Milton Viorst has done more than one could have imagined possible in pulling together this collection of thoughts and reflections by and about those who have really made a difference, for the Peace Corps and for the nations they served. To each of them and to Milton, we at the Peace Corps are profoundly grateful.

And, of course, the book would not have been possible in the first place were it not for the more than 120,000 Americans who have served in more than ninety countries around the globe. Each has begun the process of laying a firm foundation upon which a real lasting peace can be built.

Loret Miller Ruppe
Director of the Peace Corps

Foreword
by President Ronald Reagan

For a quarter of a century, Peace Corps volunteers have been offering their time, their talent, and their training to help people in developing countries around the world make a better life for themselves and their children.

In a troubled world, the Peace Corps is waging peace. Every day in Africa, Asia, and Latin America, they answer the cries of hunger, disease, poverty, and illiteracy by showing America at its best.

Peace Corps workers save lives by helping those who suffer from malnutrition and starvation. They improve the quality of life by teaching mothers how to prevent disease. And they have helped create new avenues to prosperity by showing farmers and fishermen new ways to produce and market their products.

Each one of us is responsible for building the society we want. Peace Corps volunteers do that with people-to-people exchanges, using their energy, their spirit, and their creativity to help solve problems.

In the South Pacific island country of Tonga, the Peace Corps helped an agricultural cooperative increase its volume nearly twelve-fold in a single year. In Swaziland, the Peace Corps designed water systems that will reach 37 percent of the population. In Costa Rica, a major nursery was established to market forest and fruit trees that thrive in that climate. And Peace Corps volunteers, working as educators, have taught more than five million people in classrooms across Africa.

This is the American way. Once we see a need, we want to serve—even when the neighbor we reach out to help is halfway around the world.

More than 120,000 Peace Corps volunteers have helped people throughout the world gain a better understanding of Americans, and in turn have helped Americans understand the people of the world. Our colleges and universities have been enriched by their knowledge and experience.

Giving, learning, and sharing is what the Peace Corps is all about. Our volunteers make us proud to be Americans.

THE IDEAL

The Vision

by Sargent Shriver

Oscar Wilde is said to have observed that America really was discovered by a dozen people before Columbus but that the discovery remained a secret. I am tempted to feel that way about the Peace Corps. A national effort of this type had been proposed many times in previous years, but only in 1961 did it become reality.

In *quantitative* terms, the Peace Corps has never been a big idea. It started the first year with a few thousand Americans being dispatched to serve in the underdeveloped world, and, though the number has gone up and down, the concept has remained essentially the same. Compared to the millions in uniform who have served America abroad, the ambition was modest—perhaps too modest. Compared to the funds our government transmits in foreign aid to countries less affluent than ours, the budget was barely visible. Still, those of us who were present at the creation nurtured the notion that the Peace Corps had a huge potential for promoting the peace of the world and the well-being of humanity. After twenty-five years, though poverty and war remain with us, I think I see some evidence that we were right. *Qualitatively,* the Peace Corps has succeeded.

My own interest in the Peace Corps idea had started quite a few years before, when I was a part of and, later, leader for Experiment in International Living groups in Europe in the 1930s. In the 1950s I visited several Asian countries—Japan, Korea, Vietnam, Cambodia, Thailand—and, when I returned, I proposed sending three-man political action teams to Asia, Africa, and Latin America. These teams were to consist of vigorous and imaginative young labor leaders, businessmen, and politicians. They would offer their services at a grass-roots level and work

---

Sargent Shriver, a senior partner at Fried, Frank, Harris, Shriver & Jacobson in Washington, D.C., was the first director of the Peace Corps.

directly with the people, contributing to the growth of the economies, to the democratic organization of the societies, and to the peaceful outcome of the social revolutions under way. When the idea of the Peace Corps emerged during the presidential campaign of 1960, it seemed to offer the possibility of realizing, in a new form, this old objective, which seemed to me more important than ever.

A month or so after President Kennedy took office, he asked me to report to him on how the Peace Corps could be organized, and then to organize it. John Kennedy believed Americans had decent ideals that were going untapped, and a physical and spiritual resilience that was being unused. He told me to make the Peace Corps a tough agency, to prove wrong those who were skeptical about the willingness of Americans, especially young Americans, to make the kind of sacrifices that the Peace Corps would require. "Go ahead," he said, "you can do it," and to do it we assembled the best people we could find from the professions, from our universities and foundations, from our corporations and unions, from private agencies and the civil service. We knew the Peace Corps would have only one chance to work. We felt like parachute jumpers: the chute had to open the first time, or we were sure to come to an abrupt end.

Within the team I had assembled, we wrestled with a hundred questions of policy, debating around the clock, in those early days of 1961. Not the least of the questions was the name we would give to the undertaking. For a while, "Peace Corps," which Kennedy had used during the election campaign, was not the first choice. Some of the President's advisers scoffed at it, arguing for a solid bureaucratic title like "Agency for Overseas Voluntary Service." Conservatives, furthermore, said the word "peace" sounded soft, vague, and weak. They insisted Communists had corrupted it by applying it to every political initiative and even to every war they were involved in. Not to be outdone, many liberals disliked the word "corps." They said it sounded militaristic.

But I thought we should try to recapture the term "peace," to liberate it, so to speak. I thought we should be able to use it without its sounding like propaganda, metaphor, or corn. As for "corps," I was not uncomfortable with conveying the militance of our purpose, at least a quiet militance. The fact was that I could not visualize the elimination of war except through the kind of effort in which the Peace Corps was to engage. Peace was our goal, and we were not embarrassed to envisage this effort as a genuine way station along the road.

We knew there were misgivings about the new Peace Corps. I was disappointed when some very distinguished Americans made fun of our conviction that volunteers could do a serious job in the developing world.

THE IDEAL

Congressmen and columnists called it a range of invidious names, but Americans were not alone. U Nu, who was then prime minister of Burma, asked me during a visit to Rangoon, "Do you think you can send me a young man from Kokomo, Indiana, who will have the dedication, determination, and sense of mission of someone from Communist China? Make no mistake about the kind of person you will be competing with." We were not so sure ourselves how well Peace Corps volunteers would work, nor were we sure that our idea would catch on, either overseas or at home. I recalled with some apprehension an African proverb I had heard, which went, "Until you have crossed the river, don't insult the crocodile's mouth."

Our Peace Corps task force worked literally day and night for weeks, readying recommendations for the President. John Kennedy had set the theme of the new administration with his inaugural statement, "Ask not what your country can do for you, ask what you can do for your country." Those were inspiring words, and at that point, many were asking, "All right, what *can* we do for our country?" We considered speed essential in order to maintain the momentum of the Kennedy theme.

By March 1, 1961, we were ready with a detailed report, which recommended to President Kennedy the Peace Corps' immediate, full-scale establishment. We rejected proposals for pilot programs or small, experimental initiatives. We asked for an independent agency, not answerable to the Agency of International Development, and we turned down suggestions to limit the mission of the Peace Corps to supplementing efforts of the Junior Red Cross, the Chamber of Commerce, or other American groups working abroad. We rejected uniforms, badges, medals, and any other distinctive clothing, along with rankings and grades. We said we wanted no special housing, food, schools, or anything else, except health services: we decided to send our own doctors to care for the volunteers. We even promised to discourage vacations in the "fleshpot" cities of the world, though many were accessible.

Yet we did not stake the Peace Corps gamble on the power of a few thousand Americans to accomplish a physical transformation of the underdeveloped world. We based our gamble on a conviction that it was not muscle power but idea power that changed the world. We did, after all, have some precedent. Religious movements have long demonstrated how ideas transform societies. Ideas were the driving force behind the Renaissance and the Enlightenment, even the Industrial Revolution, movements that gave the West a new, a more dynamic social character. The idea of the American Revolution, born more than two hundred years ago, continues to resound with explosive force throughout the world.

I shall always remember a visit I received in India in early 1961, while

I was exploring the prospects of sending one of our first contingents for service there. Ashadevi Aryanayakam, an extraordinary woman who had been an associate of Mahatma Gandhi, traveled three days and nights on a train to see me in New Delhi. "Yours was the first revolution," she reminded me. "Do you think young Americans possess the spiritual values they must have to bring the spirit of that revolution to our country? India should not boast of any spiritual superiority. There is a great valuelessness spreading around the world. Your Peace Corps volunteers must bring more than science and technology. They must touch the idealism of America and bring that to us, too. Can they do it?" I was stunned by the question, but inspired, too. Later, in describing the experience before the Senate Foreign Relations Committee, I said, "Our answer, based on faith, was yes."

It reminded me, of course, that an idea, to conquer, must fuse with the will of men and women who are prepared to dedicate their lives to its realization. We had a sense twenty-five years ago that there were such men and women in America waiting to be called, impatient to carry the idea of service to mankind. As it turned out, I think we underestimated both their numbers and their dedication. Thousands responded when we first raised the Peace Corps banner, and thousands have been responding in every succeeding year. Therein lies the true grandeur of our country.

Since 1961, the Peace Corps has sent more than 120,000 Americans to serve overseas. They are patriots, committed to the special vision upon which the Peace Corps was founded, and they have helped to disseminate this vision far and wide. As Americans in service abroad, they have gone beyond Cold War competition, beyond careerism, beyond fun and adventure, to dedicate their best efforts to the idea of raising up humanity. And there could easily have been a quarter-million or a half-million of them by now, if precious tax dollars had not so often been squandered on programs of violence, vengeance, and vituperation.

The Peace Corps is unique among American institutions. Though it is an agency of government, it is profoundly nonpolitical. That does not mean the Peace Corps is indifferent to the national interests of the United States. But it was conceived to reach beyond domestic political goals, and beyond international rivalries, to touch the deepest hopes of man. Without trumpets, banners, or weapons, the Peace Corps serves America abroad. It renders this service to our country by promoting an idea of an America that is caring and humane.

I remember an Asian prime minister many years ago summing up the vision of the Peace Corps for me, after reminding me that the arrival of the first twenty-one volunteers in his country had provoked Communist

THE IDEAL

protests. A bit impudently, I asked him whether the protesters thought the volunteers were spreading germs. "In a certain sense, yes," he told me. "If these volunteers were simply twenty-one more Americans, there would be no interest in them at all. But these volunteers come representing an idea, the Peace Corps idea. That is why there is opposition." Those twenty-one Americans were a microcosm. They represented a working model of the kind of world—a world of commitment to freedom, to human well-being, to personal dignity—that we wanted our own children, and children everywhere, to live in. That is the message the Peace Corps has carried to foreign lands.

Knowing what we wanted to convey, we made some deliberate choices in 1961 about the composition of the body of volunteers. What we envisioned was a microcosm not so much of what America was as what we thought it should be. These choices, I am glad to note, have since become the norm of our society. But back then, if I may say so, making those choices took a bit of audacity. We knew that most of our volunteers would be young college graduates with liberal educations. But we also encouraged people who were older, more mature, and more experienced to join us, and we enlisted superb volunteers in their fifties, their sixties, and even in their seventies. More controversial was the decision to give women the same opportunity as men to serve. The conventional wisdom held that the Peace Corps inevitably had to be a man's world. We said it would not be, and since the first days, nearly one out of three volunteers has been a woman. The role of the two genders has been exactly the same throughout the Peace Corps' history.

We also chose to take a positive position on the race issue, which in the 1960s was a powder keg, threatening the cohesion of our society. We considered it vital not simply to *accept* blacks and other minorities into the Peace Corps, but actively to recruit them. And blacks responded to the call. I recall being told the story of four volunteers, living and working together at a small college in Nepal, visited one evening by a young Marxist who was prepared to denounce the Peace Corps for its American-style racism. The Marxist, however, could not reconcile his beliefs with the fact that he found one of the four to be black, and a graduate of one of America's best universities. The volunteers never denied that racism existed in America, but after several visits, the Marxist was persuaded that a change in our country was under way.

To me, that story illustrates the new politics which the Peace Corps was meant to represent. The foreign minister of Thailand once told me he considered the Peace Corps "the most powerful new force in the world today." In this age when nuclear stalemate and the danger of total devastation limit the use of military power, he said, we must rediscover and use a power that often seems to have atrophied from disuse. "The secret of your greatness," the foreign minister said, "is the power of American ideas and ideals." It is a secret which, he said, the United States has not adequately shared with the world. I agree with him. In every country, we are famous for our bombs, our high-powered technology, our capacity for organization, our wealth. "How many of us in foreign lands," the foreign minister said, "know that in the United States ideas and ideals are also powerful?"

I suspect the reason so few people appreciate our ideas and ideals is that we ourselves fail to understand our potential in this area. As a result, we consistently sell ourselves short. When we hear of a "secret" American power, our minds seem to turn automatically to killer devices. It is true that our weapons and our wealth are what is most clearly visible to the majority of the world. But our real "secret" power, I believe, is the vitality of our democratic life. I would like to quote David Crozier, who lost his life in an air accident while serving as a Peace Corps volunteer in Colombia. In a sadly prophetic letter to his parents, he said, "Should it come to it, I would rather give my life trying to help someone than to give my life looking down a gun barrel at him."

How much does the world know not just of the Peace Corps but of the great network of our private voluntary agencies, community organizations, labor unions, service clubs, or philanthropies? Do we not fail to convey our real pride in such federal programs as the TVA, VISTA, the National Institutes of Health, Social Security, and Head Start, in our individual liberty, free speech, and free elections? In fact, I think we take them for granted, leaving the world too intimidated by the power of our weapons and insufficiently aware of the power of our democracy. It is the humanity and concern of our system that the Peace Corps represents.

But let me assert the Peace Corps is no naive organization, aiming to do good while indifferent to the existence of evil in the world. We know the United States is involved in a contest of ideologies being waged in many arenas, not the least of them the underdeveloped nations. The Peace Corps plays a role in this struggle. But let us be clear that its role lies not in its solicitation of these nations' support for America's political positions, much less our alliances. The role lies in the contribution the Peace Corps makes to *their* success. If these countries succeed in their plans for economic, social, and political progress, it will not matter much whether they agree with us on a given issue, or even whether they like us. If they become healthy, democratic societies, they will not be a threat to world peace. That is what matters.

The arena in which the Peace Corps makes its stand for America is in the nations where a peaceful outcome to the world's ideological struggle remains possible. Most of the African continent meets that test, as do Latin America and East Asia. But I exclude no region of the world. We must not let our preoccupation with the Cold War and military confrontation blind us to the opportunities waiting for us throughout the globe. Though the Peace Corps volunteers carry no rifles to battle, they serve their country on fronts that are vital to the peace of the world. They serve in the Third World, home for hundreds of millions of people whose only ideology is to create a decent life for themselves, a life that measures richness with dignity, that is free of fear and instability. The time to reach them is not when military action becomes necessary, when war or violent revolution is impending. Peace Corps volunteers are not trained to deal with enemies bearing arms. Their enemies are hunger, ignorance, and disease. By forcing these enemies into retreat, the Peace Corps serves humanity's interests, and America's.

It seems a paradox to say that Peace Corps volunteers make their contribution to American foreign policy by staying out of the foreign policy establishment, but it is true. Peace Corps volunteers are not trained diplomats, not propagandists. For the most part, they are not even technical experts. They represent our society by what they are, what they do, and the spirit in which they do it. They scrupulously steer clear of intelligence activities and local politics. The Peace Corps' strict adherence to these principles has been a crucial factor in the decision of politically uncommitted countries to invite American volunteers into their homes, and even into their classrooms to teach future generations of national leadership. In an era of sabotage and espionage, Peace Corps volunteers have earned a priceless but simple renown: they are *trustworthy*.

When the Peace Corps goes abroad, it spreads the ideal of a free and democratic society. Its strategic premise is the sense of concern that every member has shown by the act of volunteering. The Peace Corps' secret weapon is example. This example proclaims that in America, the color of a volunteer's skin, or a human's religious or political beliefs, do not determine personal dignity and worth. We have sent black Americans to white men's countries, white Americans to black men's countries. We were told that we could not send Protestants to certain parts of Catholic countries in Latin America, and that we could not send Jews to Arab countries. But we sent them. Rarely have these decisions spawned discontent. Far more often, they have elicited admiration and, if I may say so, even envy. On a practical level, what a volunteer has left behind may be a well, or a proficiency among a few students in English, or a better way to raise corn. But he or she has also left behind the germ of the Peace Corps vision, and it is a germ that inevitably spreads. I believe there are few more important contributions to be made.

We never meant for Peace Corps volunteers to go abroad as promoters of a particular political theory or economic system, much less a religious creed. But that did not mean they were without a mission. The volunteer goes overseas as a willing and skilled worker. He also goes as a representative of the ideals that America, with all its imperfections, embodies better than any society in our time. It is the idea that free and committed men and women can cross, even transcend, boundaries of culture and language, of foreign tradition, and great disparities of wealth and culture, to work in harmony with one another. The Peace Corps has a commitment to overcome old hostilities and entrenched nationalisms, to bring knowledge where ignorance has dominated, to challenge traditions that may enslave, even as it respects the societies from which they emerge. The Peace Corps was designed for different cultures to meet on the common ground of service to human welfare and personal worth, so that men and women might share what is valuable in the spirit of each.

Those of us who were around at the beginning conspired in sending volunteers off on assignment as free men and women. I say "conspired" because what they secretly carried in their baggage, along with the books and clean socks, was the Peace Corps ideal. As Americans, they were free to travel, to write, to read, and to speak as they chose. They were surrounded by no wall of censorship, nor constrained by any authoritarian code of discipline. They were trained to work with people, and not to employ them, or use them, or give them orders. Volunteers from the start were instructed to do what the country in which they served wanted them to do, not what they, out of some sense of cultural superiority, thought was best for their hosts. That does not mean volunteers did not often have to rely on their own initiative to make best use of their time and talent. The Peace Corps encouraged their initiative. The staff provided the framework and then relied on the creative energies of dedicated individuals to fill in the spaces.

Let me quote a few lines of a letter I sent to President Kennedy in December of 1961, shortly after we dispatched the first contingent of Peace Corps volunteers to their destinations. I wanted to make clear to him that we were serious about the objective of showing that Americans were not soft. "Volunteers are expected to live simply and unostentatiously," the letter said. "We believe it will make their work more productive and effective. They have a twenty-four-hour-a-day job. They receive little or no pay and accept substantial hazards to their health and even to their safety. . . . The Peace Corps is not just a job. There are no 9:00 to 5:00 days in our operation. There will be little tolerance of a 'tomorrow' philosophy or an 'it can't be done because it hasn't been done before' attitude. We know the American people are behind us."

For a quarter-century the Peace Corps has remained faithful to this vision. Very early, the Peace Corps perceived the trap of neocolonialism, and volunteers understood that they must, if necessary, go out of their way to avoid it. They have lived not in some figurative house on the hill, not in isolated compounds or chic neighborhoods, but physically among the people they have served, in intimate contact with them. A visiting Ghanaian once said to me, "Peace Corps teachers in my country don't live so badly. After all, they live as well as we do." We did not inflict discomfort on the volunteer for discomfort's sake. Rather, by their way of life volunteers have shown that material privilege has not become the central and indispensable ingredient in American life.

From the beginning, Peace Corps volunteers have not only lived sparely but have eaten the food and talked the language of rural villagers, of dwellers of the barrios, of communities of seaside fishermen. They shopped for bargains in the marketplace and rode in buses or on bicycles. They enjoyed no diplomatic immunity and observed the same local laws as everyone else. They received modest living allowances in the field, sums fixed to match local conditions, far from conventional American salaries. They sweated in hot climates without air-conditioning and made their own fires in wood stoves when the weather was cold.

One of my favorite letters was from a volunteer who said, "For the last four months I lived with a Filipino family who were my friends and my companions. I soon forgot that I was an American and they were Filipinos. They treated me as one of the family. All of us, as human beings, have the same basic needs and desires and a common yearning to be understood and respected." I doubt that any young officer of a colonial administration ever wrote a letter back home like that. What it reflected, I think, was the volunteer's understanding that his service in the Peace Corps was not a one-way channel of communication, not a mission to a lesser people. He knew he had something important to contribute, but he also knew that the land and the people he was assigned to serve had something important to give him.

Living in the developing world, the Peace Corps volunteers have learned new facts of life. They have escaped from what is all too often a kind of cultural imprisonment, brought on by American affluence, and exposed themselves to the reality of life in much of the world. This is a world which, for all of its richness of culture, often still lives on the edge of survival. I could feel the suffering of the Peace Corps volunteer who wrote to me from East Africa, "People die here for want of so little." How many Americans have the painful privilege of learning that lesson?

The volunteers who brought back from their experience abroad a revised sense of the human condition also acquired an appreciation of the fact that answers to its problems are generally much more complex than they appear at first glance. Those who think there are panaceas for the ills of emerging nations, who believe all that is needed is more money or more schools or a few more dams, or even more democracy or more private enterprise, never served in the Peace Corps. The wisdom that volunteers brought back with them has added to the reservoir of compassion and understanding in America. It has provided our nation with insight into the thinking of the great majority with whom we share the globe. But Peace Corps volunteers, because they were toilers and not just observers, also learned that they need not sit by impotently while others suffer. That, too, is an important lesson for America.

So, in 1986, we look back across a quarter-century of soul-filled history. We have known the summer heat of the Sahara, the biting cold of the Alte Plano of Peru, the endless rain of the Asian monsoons. We have often overcome the obstacles of the federal bureaucracy, only to stumble over our own mistakes. But we have survived, and precious gifts have been bestowed upon us. We have seen the smile on the face of a child whom a volunteer has taught to read. We have been grateful that a volunteer has had a hand in building a feeder road, establishing a credit union, forming a cooperative for buying a tractor or marketing fish. We have marveled at the energy of a people in a dusty village after a volunteer has persuaded them to lift the dead hand of hopelessness.

In twenty-five years, the Peace Corps has made a start. The idea is in the air, a seed being carried on the breeze of human contact to people and institutions throughout the world. I do not know how many converts the Peace Corps has made, but I would like to think it has dealt a solid blow to ignorance and hunger. I want to believe it has moved human dignity to a higher plane. I pray it has moved peace a trifle closer, while chasing the shadow of nuclear war to a more distant reach.

Regretfully, I acknowledge it will require more time and still greater effort for the vision of the Peace Corps to win the world. That a pugnacious nationalism seems once again to be sweeping over our country does not so much mean that the Peace Corps has failed as that it has not tried hard enough. I know that, even in its brief life, the Peace Corps has emitted a glow, faint though it may be, that has helped light the way to a better and more peaceful life over a great area of the earth's surface. I take its triumphs, however, not as a cause for congratulation, but as a challenge. After twenty-five years, the task ahead is clear: to bring the Peace Corps and its ideals back to the top of America's agenda.

Passing the Torch

by Alan Guskin

When my wife, Judith, and I think about the letter we wrote that began the student Peace Corps movement, it still surprises us. We were not letter writers, nor were we even student activists on the University of Michigan campus. But there we were in the basement of a greasy-spoon restaurant, composing on a napkin a letter to the editor of the *Michigan Daily* that expressed our personal commitment to serve and that urged others to do the same.

As we began to write the letter, we thought about what John Kennedy had said and what Chester Bowles (Kennedy's foreign policy adviser and, later, his undersecretary of state) had more or less repeated on our campus. We had been only two out of the ten thousand students who had heard Kennedy at 2:00 A.M. on that chilly fall night of October 14, 1960, and had joined five hundred students who had heard Bowles a few days later. We wrote the letter wondering whether others felt as excited as we did about the idea. We ourselves had not seriously thought of serving abroad before that week, and we did not know anyone who had done so. Yet Kennedy had inspired us, and we were ready to make a commitment. Perhaps others were, too. Still, we never expected what was about to happen.

John Kennedy had come to the Michigan Union to get a good night's sleep, not to propose the Peace Corps. He had just concluded the third debate with Richard Nixon and was about to begin a hectic whistle-stop tour of the state the next day. He was said to have been surprised by the crowd and did not have a prepared speech. The press, having been told nothing was going to happen, had gone to bed. No major newspaper or wire service reported his remarks. Yet what he said touched deeply many of the students who waited for him, and especially the two of us.

Alan Guskin is president of Antioch University.

Why would ten thousand students wait until two in the morning to hear a few words from a presidential candidate? Curiosity has its limit, usually about midnight on a cold night. To understand why we waited to hear Kennedy, and the response that followed his talk, it is important to look at the world of twenty-five years ago through student eyes.

There was excitement surrounding the presidential campaign of 1960. It was not so much the issues discussed—proposals on the Cold War and the arms race conveyed little excitement—as a feeling that students had a role to play, that the torch was, indeed, being passed to a new generation. Change was in the air, and students at Michigan and elsewhere sensed that they were to play an increasing role in making it happen. The civil rights movement, begun in the South, was advancing to campuses in the North. Students were organizing politically to influence their own education. In Ann Arbor, students were collecting canned food to send to a tent city, picketing local stores of national chains that didn't serve blacks, creating a student political party called Voice, and planning a major conference on the state of the university.

Most significantly, John Kennedy's words that early morning seemed to present to students on our campus a way to live our idealism, an opportunity to commit ourselves to the service of others. When Chester Bowles, probably unaware of what Kennedy had said a few days earlier, described how his son and daughter-in-law were serving in an African village, he inadvertently triggered a ground swell of enthusiasm among his restless listeners. What he described was much like what would later be the Peace Corps.

Bowles had given substance to the idea that Kennedy introduced. There were, indeed, people in their twenties living and working in Africa. If they could do this, why couldn't we? Maybe we could make a difference, not only by contributing to economic development but also by helping to create world conditions that could lead to peace and disarmament. After exciting discussions with some of the students in the room where Bowles had just spoken, Judith and I sat down to write our letter. It appeared in the *Michigan Daily* on October 21, 1960:

> . . . Representative Chester Bowles and Senator Kennedy in speeches to the students of the University of Michigan both emphasized that disarmament and peace lie to a very great extent in our hands and requested our participation throughout the world as necessary for the realization of these goals.
>
> In reply to this urgent request, we both hereby state that we would devote a number of years to work in countries where our help is needed. . . .
>
> We also would like to request that all students who feel that they would like to help the cause of world peace by direct participation send a letter to this paper and/or our address. These letters will be forwarded to Ken-

nedy and Bowles as an answer of the students of the University of Michigan to their plea for help. If it is at all possible, we would like students to start asking others in their classes, dorms, sororities, fraternities, houses, etc. to send letters expressing their desire to work toward these goals. We also request that those who have friends at other universities write to them asking them to start similar action on their campuses.

With this request we express our faith that those of us who have been fortunate enough to receive an education will want to apply their knowledge through direct participation in the underdeveloped communities of the world.

The campus was energized overnight. The phone in our apartment rang constantly, spontaneous discussions dominated the campus, and we did what we could to organize response. We founded a group called Americans Committed to World Responsibility. In less than two weeks, eight hundred students had signed petitions committing themselves to spend several years of their lives serving in developing countries, most of them students who had never previously been involved in campus activism of any kind.

The organizing group sensed that this was a rare moment in which students could have a considerable impact on the formation of a major governmental program. We were right. Millie Jeffrey, a union official who was Kennedy's campaign director in Michigan, heard about the enthusiasm of the students and contacted Ted Sorensen, Kennedy's chief aide and speech writer. Sorensen talked to Kennedy, and a few days before the election, the candidate—describing the response on the Michigan campus—proposed the Peace Corps in a major speech in San Francisco's Cow Palace.

The next day, we were part of a small group that met with Kennedy at the Toledo airport. When Kennedy was challenged about his intentions on the Peace Corps, he answered, "Until Tuesday [Election Day] let us be concerned with this country. After Tuesday, the world."

For us, it was an intoxicating three weeks from Kennedy's speech on campus to the promise of the Peace Corps. Meanwhile, information was pouring into Michigan—and Washington—about student excitement elsewhere. We received petitions from students at Antioch, heard of activity at Princeton and Harvard. The two of us gave speeches on other campuses. On December 9th and 10th, our group in Ann Arbor held what would later be called a teach-in, in which students and faculty members discussed the potential work of the Peace Corps. The conference organized ongoing seminars to prepare papers on the Corps' potential requirements. Their work became a report that later shaped the agenda of a national conference.

Still, we worried that Kennedy might renege on his promise, so we decided to go to Washington for a conference on economic development. We met with Phil Hart, a sympathetic senator from Michigan, who disappointed us by saying he could not publicly support the Peace Corps without Kennedy's endorsement. The next day, however, *The Washington Post* reported that Hart was urging creation of a Peace Corps. Our disappointment turned to elation!

At the conference itself, we found skepticism about the willingness of American youth to serve in the Peace Corps. Convinced that the passivity of college students that had characterized the 1950s was still with us, the panelists urged a small, limited, experimental effort. I challenged those present with the evidence of the previous two months. Students were willing to serve, I argued, and were committed to aiding the developing world. Mrs. Chester Bowles came up to us after the session and spoke fondly of the work done by her son and daughter-in-law in Africa.

In Washington, we also learned of a group at American University that wanted to run a national conference on the Peace Corps. Here was an opportunity to have collaborators, resources, and a Washington site. The conference took place in March 1961, a few days after Kennedy created the Peace Corps by Executive Order 10924. Its sponsors were our Michigan group, the students at American University, and the National Student Association. Representatives from some four hundred universities attended.

Senator Hubert Humphrey, generally considered the father of Peace Corps legislation, delivered a forty-five-minute extemporaneous talk. Sargent Shriver gave his first public speech as Peace Corps director.

The conference, originally planned to lobby the President and Congress to establish the Peace Corps, became a major national meeting to demonstrate the depth of student commitment to Peace Corps service. The Washington meeting was followed by many others like it around the country. In the months that followed, the Kennedy administration was deluged with offers from tens of thousands of young people who wanted to serve in the Peace Corps.

Why did this happen? The 1960s was a time in which students like us were consumed with concern for social values, as well as strategies for change. We were determined not just to participate, but to have an impact on the events that affected our lives. When Kennedy came to Michigan on that night in 1960, the message he left behind was that young people could make a difference in helping to create a better and more peaceful world. He told us we had skills that were useful and ideals that could serve the future of our country. We responded.

Kennedy was forty-two at the time, and many of his advisers, including those involved in planning the Peace Corps, were even younger.

Around the world, young leaders, having fought for independence, were taking on the responsibilities of government in more than forty new nations. At home, young men and women were leading the confrontation with racial discrimination, the most critical domestic issue of our time. The older generation in America had not done very well on this issue, and on others related to questions of war and peace. Kennedy wanted a new beginning for the United States, and we wanted to help him.

That was twenty-five years ago, and in retrospect we are said to have been a generation that was uniquely idealistic, self-sacrificing, active. Today's young Americans are often described as materialistic, asking not what they can contribute to society but what they can get from it. Judith and I sometimes have to remind ourselves that in the 1950s, on the eve of the Kennedy era, our generation, too, was described as passive and self-centered. What explains the fact that the Peace Corps is still alive and well, that thousands of Americans continue to volunteer for service every year? How bad, how indifferent to others and to their countries can this generation be? Has it lost all sense of service? Perhaps, like ours, it is waiting only to be asked.

In the summer of 1961, the two of us were invited to serve as Peace Corps selection officers in the headquarters in Washington. Shortly thereafter, we volunteered to serve in Thailand and entered a training program. On January 18, 1962, we left with the first group of volunteers for Thailand. We served for two and one-half years as teachers at Chulalongkorn University in Bangkok. These were among the most gratifying years of our lives.

LBJ and the Bureaucrats

by Bill Moyers

When the Peace Corps was about to be enacted back in 1961, the old-line employees of State and AID coveted it greatly. It was a natural instinct: established bureaucracies do not like competition from new people. There was another, slightly more idealistic, if still myopic reason: folks who had been presiding over foreign aid all those years simply thought they knew best how to do it, and they pooh-poohed the idea that volunteers could contribute to a field which had been dominated by professionals.

This was, of course, the fundamental fallacy in their perception of the Peace Corps. It was not to be economic assistance in the traditional sense. Money and goods were not to change hands. The Peace Corps wasn't even to be "technical assistance" in the way the term was used by the experts. It was to be a sharing of people. Their experiences, talents, personalities, and eventual contributions were so diverse that to shoehorn them into the existing job descriptions—which the bureaucracy wanted to do—would be to diminish, tame, and finally extinguish the purpose and enduring value of the program.

The very idea of the Peace Corps thus scared the traditional managers of the foreign assistance sector of government. But they couldn't oppose the Peace Corps outright because it had such high visibility with the new President. So they did the next best thing: they sought to absorb it. The result, we knew, would be anonymity for an organization that needed to be publicly conspicuous to attract and excite volunteers, and stifling regulation of an idea whose great virtue was that it was by the government but not for the government. We could not, or so it seemed to us, pour new wine into an old bottle.

By "we," I mean Sargent Shriver, myself, and our colleagues. I was

---

Bill Moyers is a commentator for CBS News in New York.

THE IDEAL

then working with them in establishing the Peace Corps, having left the service of my mentor and friend, Lyndon B. Johnson. It occurred to me that we should seek the counsel of the new Vice President, who had not only had long experience combating the Washington bureaucracy, but as a young man had been a director of a program not unlike the Peace Corps—the New Deal's youth corps. Shriver and I called upon him. His argument went like this:

"Boys, this town is full of folks who believe the only way to do something is their way. That's especially true in diplomacy and things like that, because they work with foreign governments and protocol is oh-so-mighty-important to them, with guidebooks and rulebooks and do's-and-don'ts to keep you from offending someone. You put the Peace Corps into the foreign service and they'll put striped pants on your people when all you want them to have is a knapsack and a tool kit and a lot of imagination. And they'll give you a hundred and one reasons why it won't work every time you want to do something different or they'll try to pair it with some program that's already working and you'll get associated with operations that already have provoked a suspicious reputation, and the people you want to work with abroad will raise their eyebrows and wonder if you're trying to spy on them or convert them. Besides, you don't have money to give out and all these other programs do, so you'll get treated like the orphan in a big family where your prestige depends upon your budget. And to top it off, they'll take your volunteers and make them GS ones and twos and you'll send little government employees marching off into the villages over there when you want those countries to accept you as American citizens and not employees of the secretary of state. And most important of all if you want to recruit the kind of people I think you want, you're going to have to ask them to do something for their country and not for AID or State.

"This boy here"—he was referring to me—"cajoled and begged and pleaded and connived and threatened and politicked to leave me to go to work for the Peace Corps. For the life of me I can't imagine him doing that to go to work for the foreign aid program. And I don't think your folks are going to write home and tell their mom and dad that they're giving up two years of their lives for the Agency for International Development.

"Earl Rudder [then president of Texas A&M] commanded the Rangers at Normandy—toughest little fightin' bunch in the war. He took a mess of gangly little country boys and turned 'em into the damnedest crowd Eisenhower let loose that day. Now, there had been a big argument in training over whether they were part of the regular forces or not, but ol' Earl told 'em they were an army unto themselves and they believed it. And I'll tell you this—when they went up those cliffs and through those hedgerows like Indians after my grandpa Baines' scalp, it wasn't for Eisenhower and it wasn't for Marshall and it wasn't for the Joint Chiefs of Staff—it was for Earl Rudder and glory.

"And if you want the Peace Corps to work, friends, you'll keep it away from the folks downtown who want it to be just another box in an organizational chart, reportin' to a third assistant director of personnel for the State Department. Who's your boss in this town is important, and as much as I like Dean Rusk, do you think he's going to have time to give to Shriver here when he has a problem that has to be worked out? Hell, he has to worry about the Russians and the Chinese and Charles de Gaulle. You'll wind up seeing his deputy's deputy. And who the hell is going to volunteer to go to Nigeria for the second deputy secretary of state? Who the hell is the second deputy secretary of state, anyway?"

Well, LBJ loved hyperbole, but his point was not lost on us. And he felt so keenly about it that he later personally called JFK and implored him to keep the Peace Corps separate and apart, with a life and identity of its own. The rest is history.

By all of this, I do not mean to disparage our foreign assistance program or our diplomatic force. At its best, foreign aid has also expressed the magnanimity of the American people. But the Peace Corps is to the American government what the Franciscans in their prime were to the Roman Catholic Church—a remarkable manifestation of a spirit too particular and personal to be contained by an ecclesiastic (read: bureaucratic) organization. It is not like anything else.

The Mystique

by Harris Wofford

From the beginning, America has been a sort of comic hero—young, idealistic, friendly, full of curiosity, ready for adventure, ripe for disappointment, never daunted. With self-government their self-proclaimed purpose and pioneering their way of life, the first Americans took the world by surprise. So did the first Peace Corps volunteers.

From Pocahontas and the presentation of the first pipe of tobacco to Queen Elizabeth I to Lindbergh's solo flight to Paris, the Old World has been fascinated by the bold ambitions, naive enthusiasm, and brash innocence of the new Americans. When Cornwallis surrendered at Yorktown, the band played, "The World Turned Upside Down." So America again intrigued the world by founding the Peace Corps.

At the beginning, however, President Kennedy took heat from critics of the new venture. It hurt politically to have his immensely popular predecessor, Dwight Eisenhower, ridicule it as a "Kiddie Corps." A respected career diplomat, Ellis O. Briggs, called the Peace Corps a movement "wrapped in a pinafore of publicity, whose team cry is: 'Yoo-hoo, yoo-hoo! Let's go out and wreak some good on some natives!' " One can be armed with a comic spirit and still not enjoy being laughed at. Yet Kennedy went ahead with the plan, and the President's presumption proved to be prophetic. As one of the first volunteers put it: "I'd never done anything political, patriotic, or unselfish because nobody ever asked me to. Kennedy asked."

To present the Peace Corps as "comic" is not to demean it. The category in which the Peace Corps experience falls is neither farce nor is it at the level of Dante's high comedy about man's spiritual destiny. It is comedy of the human kind, from which one laughs and learns. A comic

---

Harris Wofford is counsel at Schnader, Harrison, Segal and Lewis in Philadelphia and the author of Of Kennedys and Kings: Making Sense of the Sixties.

hero may fall on his face, but the complications and contradictions that trip him can be both entertaining and instructive.

The Peace Corps is "comic" in the spirit of Mark Twain, and just as American. Like Huck Finn and Jim rafting down the Mississippi, Peace Corps volunteers were being sent down larger rivers to deal with dangers more complicated than rattlesnakes.

On March 1, 1961, the President signed an executive order establishing the Peace Corps on a trial basis, a bold step in the absence of any congressional authorization. More than 25,000 people had already asked for applications. Congressional hearings on the proposed new program were soon to begin. But no clear-cut requests for volunteers had yet come from any country. Shriver and the President would surely fall on their faces if volunteers were ready with no place to go.

So Shriver went to talk with some heads of state. As President Kennedy's special assistant for civil rights, I was lucky enough to go along on an expedition to Ghana, Nigeria, Pakistan, India, Burma, Thailand, and the Philippines. The most crucial moments of that seven-country "fishing trip" were Shriver's meetings with Kwame Nkrumah of Ghana and Jawaharlal Nehru of India, two leaders of the Third World whose reaction could open or close the doors in many countries.

"We've come to listen and learn," Shriver said upon landing in Accra. This was a good note to strike with Nkrumah, a graduate of Lincoln University in Pennsylvania, who wanted to lecture Shriver on American shortcomings, some of which he had experienced firsthand in the days when Jim Crow practices prevailed in much of our country.

After some suspense, Nkrumah's response to the Peace Corps was affirmative, with qualifications. In more or less these words, he said:

> Powerful radiation is going out from America to all the world, much of it harmful, some of it innocuous, some beneficial. Africans have to be careful and make the right distinctions, so as to refuse the bad rays and welcome the good. The CIA is a dangerous beam that should be resisted. From what you have said, Mr. Shriver, the Peace Corps sounds good. We are ready to try it, and will invite a small number of teachers. We could use some plumbers and electricians, too. Can you get them here by August?

The Peace Corps had at last been invited, in person, by a head of state! Shriver vowed that he would break the bureaucratic bottlenecks that had slowed transmission in most U.S. aid programs and left expectant countries waiting for a year or more. The volunteers would be there by August.

Then Nkrumah teased Shriver: Why just one-way traffic? Didn't he

THE IDEAL 35

want some young Ghanaians to volunteer for service to America? In the same half-serious spirit, Shriver said yes, he would welcome and find worthwhile assignments for some volunteers from Ghana. That pitch for reciprocity was repeated by others we met on the trip, and planted the seed for a small experiment a few years later, a reverse Peace Corps of volunteers to America. But that is another story, as is the fall of Nkrumah, who was overthrown in 1966 by a military coup that he charged was aided and abetted by the CIA.

In New Delhi, with his customary red rose in his lapel, Nehru created a different kind of suspense: he seemed almost to fall asleep while Shriver talked. But then he roused himself and said:

> For thousands of years outsiders have been coming to India, some of them as invaders, sweeping down the plains of the Punjab to the Ganges. Many of them stayed and were assimilated. Others went home, leaving India more or less the same as it was before they came. India has usually been hospitable to these strangers, having confidence that its culture would survive, and that it had much to teach the newcomers.
>
> In matters of the spirit, I am sure young Americans would learn a good deal in this country and it could be an important experience for them. We will be happy to receive a few of them—perhaps twenty to twenty-five. But I hope you and they will not be too disappointed if the Punjab, when they leave, is more or less the same as it was before they came.

Though the words were patronizing, this was the green light the Peace Corps needed. Even more significantly, Nehru's approval was an encouraging signal to countries of the nonaligned Third World.

In the fall of 1962, when 225 volunteers stepped out of three planes at the Addis Ababa airport, the Ethiopian minister of education said, "I haven't seen anything like this since the Italian invasion." The volunteers were the first of 500 invited by Emperor Haile Selassie to teach in all the high schools of that spectacularly stark and beautiful mountain country.

They were the largest contingent to go to one country at one time. In a single swoop they doubled the number of college-educated high school teachers in Ethiopia and enabled thousands of additional students to be admitted to studies in the fall. Having resigned from the White House a few months earlier to become the Peace Corps' special representative to Africa and director of the Ethiopian program, I was there to welcome them.

I was also drawn by the unique challenge of the Peace Corps. After the adventure of organizing the Peace Corps' African programs in Togo and Nyasaland (now Malawi), my desk in the old Executive Office Building never seemed quite the same. President Kennedy appeared to appreciate my work in the White House, where I served both as advocate for civil rights and buffer against some of the pressure of the civil rights movement, but I wanted to work on the larger frontier of world integration. Though he had sired the Peace Corps, Kennedy seemed puzzled by its peculiar appeal. Even in giving permission for me to accept the Peace Corps post, he asked, "Wouldn't you rather go out as an ambassador?"

We staff members *were* ambassadors of sorts, as were the volunteers. Open sewers openly arrived at were the first sight to strike the new Peace Corps contingent in Ethiopia as we were bused to the Imperial Palace. The second was the gorgeous mountain scenery.

Fortunately, no one described the scene on a postcard. By now, every volunteer knew what had befallen Margery Michelmore, the *magna cum laude* graduate of Smith College who was expelled from Nigeria for writing an indiscreet postcard home. (When President Kennedy bid goodbye to me, he said, "Keep in touch—but not by postcard!") A somber section of the *Peace Corps Handbook,* entitled "Living in a Goldfish Bowl," had warned volunteers: "You never will have real privacy. . . . Your every action will be watched, weighed and considered representative of the entire Peace Corps." One earnest volunteer teacher, sensing her full ambassadorial responsibility, took as her cautious motto: "Don't smile till Christmas."

Most volunteers, however, smiled soon and often—including at Christmas, when they were invited to visit the emperor to sing carols. During the visit, Haile Selassie told them he had favorable reports on their work from every province and said he had visited the classrooms of a number of Peace Corps teachers. He seemed to enjoy the informality of the volunteers, and at the Christmas party he got a taste of the rambunctiousness of the children of Peace Corps staff. As our own three-year-old son chased a tiny imperial Pekingese between the aging autocrat's legs, the amused emperor said, "If you help us to do away with some of our unnecessary protocol, that will be another of your contributions to my country."

Indeed, the volunteers' contributions were many, in the classrooms and in their communities, though in the schools, ironically, their friendly informality was not as well received as in the Imperial Palace. Teachers complained that the Peace Corps style undermined traditional authority, and students, too, were at first disconcerted. Headmasters warned volunteers to wear ties, not sit on desks, and keep their distance from the students after school. "We want to bring the young up to our standards, not lower ourselves to theirs," was one frequent refrain from Ethiopian educators. Ethiopians, as well as the many Indians in the teaching force,

THE IDEAL

envied the freedom of the volunteers, who were not dependent upon their jobs for their future livelihood. Within limits, the Americans could say what they wanted to say and do more than the career teachers dared to do—or wanted to do. Moreover, with only two years to serve, the volunteers had more reason than lifelong career teachers to exert themselves and try to make their marks in a hurry.

Some of these marks were, of course, intangible, while others could be observed and measured. Ethiopia's choice of English as its language for all higher education made it essential to have teachers whose mother tongue was English. The Peace Corps provided a massive infusion of such teachers, and the students' level of proficiency in English, as measured in both tests and conversation, soared.

Another bottleneck to Ethiopian educational development that volunteers helped break was the centralization of teaching resources. The best schools were located in Addis Ababa, the capital, and Ethiopian and Indian teachers generally considered provincial assignments a purgatory from which they hoped to escape. Peace Corps volunteers, on the other hand, usually sought to go to the most arduous outlying posts. With more than three-fourths of the volunteers teaching in provincial schools, where they often constituted about half the staff, they brought about a rapid broadening of Ethiopia's educational base. This conveyed prestige to the provincial schools, which in turn made them more attractive to Ethiopian teachers.

Outside the classroom, the volunteers were no less audacious in shaking up the traditional school system. Before long, in schools that had previously had almost no extracurricular life, student newspapers, forums, debating societies, drama clubs, glee clubs, handicrafts, scouting, and many kinds of sports were under way. Volunteers taught night courses for adults, especially English for the elementary school teachers. In one town, volunteers advertised courses by beating drums in the marketplace.

In the provincial capital of Dese, U.S./AID had sent the school violins, cellos, clarinets, saxophones, trumpets, trombones, and drums, along with a piano and a record player, but before the Peace Corps, there were no music books and no music teacher. Two volunteers organized a music program for hundreds of students. Soon, amidst excitement in the school and town, the forty-member Dese marching band, with uniforms donated from the United States, was called to play before the emperor on his birthday. The school's pop orchestra, featuring Ethiopian songs, was called to Addis Ababa for national holidays. Soon, a Peace Corps volunteer far to the south at Harar entered the competition, organizing the loudest student band that side of the Nile.

In another provincial capital, volunteers forcibly broke a logjam in the distribution of textbooks, which a custodian kept hidden in the school warehouse "to keep down wear and tear." Each year, the custodian proudly reported that not a single book had been lost, damaged, or destroyed. Almost everywhere, in fact, local school librarians made their lives easier by refusing to lend books, or by keeping the libraries closed most of the time. In most provinces, volunteers fought the "battle of the books" diplomatically, but in Debre Markos, they actually stormed through the warehouse door and seized the books for distribution.

In the little town of Ghion, an independent-minded volunteer named Paul Tsongas—who was later to become a U.S. senator—rented an Ethiopian-style house and invited some of his students to move in. Coming from villages miles away from the town, from which they had commuted every day on foot, many did. Later, Tsongas enlisted a brigade of students to work with him in building a hostel—a one-story dormitory with electric lights that allowed the students to do their homework at night. It became a showpiece of the town and of the Peace Corps, and in due course received a visit and an enthusiastic blessing from the emperor.

The presence of women among the volunteers—more than one out of three of the original contingent—provided an even greater challenge to local traditions. Before the Peace Corps came, virtually no women taught in provincial schools, and Ethiopians could not understand why a young woman would come so far from home to live in a foreign land. They suspected the worst. Faced for the first time with female teachers, boys would grumble that a woman's place was in the home, and then (sometimes) flock to their classes. When a particularly attractive volunteer offered an additional course in French, she was overwhelmed by three hundred eager male applicants. Some Ethiopian male teachers found it difficult to maintain a friendship with Peace Corps women that did not include sex, and unpleasant incidents occurred more than once. But the volunteers held their own, and not one woman quit because of these difficulties.

In fact, after the early problems of adjustment, women volunteers usually earned the respect of their Ethiopian colleagues and students. They took special satisfaction in the influence they had on female Ethiopians, many of whom had never imagined, much less seen, independent women.

Often the triumphs were as simple as that. In fact, what most irked volunteers was the overblown publicity in the United States about their hardships and "sacrifices," as well as the exaggerated accounts that were published about their allegedly exotic experiences and dramatic successes. The story that ought to be told about them, one volunteer wrote, was "not of high adventure *à la* Conrad or Saint-Exupéry—but of dullness." He said volunteers needed a "philosophy which will satisfy our

THE IDEAL

craving for accomplishment and a certain nobility, while we are faced with tedium, fatigue and the desire to sit down and dream."

Yet there were exotic—and comic—moments:

- A volunteer who taught school in the port of Mesewa on the Red Sea lived on a houseboat and was awakened every night by the mullahs calling the faithful to prayer. During the day, he endured the camels that poked into his classroom their not-very-intellectual noses, which he would push out the window with a broom.
- Far to the south, at the opposite end of the empire, a volunteer and staff member were driving a jeep that hit and killed a female camel, forcing them to flee angry Somali nomads who chased them with spears. Later, they settled their liability for $100.
- As Washington headquarters cut down the number of Peace Corps jeeps, in response to Congressman Otto Passman's goading of Shriver about "those blue jeeps roaming the roads of Africa," volunteers turned to other modes of transportation. Once Shriver told this fabled congressional penny-pincher: "I'm happy to report, Congressman, that the donkeys are up and the jeeps are down."
- Five volunteers in the northern province of Eritrea nearly died when they drove a Peace Corps jeep down to the sea for a three-day vacation. After a wrong turn and two flat tires, they found themselves marooned, fifty miles from the nearest village. With a pint of water, a peanut butter sandwich, and jovial recollections of Lawrence of Arabia, two of them set out for help. After walking all day and most of the night, they collapsed in the next day's noon sun. A Bedouin finally came to the rescue, with some sour milk from his goatskin bag.
- One volunteer got caught up in a dubious project started as a semi-jocular proposal when he was driving Shriver around Addis Ababa. Pointing out the confusion caused by the lack of street signs, he boasted to his VIP visitor, "We could make and put up signs in a week." Hearing about the boast, the mayor assigned the volunteer a crew of city workers and told him to go ahead. It took longer than expected, since they had to wait until the city named some of the streets.
- A more presumptuous project—my own—took the Peace Corps to the edge of the politically permissible in that feudal society. We knew the emperor was being pulled in two opposite directions. Younger Ethiopians were urging him to move faster with reform; the old guard was warning him to go slow. The Peace Corps itself was a point at issue. Several of the largest provincial landholders were arguing that the volunteers, by both word and example, were making students dangerously restive. Haile Selassie's better judgment pointed toward reform, and so did many of his statements, but his actions were ambiguous.

After an attempted coup in 1961, the emperor had approved a five-year plan to secure "the advance of our Nation at the fastest possible rate." The programs in that plan—such as universal public education—"are in themselves revolutionary," he said. When the volunteers arrived, they were given the five-year plan, which they considered an eloquent document. But they soon discovered that almost no Ethiopians had ever read it.

The problem was that it had been printed in very limited numbers. When we proposed to the Ministry of Education that it be adopted as a text in English classes, the Ministry approved, on the condition that the Peace Corps reproduce and distribute it. We did, and soon thousands of copies were being read and discussed by students in nearly every province.

Later, Ethiopian friends—some of them in very high places—urged me to exploit the special non-diplomatic status of the Peace Corps to reach the emperor and encourage him to move faster with reform. So, as our two-year term was coming to an end, I included in my formal report on the experience a section entitled "The Emergency," which I wrote with the emperor very much in mind.

A "state of Emergency . . . exists in any country where there is one child without a school or without a teacher or without a textbook," I wrote. The report then went on:

> The Peace Corps was created as an instrument to help interested countries meet this Emergency. It was not designed as a token for countries wishing to give merely the appearance of progress—for countries not prepared to move at the emergency pace required. . . . With millions of children requiring education, a few hundred teachers is a drop in the bucket of Ethiopia's needs. But if the dropping of several hundred American teachers out of the sky becomes the occasion for a far better and massive training and utilization of Ethiopia's own manpower, if the coming of the Peace Corps causes or encourages Ethiopia to double and triple the number of teachers and students each year, then we will have contributed to meeting the greatest need of Ethiopia.

Later, without comment, the emperor thanked me for the report, but on only one front did he take any new action that could be viewed as a response. He endorsed the idea of organizing a domestic counterpart of the Peace Corps to work in the Ethiopian provinces. "If Americans can come all this way to teach and work in our most difficult areas," Haile Selassie remarked to me in one of our last meetings, "how can Ethiopians not do so?" Soon the university was to require Ethiopian students, as a condition for a degree, to serve for a year as teachers in provincial schools. For many of us, the formation of the Ethiopian University Service was the high point in the saga, to paraphrase Mark Twain, of the volunteer Yankees in Haile Selassie's court.

It should be added, though, that these Ethiopian students, radicalized in the countryside, were to play a significant part in the emperor's overthrow a decade later. As I flew out of Ethiopia in 1964, I knew that the students whom Peace Corps volunteers had taught, and the student-teachers in the countryside, were impatient and restless. But no one foresaw the kind of revolution that was to come in the next decade.

The Peace Corps survived and even thrived in Ethiopia for a few years after we left. New volunteers came to add to the group, and to replace departing members. Each new arrival was invited to the Imperial Palace and personally welcomed by Haile Selassie.

But the day came when Haile Selassie, by then almost alone in his palace with his tame lions and his tiny Pekingese, was driven away to a dungeon and to death. Thousands of the students whom our volunteers had taught were also to die. So did other friends and colleagues, including the minister of education, the mayor of Addis Ababa and the president of the university, who launched the program to send students to work in the countryside.

That was a long time ago and in another country. Years later, Senator Paul Tsongas revisited Ethiopia to talk with the head of the revolutionary military government. When he returned to the town where he had taught and had built a hostel, he found few traces of his work. Late at night in his hotel in Addis Ababa, however, there was a knock on the door. Two of his former students were there to tell him how much he had meant to them.

By 1977, when the Peace Corps was forced to withdraw, more than three thousand volunteers had served in Ethiopia. When the former volunteers meet, as they do, they remember small lessons learned and large hopes. But no one can measure how much their teaching and friendship meant to a half-million or more young Ethiopians—or when the seeds of self-government that they planted will mature and flower. There is no telling what Americans will discover through the Peace Corps. But through the men and women who have served, the world has been rediscovering the mystique of America.

An Exchange Between President Kennedy and Tom Scanlon

President Kennedy, in a speech, June 20, 1962:

Recently I heard a story of a young Peace Corpsman named Tom Scanlon, who is working in Chile. He works in a village about forty miles from an Indian village which prides itself on being Communist. The village is up a long, winding road which Scanlon has taken on many occasions to see the chief. Each time the chief avoided seeing him. Finally he saw him and said, "You are not going to talk us out of being Communists." Scanlon said, "I am not trying to do that, only to talk to you about how I can help." The chief looked at him and replied, "In a few weeks the snow will come. Then you will have to park your jeep twenty miles from here and come through five feet of snow on foot. The Communists are willing to do that. Are you?" When a friend saw Scanlon recently and asked him what he was doing, he said, "I am waiting for the snow."

Scanlon, in a letter dated July 14, 1962:

It was a great surprise for me to hear that you had singled me out for my spirit of dedication. I am certain that in many parts of the ever-increasing sphere which the Peace Corps encompasses there are many who have had their dedication tested more than I. I have yet to be sick, whereas one-fourth of our group has had hepatitis. My living conditions are clean and comfortable, and I am sure that in other continents, such as Africa, the daily circumstances of life are much more difficult than they are in Chile.

Your mention was an undeserved honor involving a flash of kind for-

---

Tom Scanlon is president of Benchmarks, Inc., in Washington, D.C.

THE IDEAL

tune which brought my name to your attention from among the many who could just as easily have been cited. Now it is my duty to respond, and I can think of no better way than to tell you more about the people and place you spoke of. Forgive my presumption in assuming you might have time to glance through the story. The main reason for telling it to you is that it has taught me something about Communism and the role of my country in the world. . . . I have been accused by the socialist press in the most widely circulated newspaper in Chile of deluding you. Here is my translation of excerpts from the article.

BEATNIK YANKEE SCARES KENNEDY WITH HIS STORIES OF INDIANS IN CHILE

Tom Scanlon is a Yankee youth of twenty-three years. He ought to have hair the color of carrots, freckled skin, drink a lot of milk, a shot of whiskey now and then, and chew one Chicklet after another. In his ranch, he never missed a television program. He likes the ones with lots of redskins.

Now Tom is in Chile. They sent him with the Peace Corps, telling him that they were modern Boy Scouts, young kids who had to act among the Indians and the Communists in Latin America. Tom told President Kennedy about his adventures. They're the same as he saw in the television programs. The grave thing is that a President of one of the largest nations in the world has believed the story of Indians and villages buried in the snow. In what television program did Tom see all this? . . .

The conclusions to the story have to do with the rivalry which now exists between the United States and Communism in these Latin American countries. My experience tells me that Latin America has more to gain by working with us. The Communist solution is a political one, and it must be presented as the political system to end all systems to a people whose natural propensity is to make one political experiment after another. Ours is more social and economic—going directly to the real problems of the people. Our solution is not a political theory which must wait to be applied, but a stimulus to processes which should begin without delay.

I am jealous, Mr. President, of our country's right to be considered a leader in the world's struggle for development. Perhaps it is a youthful idealism to imagine that our whole nation would act in a humanitarian way even if the fear of Communism were not prompting it to do so. I believe it is no more impossible than democracy or human compassion themselves. It could be that this is our most important responsibility as Peace Corpsmen—the education of our people in their possibilities for doing great things in the world.

If this is our responsibility, we have not begun well in fulfilling it. The press reports on the Peace Corps have stressed our early successes rather than the problems that required our presence here. They make it seem we've already made a great contribution when, in fact, we are struggling toward a beginning. I fear the ballyhoo, Mr. President, the self-congratulation of the American people when they praise their own Peace Corps.

When I am working with the *campesinos* and Indians, I regard myself as the extension of the interest of the American people in my involvement in their problems, and when I return to the United States, I hope to hear more questions about their health than my own. Then I will know that my country, of which I am overwhelmingly proud, is ready to take the place of leadership in the world which belongs to it.

THE PEOPLE

The Volunteer

by Jody Olsen

The car was covered with mud as we pulled into the African village. We had driven for three hours over unpaved roads from the Atlantic coast, passing through countless groves of palm trees and neat family compounds, past roadside markets and lovingly tended gardens and farming plots. The young woman beside me was a Peace Corps volunteer, tense but consumed by a sense of anticipation. Since she had learned nine months earlier that she would be assigned to Togo, she had imagined this moment. In this village of five hundred, she would spend the next two years teaching health in the local primary school.

When we brought the car to a stop in the village center, a few people came near, smiled a welcome, and pointed to her new home, a two-room mud-brick hut with a thatched roof, surrounded by a neat fence of dried grass. Children peered shyly at her from behind the fences of their own houses as she moved in her baggage. Thus another Peace Corps adventure began.

I recalled at that moment, and I think often of it still, the start of my own Peace Corps adventure, when, nearly twenty years ago, I first saw my town in Tunisia. It was night, and I was confronted with high walls and veiled women. Since that day, part of my identity has been fixed to that town, and to the Peace Corps. Not far away from my sight, a group of Americans from the Agency for International Development worked as agricultural specialists, retreating each evening into large houses to resume their American ways. It was apparent to me that their technical competence far exceeded my own. My own self-esteem was to come from being part of the town itself, and of its caring people.

One of my responsibilities was to teach child nutrition, using Dr. Spock's *Baby and Child Care,* as it was the only book I had available. I remember

---

Jody Olsen is vice president of programs, Youth for Understanding, Washington, D.C.

an early lecture that I had worked so hard to prepare, on what to do for diarrhea. After I had proudly presented my lesson, an older mother raised her hand and said succinctly, "Give the child rice." I realized that there was a basic wisdom in that community, unsophisticated as it may have been, which I would have to learn to appreciate before I could really teach and be useful.

I am still not sure what I brought to my Tunisian community in the two years I lived there, though I did my best to teach English and family planning, and convey some modern notions of child nutrition. But I have a pretty good idea of what my town brought to me. Twelve years after I left, I went back for a visit, and the family I lived with embraced me as if we had never been separated. My own love for this family even today is as strong as for my family in the United States. In seeing my Tunisian family again, I understood and appreciated how I had grown, and how much I had learned from them, while I was a part of a very special people.

So I knew what the young volunteer was feeling as she reached her village in Togo, where I was then the Peace Corps' country director. I wondered what I could tell her to make her task easier. How could I share my own experiences with her? She had done well in training, but I knew formal training could only help her begin. The Peace Corps adventure is such a personal thing that each volunteer must handle it with the resources of a private, internal spiritual reservoir. It eludes generalizations, textbooks, even words.

I knew from my own experience that the Peace Corps was an adventure based not just on exposure to unfamiliar geography and cultures. That was the easy part. In my own case, the more important exposure was to a segment of my own psyche that I had not previously known. What excited me most as a new volunteer was the challenge of keeping an open mind, of trying out what I had never tried, of resisting the temptation to measure my experiences against what I had done before and was comfortable with, and of adjusting to a psychological insecurity brought on by the requirement to respond to a constant intrusion of the unfamiliar.

In time, the pride I took in myself as a volunteer was in knowing I had the ability and the self-confidence to cope not just with the different, but with the unusual, knowing I could survive. At one point during my first year I wanted to stay in bed to keep away from all the differences, and I got up at six every morning in the cold and did exercises just to force myself to get going. But I made it, and life became better and better. I knew I could give the young volunteer in Togo a few technical tips. But in joining into the life of her village, she was on her own. That is the experience that makes the Peace Corps special.

People in the Peace Corps have given a great deal of thought to the question of what makes a good volunteer, without ever settling on an answer. Aside from self-confidence, the volunteer must have common sense and a feeling for what is practical. I also think that a volunteer cannot succeed without being idealistic. As much as anything, volunteers must *want* to make things better in the community to which they are assigned. But, in equal measure, the volunteer must also have patience, a commodity often in short supply among Americans, especially the young ones.

In most communities in the developing world, the same work patterns have been in place for generations, and volunteers are likely to be dismayed at the desultory pace of change. Peace Corps volunteers usually arrive feeling that two years is all the time they have to make a difference, and that every day counts. Characteristically, they go through a low period, after the initial exhilaration but before they have really mastered either the local language or the customs, when they wonder whether what they do really matters. After that, they begin building friendships, while acquiring a sense of what is possible and what is not. Finally, they feel a part of the community and its reality, and stop worrying about what they cannot do. The best of the volunteers know how to make time pass in a positive way, while they are waiting for events to happen. They are dogged, without being impatient.

But volunteers must also know how to communicate their care and concern. They must know how to establish a trust between themselves and their community. In practice, they must know how to listen and how to detect differences between their own values and those of the community. Furthermore, they must be tolerant of these differences, accepting them as a base from which they may then introduce new ideas to make the community's life better. The volunteer who sees virtue in introducing oxen for farming, new vegetables for family gardens, or inoculations for child health must frame the proposal in a way the community understands and can accept. The success rate is low for new ideas that offend old values. Volunteers must be able to put aside their own cultural system to work in another. In its twenty-five years of experience, the Peace Corps has learned that this is not a capacity given to every volunteer.

Ever since its beginning, the Peace Corps has been trying to determine what makes a successful volunteer. There was apprehension in the beginning years that, unless some more or less scientific method was established to predict success, the Peace Corps would suffer from an excessive proportion of failures among volunteers. The early period was famous—and to some degree infamous—for stories of trainees taking standardized personality tests and drawing sociograms while being counseled and assessed by professional psychologists. This led to "deselection" of those whose inadequacy was predicted, with furtive departures from training that were embarrassing and often damaging. Furthermore, there was never much evidence that the psychological tests were particularly valid. So when pre-service training was moved from the United States to host country sites in the late 1960s, the tests were abandoned.

Now most candidates, having been selected on the basis of academic or professional record, more or less screen themselves out in the course of "in-country" pre-service training. The system is geared to those who *want* to become volunteers, and, empirically, that desire has proved as valid a psychological test as any. When the Peace Corps has had a failure, it has as often been the result of the inadequacy of a project as of the inability of a volunteer to adapt (on an average, about 28 percent of volunteers do not complete their two-year assignments).

There is surely no single reason that Americans decide they want to become Peace Corps volunteers. There has always been a mixture of motives, fusing idealism and practicality. It seems fair to say that a good volunteer must have this combination. It is hard to imagine a successful volunteer who is totally visionary, any more than one who is completely self-serving. In the early 1960s, idealism seemed to be the key, reflecting the mood of the Kennedy years. Recruitment emphasized service over technical skills. In fact, the Peace Corps has from the beginning been quite successful in imparting to generalists in its training programs the basic technical skills needed to provide useful service. On the whole, volunteers have responded ingeniously in adapting the skills taught in training to the needs of the communities in which they have served. Thus, from the start, the Peace Corps felt confident in adhering to the principle that a volunteer's most important attribute was commitment.

Nonetheless, by the beginning of the 1970s, there was a shift in the design of Peace Corps programming, which led to a heavier emphasis on technical skills in the recruitment of volunteers. The Peace Corps began to think of itself as a more conventional development agency and shifted away from volunteers with capacities for improvisation to accommodate volunteers with existing technical training. This, as it turned out, was probably the least successful era in the Peace Corps' history.

The end of the 1970s saw a shift back to an interest in generalists, and in volunteers with high levels of motivation who could be trained in the field. At the same time, the host countries of the Third World—a little older now, and with citizens of their own with advanced levels of training—were requesting volunteers with greater specialization, particularly

THE PEOPLE

in the areas of mathematics, science, forestry, engineering, and agriculture. The result, relative to earlier periods, has been an effort to recruit volunteers with "practical idealism," a combination of generalist background with some technical specialty, but more important, an ability to acquire the needed technical skills in the three months of training without ever losing the desire to make a difference. As it happens, the Peace Corps does not seem to have difficulty recruiting volunteers with these attributes.

What explains why an American will volunteer to serve two years away from family and home, often in some physical discomfort, at no pay, frequently in conditions of considerable loneliness? It is a question routinely asked by the Third World people among whom Peace Corps volunteers serve. In some cases, the question reflects suspicion. Some local people simply cannot believe that volunteers would willingly give up American comforts for their more basic way of life. But more often, the question emerges out of the bewilderment of people who may love the Peace Corps volunteers who have come to their community, but who consider estrangement from family and home the worst imaginable punishment.

I specifically remember wanting to join the Peace Corps long before I could give it a rationale. I wanted to go to another country, live in a new environment, test myself on the unfamiliar terms that I knew I would encounter. I knew I wanted to "make a difference," a notion that seems to be a recurring theme among Peace Corps recruits. Who knows where this motivation comes from? In one way or another almost every volunteer has it, combining a fundamental idealism with a practical objective.

For some, the motivation is simple curiosity, the desire to discover another country, experience its food, dress, customs, language. The Peace Corps is, after all, an exposure to the unfamiliar and, to a degree, the unpredictable. The presence of this objective seems to explain why the more exotic countries that the Peace Corps serves, those whose cultures are most far removed from our own—Nepal, for instance—are traditionally those most sought after by volunteers for assignment.

The practical counterpart of this idealism is the prospect, apparently entertained by increasing numbers of volunteers, of using the Peace Corps experience as a springboard into an international career. Twenty-five years ago, this prospect was absent, because there was no precedent, but international organizations have since learned to appreciate the attributes that Peace Corps volunteers possess. Returned volunteers are recognized as having a unique sensitivity to other ways of life and other cultures, and they rate high marks compared with other Americans for their language ability. Peace Corps volunteers, after all, are trained and work in some two hundred languages. It is no exaggeration, furthermore, to say that the energy and adaptability of the volunteer working abroad have become legendary.

Over the past twenty-five years, returning volunteers have become involved in every kind of international work—banking, charity, business, education, and, of course, diplomacy. Currently the Peace Corps is the chief recruiting ground for the State Department and the Agency for International Development, which have on their rolls more than a thousand former volunteers. The World Bank, CARE, and Chase Manhattan Bank provide similar reports. Increasingly, international organizations have revised their job requirements to recruit returned Peace Corps volunteers.

Prospective volunteers also see the Peace Corps as the opening to careers other than international. Graduates of the social sciences and the humanities often consider the Peace Corps a way to spend two useful years while they define their life goals. The Peace Corps is virtually unsurpassed in teaching the use of a foreign language. It has proven important to volunteers in learning or sharpening skills in agriculture, forestry, public health, architecture, and engineering. Many returned volunteers build upon their foreign experience to go into higher education, government service, and even electoral politics. Getting away, having time to think, serving while making personal decisions, and absorbing the meaning of new experiences have all become reasons for joining the Peace Corps.

The rising age of volunteers in recent years suggests that more and more recruits are motivated by divorce, retirement, the loss of a job or the death of a spouse. The 120,000 Americans who have served in the Peace Corps clearly represent a reservoir of information, upon which applicants from every sector of the nation's life feel free to draw. Peace Corps service is becoming familiar—and surely less intimidating—to increasing numbers. The recruiting forecasts of the Peace Corps itself are based upon a belief that, in the coming years, volunteers will be drawn from an ever wider circle, chronologically, geographically, socially.

Still, though every American over the age of eighteen is eligible to join the Peace Corps, it is clear that the pool of available recruits is much narrower. Those wanting to volunteer, for example, must be able to set aside personal and professional activities for a minimum of two years. They must be able to support themselves without compensation other than a stringent monthly allowance averaging $325, and a $4,000 "readjustment" payment after successful completion of the two-year term of service. The financial costs thus tend to exclude the poor, as well as those with family or professional responsibilities.

THE PEOPLE

There is further exclusion in the requirement that all Peace Corps volunteers have a four-year college degree. The only exception is for a few technical posts, but even for these assignments, preference goes to degree holders. Volunteers, furthermore, cannot take children with them, and spouses can go only if there is a position for both husband and wife. Since the Peace Corps currently accepts only about one applicant out of four, the preference inevitably goes to those with the highest levels of education, substantial previous travel experience, a proficiency in languages, and specific technical skills.

The built-in bias in favor of Americans from prosperous origins explains the relative failure of the Peace Corps to bring in minority volunteers. Members of minority groups are less likely to be able to afford the luxury of volunteering. The number of Hispanics who have applied has increased in the last four years, while the percentage of applications from blacks has remained steady. The percentage of blacks who are accepted, however, is less than 3 percent, a fourth the ratio in America.

In fact, the Peace Corps made special efforts to recruit minorities long before the practice was adopted in the United States generally, and it continues the effort. Yet, despite its many recruitment programs, the representation of minorities actually dropped to less than 6 percent in 1985. From the ethnic perspective, the Peace Corps has failed to represent the United States in its full diversity. It is probably the Peace Corps' misfortune that service in its ranks is a privilege of the relatively rich in our society.

In respect to gender, however, the Peace Corps has done substantially better. When the Peace Corps began, 63 percent of the volunteers were men, that figure rising to 69 percent by 1970. Since then, the ratio has dropped to almost fifty-fifty. These numbers come close to representing not only the balance in society but, more pertinently, the balance among college graduates.

Traditionally, the Peace Corps has tended to typecast women in their assignments. Men were generally given jobs in agriculture or construction; women were assigned to teaching or social work. In recent years, however, this has begun to change. It is true that most Third World communities expect men to do the work in forestry or fisheries or in building water systems, but it seems likely that the involvement of women in this work has had a positive impact, not only on women in the Third World but on development itself.

The growing role of women, besides reflecting an important change in our own society, is the product of deliberate Peace Corps policy. Despite the reluctance of individual countries to accept women on certain projects, the Peace Corps has encouraged them to compete for any assignment. I remember the looks of amazement when one of the first female volunteers showed up in a village in Togo on a motorcycle with tools and seeds in hand, ready to work. The Peace Corps assigned a woman as its country director in Oman, a very conservative Islamic nation, and women have become part of a range of projects in many Arab countries. Such women have become important role models in developing societies.

The shift in roles has exacted its price from women in the Peace Corps, as it has in some cases at home. A woman who performs what has traditionally been a man's work has characteristically had to do it better, and with significant community surveillance and harassment. In my own case, working in an Arab country, I waited months before I felt that my contributions were recognized. At that point, I was made to feel I had become the "third sex," playing neither the traditional male nor the traditional female role. The success of one woman usually makes it easier to place other women in "male" jobs, though the sense of unease often remains. But the Peace Corps has committed itself to a principle, and in projects from Liberia to Tonga it has encouraged female volunteers to take the lead in promoting a position of equality for women in development.

"Senior" volunteers are also becoming more common. A husband and wife who had run a restaurant for twenty-five years transferred their experience to an entirely new setting to become food co-op leaders in Fiji. Though a smaller percentage of older volunteers has completed college, they offer years of professional experience in its place. Older volunteers are usually well received in communities in host countries and, in fact, often become community leaders. One recent widower, who became a boat builder and educator on a small Pacific island, so engaged the concern of his neighbors that they regularly offered him candidates for marriage. Another older volunteer told me she had sat around despondently for a year after her husband's death, finally responded to a Peace Corps recruiting advertisement, then left her children and former life to find happiness as a nutrition educator in the Philippines.

When I went back a year later to the village where I had left the young health education volunteer, I found her in her hut with two Togolese "sisters" by her side, playing a flute sonata. She was waiting for me with a special Togolese meal, jointly prepared with her family. Afterward, she excitedly took me on a tour of her village, calling to each person by name. She also described to me the special village rituals and traditions, achieved only by knowing the language. She talked of health issues and of the new well she and the village had just found the money to build. It would be completed before she left.

In her first year she had struggled, had questioned her purpose, had wondered why things moved so slowly. She had received some discouraging letters from home and had cried a little. But now she was happy, was learning, and, more important to her, knew she was making a difference, at least to the families near her. After completing her tour in Togo, she came home to make new decisions about what really mattered in her life. She typified the Peace Corps experience, one we all share. It ties all of us together, no matter when or where we have served.

Letter from India (1962)

I am sure that in some ways my experience differs from that of other volunteers because I am one of two Negroes serving in south India. Few people here have any idea what a Negro is or looks like, and even fewer have ever seen one. Thanks to the movie industry, the common belief is that all Americans are fair-skinned, rich, and polygamous. Fortunately or unfortunately, I don't fall into any of those categories. Whenever someone asks, "Where is your native place?" and I answer, "The United States of America," I encounter undisguised expressions of disbelief. As the conversation progresses, I am again asked the same question, followed by, "And your father's native place?" The same answer again serves to convince my inquirers that I am the world's greatest liar.

My first experience at the village barber angered me until I remembered my uniqueness, and then the situation became comical. As soon as I sat down in the chair, runners were sent out in all directions. When most of the villagers had touched and inspected my head—as the barber stood aside, beaming with pride—my haircut proceeded. I'm sure the first strands never hit the floor, as there was a mad scramble for souvenirs.

At present, I am lecturing in English, world civilization, health, and sanitation, and supervising a physical training program at a rural institute. Two or three nights a week I spend in villages showing educational films in the local language.

So far, my life here has been without any unfortunate incident pertaining to race and color. Hardly a week passes when I don't receive an invitation to attend some social function or to visit someone's home. I feel somewhat of a hypocrite when I speak of the glorious and wonderful life of an American, the free and advanced educational system, job opportunities, politics, and social life. I praise these institutions knowing that this life is not enjoyed by all Americans. I often wonder what thoughts occur in the minds of volunteers who, in the U.S., live in places where to extend similar hospitality to a Negro would mean sure social ostracism and possibly economic reprisal.

THE PEOPLE

Words fail me when I try to express the feeling I get of living in a country where I am free to come and go as I choose, without that nauseating feeling that occurs when you sense you will be denied service in a restaurant. In some ways, it is ironic: I am enjoying, in a country thousands of miles from my own, a way of life that every male in my family has served in the U.S. armed forces to protect. It is an ordeal to explain how the black man came to be an American. Describing the Civil War in a new and strange language is no easy feat. Even with thoughts of this and of life in the southern U.S., when I am asked to name the country I would prefer to live in, I do not hesitate to say America. With all its faults, I sincerely believe that I can one day share in the wealth and glory of what I think is the world's greatest government and people.

Letter from Iran to the Peace Corps Director (1965)

This letter concerns something which I have strongly come to believe. If I didn't feel a sense of responsibility for the work of Peace Corps everywhere, but especially in Iran, I wouldn't bother to write you. I've been here a little over nine months, and it is my conviction that unmarried girls shouldn't be included in a Peace Corps project in Iran. I write this not as a volunteer serving in a small provincial town, but as one who teaches in a university in a large provincial city. One would think, therefore, that we have had a chance to meet many Iranians, relate with them, discuss ideas with them, and in general get beyond the scope of "teaching English." This is not true. All of our colleagues are older men who couldn't speak with us other than good-day pleasantries for fear of breaking social customs. Never could we have been invited into their homes. The only exception was a young Irishman hired to teach English with us and who formed our sole basis for intellectual and social activities at the university.

We attempted to make up for this lack by starting an English club for our students, getting to know those Iranians who make an effort to be friendly, and meeting other Westerners in town. Our English club was the one thing that the students had which resembled a group working situation—not for grades but for fun and pleasure. But this evidently upset some of the other professors and our dean, who saw a breakdown of the traditional teacher-student relationship. It also caused unfavorable comment about our conduct.

We've received no reaction whatsoever from our teaching activities, except an unfavorable one from the fact that we spoke pleasantly in the halls to our students or answered their questions between classes in the school commons. As for meeting Iranians who were largely educated abroad, we've found out now that these fellows haven't a respectable reputation in town. That we were seen talking to them (not dating, mind you) caused comment enough for us to be censured by the dean.

We never considered the consequences from our meeting and associating with other Westerners, who turned out to be our *only* social contacts. This isn't particularly desirable in light of the Peace Corps ideal of living with the people. It also classes us with other Westerners who live and work here, and that may be bad. I don't know yet.

Every action we've taken has been scrutinized. We bother Iranians who can't fathom why unmarried girls would leave their homes to come here and live alone. Their conclusion is that such girls are up to no good. No one bothers to understand our motives, least of all the average man in the street, who takes advantage of an un-*chadored* girl to say dirty phrases to her, brush up against or bump her, or even actually deliberately run into her on a crowded street. All these actions, without exaggertion, have happened to me *every day*. In addition, the taxi drivers make unpleasant comments. Why? Obviously, we've given them cause to think they can be familiar—we come and go at will to our classes, some of which are at night, are seen visiting the homes of our friends later than nine-thirty or ten in the evening, make business trips to Tehran alone, and give parties in our home.

It is my contention that our mere presence here is hurting Peace Corps' image. True, we aren't here to be like other Americans. But I don't think it's necessary to become "just like an Iranian." Men are allowed much freedom in this double-standard country. As far as Peace Corps is concerned, this means a male volunteer is freer to be himself, to relate with other men, to get to know them and their country. I feel hampered, though I shouldn't be, for I feel I was told what would happen by many, including two earlier volunteers in Iran who were at our training site. All of it just didn't sink in. Much has happened to me that has been wonderful. I wouldn't trade places with anyone. I didn't expect it to be easy. But I didn't understand what it means to be a second-class human—a female.

Letter from Mauritania (1985)

As an American, I can never really forget that I'm in a developing part of the world. Nothing could illustrate that better than my life here in my village, N'Gawle. At the same time, because I am so immersed in the culture, in the timelessness of this life, for the most part it has come to feel very natural. Yesterday, for the first time when I demonstrated my skill, women actually told me I *could* pound rice! What an accomplishment.

There's a fatalistic, *Allah jebbi* (If God wills it), things-take-time attitude here. It really permeates the whole country. Partly due to Islam and the absolute omnipotence of Allah, but also I think related to the different perspective of Africans. The concept of progress is so ingrained in us as Americans—your children should do better than you. That drive is pretty absent here. It's more of an honor for the kids to be Koranic students, and beg for money and food for themselves and their teacher, than to go to school and learn French. It really gets me crazy when I think about the fact that none of these kids ever reads books—maybe they have one school book but, beyond that, nothing. Things are oriented much more toward the land, the status of the rice harvest, where the money for oil for that day's lunch will come from. Life here on the banks of the river is the life they've lived for centuries. A Yale education didn't prepare me for a lot of the challenges I face here.

At times, identifying and clarifying my role in the village presents the toughest obstacle. There will always be resistance to me, perceptions of me as a *tubok* (foreign, white person), as a patron (source of money, gifts), even as I eat what they eat, live as they live, dress as they dress, speak their language. Similar constraints hamper my work. I'm working on opening a health center, where I can give lessons, weigh babies, dispense the village medications. But they have no real reason to listen to me— they have done things the same way forever. If I don't have any medicine or shots to hand out, what possible good am I? The people here welcome me into their homes, but the health education I try to dispense is too foreign an approach. Every day I have to remind myself that change takes a long time. And they'll tease me about not being married and pester me to pray to Allah five times a day until I leave.

Although I am a bit low now, and thus aware of the loneliness and isolation that goes along with all this, I continue to marvel at the experience. But if I enjoy it so, and feel so myself here, why do I choose to cram into that bush taxi and, every few months, ride away from it all? I long and long for the escape to Nouakchott [the capital], for that submersion into Americana. Shouldn't that yearning tell me something? In Nouakchott I feel dispirited about my work, but I get into that taxi, and after, onto the sacks of powdered milk in the back of a pickup truck that takes me the windy last three hours to N'Gawle, because I expect it of myself. It's what I came here to do. And the joy of it is that after the initial readjustment, I am *so* happy to be here. I know that I have come home.

Reports and Letters on Life, Work, and Love in the Peace Corps

MALAWI

This afternoon I got out our trusty dull hatchet and killed a chicken—mmm! We cooked a fried chicken, hot-water cornbread, tomatoes, other vegetables such as eggplant and squash. Well, after we finished eating, here came the chief's daughter with plates of food. So we ate a bit, bursting at the seams all the while. After we had eaten that, we sat around and groaned and wished for milk of magnesia when here came Modesta's son (Modesta is one of the chief's daughters, who is married and has about six children)—with a big bowl of bean soup! It was delicious, but I was too sick to appreciate it.

Last night we went to Mwanje, about two miles away, to a Youth League dance. The League is the compulsory organization that all Malawi young people must belong to who are not in school—which is most of them. It is a political organization. They march for three hours four days a week. I don't know why, but they do—girls and boys. They march and run and sing political songs. They are organized by the Young Pioneers, a tough young bunch of men, and not to be fooled with since they have been declared as a legal police force with the power to arrest and even shoot anyone suspected of plotting against the government. A great responsibility for young men with little or no education and only some training in marching and military maneuvers. These Youth League dances are held every Wednesday night and Saturday in each district, and no dances can be held in the villages when a Youth League dance takes place. You see, the admission fees go to the party organization.

When we entered the dark hall, lit by a kerosene lantern at one end, the crowd parted before us, and we were led to the front of the hall, where chairs had been placed for us as guests of honor. I was so embarrassed! They were trying to be very kind to us, but I would rather they had just gone ahead as if we weren't there. But it was not possible. The dance was enjoyable, and we danced much. Around midnight we left. The two-mile walk home in the moonlight was beautiful, although as were descending one hill, on the gravel, I slipped and fell and cut my leg a little. Nothing serious, though.

We are really beginning to feel a part of the village now, because the babies don't cry anymore when they see us—in fact, miraculously enough, a couple of them will even let us hold them without screaming, although they do keep an eagle eye on their mothers to make sure they are not being abandoned to these bleached persons. We are slowly getting to know the names of some of the children. They are beginning to become personalities, and are nearly all little characters and show-offs. They've taught us some Nyanja songs, and we've taught them some American ones.

TUNISIA

Endurance, patience, and determination are necessary for a volunteer placed in an ill-defined job that he is all too often technically ill-qualified for. He needs these characteristics to stick it out until he can get across to the strangers around him who and what he is and what he is trying to do. This can be a discouraging task, and sometimes, when his and the Peace Corps' concept of the job is out of kilter with local reality, it is an impossible task. In the latter case, he needs these qualities to avoid defeatism as he either modifies his concept of the job or seeks a different one.

Take Marilyn, a girl whose humility keeps her from standing out in a group. When she arrived at Hammam Lif to take up her physical education assignment, she related, "They asked me what I was and why I was there. It was depressing to get such a reception." When she explained her assignment, they put her to work right away, but mostly at making beds and keeping the kids quiet during endless idle hours. "I was overburdened," she said, "but with things any moron could do." She worked with two shifts of girls at the Bourguiba Village, four hours with each shift. The girls got their physical education at the school they were taken to in town. Marilyn's job was to occupy their spare time. She supervised games outdoors in good weather and organized projects like puppet shows indoors in bad weather.

Marilyn's problems were made harder because the directress of the village was indifferent and stayed away from it as much as possible, and because troublemakers from other villages were transferred there. The directress never bothered to get equipment, not even shorts, which Marilyn finally bought out of her own pocket.

Inevitably, she said, "I ran out of things to do, and the novelty wore off for them. By the end of the school year, I was really fed up." But she met many Tunisians, and these friendships, she said, were what made life bearable. In her second year, she doggedly diversified her mission. She persuaded the directress that four hours a day of spare-time minding was too much for the village girls as well as for herself. So she works at the village only in the mornings now. Four evenings a week she teaches English at the Bourguiba Institute in Tunis, commuting by train and bus. Saturdays she spends teaching at a school for the blind. Weekday afternoons she prepares for her night classes.

"I'm really enjoying this year," she says. "All three projects are challenging. But I believe the change from last year is more in me than in the situation. I've grown up a lot and learned a lot about myself."

PERU

Kitty and Sue have developed their programs within urban Arequipa. Kitty, an arts and crafts worker, has established contact with local producers of small articles and is working, particularly with ceramics producers, to help them improve the quality and design of their products. Sue has organized a local choral group which recently won second prize in an area competition. She has found there is a great deal of interest in music within the *barriadas*. She discovered her own counterpart in a music teacher who is assigned to the general Arequipa area. She is now forming a boys' choir in an orphanage. Out of 100 boys she got 100 percent turnout. Her own vitality and interest serve as a spark to her activities. She is well-received in the communities, and is well-liked by the young children with whom she works.

Jim and David are interested in the small-industry approach to manual arts. In addition to their classes, which have reached 250 persons, they have been holding meetings with local artisans and encouraging discussion of their problems of production and marketing. The manual arts group has high hopes of being successful, and I believe this project can contribute greatly to the development of the community, if its members are content to settle on one or two activities and keep the project within the local context.

THE PEOPLE 65

SIERRA LEONE

Barbara, Jack, and Eleanor have taken the town and the school by storm. Barbara runs the library; Eleanor operates what amounts to an outpatient clinic; Jack took over the training of the school track team. Jack does carpentry with the villagers; Barbara gave a huge party for her cook's wife (featuring dancers from the women's secret society); the three have started raising chickens and vegetables. But their splashiest project was the library for the primary school.

During the Christmas vacation, the group invited a large number of Peace Corps volunteers to Jimmi to build a library. Volunteers swarmed to Jimmi. Without much Sierra Leonean help, they made the blocks for the building and began to put up the walls, leaving it unfinished to return to their jobs. The volunteers, doing something different and tangible, were most enthusiastic about it. The paramount chief and the principal were gratified and impressed. Jimmi Bagbo had never seen anything like it.

After the volunteers left, local people slowly began to work on the unfinished building, which will soon be opened and dedicated. The project was spectacular but would have been worthless if the villagers had not finished it. Why they did hasn't been fully explained. The only explanation I can offer is that after two years, the town has come to identify with the volunteers, as the volunteers have identified with the town. If the same project had been started when the Peace Corps arrived, the building would still be unfinished.

NEPAL

I think I may have solved, or at least partially solved, the problem of students making disruptive noise while I teach. The other teachers told me how to do it. "*Tapaille le bademas haru lie pitnu parcha,*" they said, which roughly translates as "You have to hit the bastards."

The mere mention of corporal punishment prompted in me the proper amount of Northeastern-white-liberal-public-school-educator reaction, as I informed my colleagues that I *never* hit students. It's just not necessary, I said. Boy, was I a stooge. It *is* necessary. People respond here only to punishments they've been conditioned to expect—and to view fear *as* punishment. Just as corporal punishment wouldn't work in Montgomery County, Maryland, noncorporal punishment doesn't work in Pythan, Rapati. I've also found that you have to give a kid a fairly good punch to make the punishment effective. They've been struck by parents, older siblings, and teachers throughout their lives, so a light shove won't do more than elicit laughter.

I hit my first kid early last week and have since struck two more. Not really hard blows (he wrote defensively, betraying the fact that he hardly feels as comfortable with the new method of discipline as he'd like to), but hard enough to keep the noise down—or at least to keep them quiet enough to run a class. It wasn't easy hitting that first kid. I actually didn't hit him, but threw him to the ground. But it was interesting how quickly I got over it. Immediately afterward, I felt like a complete schmuck. I was the guy friends have said makes Mahatma Gandhi look like Caspar Weinberger, and here I was betraying everything I believed in. Or so I thought. But as soon as I resumed the lesson and hit my stride, I forgot about it.

Adaptation isn't a matter of choice out here. You simply have to do it, and this includes the adaptation (adulteration?) of your most strongly held principles. A lot of the Peace Corps literature they send you before you join is bullshit, but the part about doing things that surprise yourself isn't. It's fact.

CAMEROON

Tony, who came here to teach English, explored the warm beer circuit in the village bars for awhile. He took walks on the beach, talked with fishermen. The picturesque coastline in both directions from Kribi is peppered with fishing villages, some of them populated by Nigerians or Togolese. The fishermen make big catches, but a very small percentage satisfies the local food demand. Although some of the balance is crudely smoked and lasts awhile longer, the bulk is left to rot on the beach.

Tony went to the prefect of Kribi. Why not organize a cooperative and transport the surplus catch to inland towns for sale? The prefect was agreeable, but pointed out that it had been tried once before and failed, mostly because the guy who ran the co-op absconded with the receipts.

"The prefect doesn't want to risk his political position on a project that might fail," said Tony. "He won't do anything about arranging transport until I can prove the project will be sure-fire. I want to start small and take a few chances but I can't until I can get some transport. It's a delicate chicken-and-egg sort of thing."

At this point it is hard to tell which will come first, but Tony has been moving steadily toward success.

First, he got himself invited out on the ocean to fish in pirogues. Next, for $8, he had his own dugout built—a *moustique* about twelve inches wide and ten inches deep. But handling it in the surf is tricky, and he gets dumped into the sea with considerable regularity. Under construction while I was there was a bigger and less tippy pirogue, which Tony had built for a flat $16. The fishermen weren't sure at first why Nutty Tony wanted to dump himself in the drink and learn about fishing, but they are all for him. They listen now, when he explains his plans for marketing their fish.

Tony has walked several miles north and south along the coastline, talked chiefs into calling meetings, proposed his scheme to fifty or sixty at first. Soon, new fishermen came around looking for him. He's made his pitch to more than two hundred, and they want to give it a go.

"I have had money offered, but won't take it until I am sure it will get back with a profit," says Tony. "Between school terms this Christmas, I'll go to Ebolowa and Yaoundé to try to get merchants there to agree to pay for fresh fish. If I can bring that assurance back to the prefect, I think I can get him to arrange the transport."

Tony had been at Kribi a little over three months when I saw him. He says he has only two years and wants to start something that will carry on after he leaves.

"For hundreds of these people on the coast, this could be an economic transfusion," he says. "For people in the interior, a whole new source of protein in their diet."

His project faces many pitfalls, but even if it fails, the Africans around Kribi won't soon forget the American Peace Corps English teacher. He's the first white man they've ever seen taking on the ocean on their own terms, walking the beach with an idea about their rotting surplus.

MALAYSIA

Are married couples more effective in community development than single volunteers? For rural Malay society, the answer to this question seems to be yes. Malay society is built around the family as social unit. The pervasive values in the rural areas are social ones. These values underlie all activities in a *kampong* [village], so in order to function naturally and effectively in the rural Malay setting, one must be accepted as a social unit, that is, a married couple. Without this social status, acceptance into the community in which one lives becomes more difficult, because the people do not know what position to assign you.

The single community development volunteer can work on the periphery of society, not necessarily becoming emotionally entangled.

However, the inherent advantage of a married couple's involvement in society carries along with it the pressures of continual social demands. The problems of acceptance and involvement are the first steps to beginning community development work. After, the question of what the man does and what the woman does arises. The inferior role is extremely difficult for an American woman to accept; yet the Malay social context places her in this position.

The wife often has periods of depression, seeing her husband go off to dig ditches, pour cement, or split bamboo. She wishes her part of the job could be so easy! By physical labor willingly given, a man can earn the immediate respect of the *kampong*. His advice is thereafter sought on various community problems.

A woman cannot easily play an influential role in *kampong* affairs. Negotiations are considered more serious when undertaken by a man. A wife can be more effective by being a good cook, housekeeper, or gardener. Her peers, the other *kampong* wives, will be curious at first about her activities, but will soon identify with her and offer their friendship. A wife in community development can also carry new ideas—family planning, sanitary housekeeping, children's education, handiwork opportunities—directly to the member of the family who can use and benefit by them the most.

To look separately at the jobs of a husband and wife in community development is to see only half of the situation. The people of a *kampong* look upon them as a unit. They complement each other in many respects, so that their work cannot be broken down into male-female categories. The husband gives his wife support by providing an authority figure for some of her ideas and projects. Married, the female volunteer has a needed identity as wife. *Kampong* women become aware of an additional aspect of her life, that of the wife actively supporting her husband's endeavors and participating with him as a unit, a couple, in community affairs. Rather than letting the world pass them by, *kampong* women may be encouraged out of their complacency to extend themselves beyond their mundane daily activities.

TOGO

The problem of sex might just as well be raised here as anywhere else. It is a problem for a variety of reasons, and the country doctor is struggling manfully to cope with it, but there is really little he can do, humans being what they are.

There is an impending marriage between a reluctant fishing volunteer

THE PEOPLE

and the daughter of a chief. There is also ample indication of affairs involving female volunteers and Togolese men. There are affairs involving female volunteers and volunteer men. There are affairs involving volunteer men and Togolese women. And there is a bit of VD.

The Togolese, I am told, take these things rather lightly. But the question of paternity suits, already noted in one African country, may well seem chronic in the course of time, and the Peace Corps may be forced to give the question of sex greater attention during training.

PAKISTAN

A few things some volunteers brought or were sorry they did not:

Food: canned meats, popcorn, candy
Film: very expensive here
Camera, radio, typewriter, raincoat
Injector blades: impossible to get here
Toothbrushes, shaving lotion
Knapsack: excellent for traveling and trekking
Iron: international model, 220V
Sears catalog, pictures of family, home, etc. Very important!
Clothing: Many of you will have clothes made here, so don't spend your whole clothing allowance before departing. Men should have a good supply of underwear, T-shirts, socks, and work shoes. I can't help the women on this topic.

RECIPE FOR HOME BREW

10 lbs sugar
3 lbs. malt (bring this from States)
1 pkg. yeast
19 gal. H_2O

Set in crock until no bubbles rise (ten to fifteen days). Bottle and let it set two weeks before sampling.

GHANA

Example of making students think: one day he took a math class out to the athletic field, divided it into groups of eight, and had each group elect a leader. He gave each group a one-foot ruler, and then handed one group an old tire, another a board, a third a crooked branch, told the fourth to find its own implement, and told them their assignment was to measure the track—and to start doing it by some method within two minutes. There were excited conferences. The kids with the tire started by measuring its diameter and flopping it end over end; then someone figured out that they could measure its circumference and count the rolls around the track. The students to whom he had given no implement decided to use a girl student's belt as their measuring rod. Each group completed the task with reasonable accuracy in short order and with a great feeling of accomplishment.

A challenge never to do himself what he can get the students to do themselves. "The Ghanaians have a clock that runs about an hour behind ours, a calendar that runs a day behind. Time and again I have to choose between letting them complete a task behind schedule or doing it myself. I force myself to let them finish it—late."

The Benefits
by Warren W. Wiggins

Once upon a time, two social philosophers named Burdick and Lederer wrote a book. They had a notion that America was sending abroad beauty-contest winners as the people's representatives: good-looking, well-barbered, handsomely dressed "cookie pushers," who stayed in the big cities, didn't travel to the boondocks, and could always be found not too far from their spacious air-conditioned houses, swimming pools, well-stocked commissaries, and chauffeured limousines. Lots of ordinary Americans read this book and agreed things abroad were a sorry mess.

The social philosophers also described a man who wasn't pretty, who lived in the boondocks and helped people build water pumps and dig roads. His trousers were striped with grease and dirt. He was devoted to helping poor rural people, so he learned their language, ate their food, and wore clothes appropriate to his work. Although he was not blessed by good looks, to the poor people he was helping, he was beautiful.

Burdick and Lederer named their book after this central character, calling it *The Ugly American.*

And the ordinary Americans who read the book said: "We need more ugly Americans overseas."

Twenty-five years and 120,000 ugly Americans later, we are faced with the question: "What has it all meant?"

We know that the Peace Corps expressed the tenor of the times. President Kennedy then symbolized a philosophy of optimism, a belief in the role of leadership, a sense of new beginnings, and an assertion that youth was to be valued for its vigor and freshness. Kennedy went further and challenged Americans to "Ask not . . ." He expected the youth of America to be participants in a revitalized, personalized, optimistic approach to overseas involvement.

Warren W. Wiggins, president of The New Transcentury Foundation in Washington, D.C., is one of the founders of the Peace Corps.

The assessment of the Peace Corps' achievements begins with the three original purposes enunciated early in 1961, though they were but one part of the new President's broad program.

The first purpose was to provide skilled manpower for some of the jobs that needed doing in the Third World. As a large-scale employment/placement agency, the Peace Corps has done a creditable job. However, as Peace Corps director *ad interim,* I was also painfully aware of French speakers assigned to Latin America, trained science teachers raising chickens, and medical technicians teaching English. Worse memories, of course, are about thousands of volunteers who never found *any* meaningful job in the course of their overseas tour.

Nonetheless, the Corps' record as a provider of skilled manpower remains good. Most volunteers attest to this, and the host countries continue to ask for these people. It is still true that all Peace Corps accomplishments begin with a solid job that needs doing, and by and large volunteers have done it well.

The second purpose was to enable people in the Third World to learn more about Americans. To the extent that the poor of the villages and rural areas had *any* prior perception of Americans, it came from the propaganda mills of the West and East via rumor and grapevine, and via odd bits of scattered images, nearly always by word of mouth.

And the one word that dominated these images of Americans was "rich." Of course, by any standard, it was a highly accurate word. But the people in Third World villages knew that "rich" always meant a blend of uncaring, overbearing, insolent, and untrustworthy. In their experience the rich were the hated landowners and employers, the tyrants and the oppressors. Rich people were different, strange, and their behavior was bad news.

But this new American arrived on a jitney, mammy wagon, lorry, or bush taxi. Sometimes the volunteer arrived on foot or bicycle, and half the time it was a young woman! Though these Americans told stories of the prosperous land of their birth, the actual volunteer came to *stay,* to live, to work, to wear the same clothes, to eat the local food, to speak the language. But most important, they came to help do the usual, regular work of the town: teach in a classroom, help build a feeder road, raise chickens and ducks, and try to market vegetables for a piddling amount of cash.

And it still remains a mystery to thousands of the world's poor *why* this young American, this *rich* young person, would want to be poor for a couple of years and would want to do one of the menial jobs so abundant in their towns.

But what happened was not a mystery. For two years their kids were taught; they daily saw this American at work on the road that would lead to a market, and they sang and played together, became friends, and above all, shared lives in an atmosphere of growing mutual understanding and admiration.

The third purpose of the Peace Corps was to increase American understanding of Third World peoples. There is little doubt that our national perceptions of the Third World, both positive and negative, have been greatly enhanced by this people-to-people program. Peace Corps volunteers not only grow enormously in their understanding of the developing world during their years of service, they also become more effective people. After the Peace Corps service, they have often ended up in positions where their increased knowledge is communicated to fairly large numbers. Many of them have substantial responsibility for influencing great American institutions.

But this understanding was not just an encyclopedic addition of the Third World's social, political, and economic features. What was learned also had to do with a growing appreciation that other peoples have different life goals, different sets of values, different dilemmas in their national and individual lives. Peace Corps volunteers grew in recognizing that *effective* help from one nation (usually rich) to another (usually poor) must truly start with understanding. And as this appreciation grew, the volunteer changed. His or her own value system was altered, his or her own framework for evaluating approaches to fundamental life issues was enlarged.

This learning process was quite remarkable. Young Americans went abroad, leaving at home the elaborate support systems that had enveloped them. Graduating college seniors came out of one of the most protective human environments ever devised. And the product of this protective environment was not considered especially susceptible to new kinds of learning, particularly the kind of learning that required a reassessment of one's value systems.

The Peace Corps "took" this graduating senior and with appropriate transitional training sent him or her overseas *without* any of these usual supports, and often without defined regular activity. The volunteer was then confronted with new customs, different food, and a goal: *to live as if he were poor*. He was to behave as if wealth, career enhancement, fame, or fortune were not motivating features. She was stripped of nearly all the trappings of American civilization. The volunteer was asked to stand naked in a strange land: somewhat embarrassed, insecure, misunderstood, without technology, and, above all, he or she was asked to be the quintessential American. On top of all this, it was abundantly clear to the volunteer that he or she had a real, ever-present responsibility to both his or her hosts and his or her own country to be effective on the job and in personal relationships.

As we assess the Peace Corps' accomplishments, it becomes clear that the purposes proclaimed twenty-five years ago have not essentially changed. What *have* changed are the times. Thomas L. Hughes, president of the Carnegie Endowment for International Peace, recently noted a shift in America's position on international involvement. "Traditional internationalist themes are no longer significant outlets for political idealism in the United States," he remarked. "Instead, they are the objects of derision and contempt." Hughes' perspective suggests that there is a clash between the Peace Corps' ideals of service and mutual learning on the one hand and "exhausted internationalist impulses" on the other.

Yet it remains manifestly clear that there is a continuing need for skilled people to fill jobs in the Third World. Further, the need for mutual understanding remains, whatever the shift in the overall national mood.

We also need to consider the developments in Third World thought that have coincided with the change in America's stance. The Third World is now telling us:

> Yes, we need your help, your dollars, your wheat, your technicians, your Peace Corps volunteers, but we don't like the way you insist on managing the whole show. Your programs are awfully slow, terribly bureaucratic, and you are so afraid of a little waste, a little personal "take" in public programs, and a little political influence in economic development issues. Because you are the "donor," you behave as if you have divine rights to manage our so-called "cooperative arrangements" with *your* people, *your* accounting systems, *your* formulations of the good economic development planning process. We prefer to be more in charge; we prefer to apply our value systems even if we achieve "less development" by your computerized standards. Please don't tell us how to balance minority rights or race relations with economic theory. Please don't tell us how women in our country are held back by our antiquated cultural perspective. Even when you come to our country as foreign AID managers or as Peace Corps representatives, remember your primary identification in our mind is as an invited guest. And don't think that because we understand you better, or because we have known volunteers, that indeed we will vote with you, adopt your values, or even like you better—though we might.

On reflection, those of us who were involved in the original design of the Peace Corps must now recognize how "American" it all was: the designers, the implementers, the leaders, the selectors, the trainers, and, most important, the volunteers—all American.

THE PEOPLE

The Peace Corps was one of many forces that helped Third World peoples to change and grow, so that from their viewpoint, the greater the success, the less relevance the Peace Corps has to their lives and to their countries. Moreover, the history of the Peace Corps and its accomplishments, as measured against its initial purpose, is of such high order that we can take heart in having launched a new enterprise that sustained itself. There is no reason that we should not be able to come up with other approaches, reconciling the new mood in the United States with new goals overseas.

In considering our future needs for new forms, a different retrospective evaluation of Peace Corps accomplishments is useful. Having rolled the dice in 1960 and 1961 and come up with a winner that has stood the test of decades, we now need to ask: how was it possible for the federal government to initiate a new, daring, even bold experiment that was well received by U.S. citizenry and the overseas developing peoples? What were the elements that enabled the U.S. government to successfully launch this new tool, this new approach? What were the significant factors that enabled the Peace Corps to be born, and to survive, when it was designed to be anti-bureaucratic; when many of its goals ran counter to civil service tradition; when many of its pronouncements indicated pride in its renunciation of some hallowed aspects of its parent agency, the Department of State?

The innovative birth of the Peace Corps is important to America as a retrospective case study, particularly now that America asks itself what will replace the old internationalism. It was not a freak occurrence; maybe there are more where it came from.

Central to this—and no doubt any future—creation was the belief of everyone involved that risk was an essential ingredient that was *not* to be avoided; minimized, yes, but not avoided. Significant risk was thought to be a positive feature. The Peace Corps was not *crucial* to anything; therefore it—and all associated with it—could be, and should be, at risk. It was valuable if it worked, but it sought only participants who could risk failure. The volunteers and staff risked their time and, to some extent, their reputations in something that might well have flopped. But while they were doing it, they were proud of the risk—it was a *positive* element of their service. With risk as an ingredient, the right kind of human resources were assembled to enhance the chances for success of the institutional innovation.

In some future time, a Third World social philosopher might say: "Since the Peace Corps happened here, not in America, I will write the sequel to *The Ugly American*." In the closing chapter of his book, he will seek an answer to the perennial question "What has the Peace Corps meant?"

He will rely first on an exchange recorded by Gerard T. Rice in his fine study *The Bold Experiment*:

> In El Salvador (which at the time of the Peace Corps was an independent nation-state) there took place the following encounter between a Peace Corps "official" and a Peace Corps volunteer:
>
> Official: How will you describe your Peace Corps experience?
> Volunteer: Well, I won't sell it. (Pause)
> Official: What will you say?
> Volunteer: I'll tell them what it was like. (Pause)
> Official: Such as?
> Volunteer: The best goddam experience a young man can have. Worth four years of college.

His second story will concern a couple. The wife decides that they—husband and wife—will do what *she* wants to do for the first time in their long married life. They are an older couple living in California, and they have always made life's big decisions based on the husband's career. He is a conservative corporate gentleman who sees no reason ever to "volunteer" his services. He wants to start his own business at age sixty-five, improve corporate management practices, and make more money. So his wife fills out *his* Peace Corps application as well as her own. She then engineers a time and place to force him to sign the application or face family embarrassment.

To avoid embarrassment, he signs the application with a hostile display of silent disdain, sure that he will *never* be invited by the Peace Corps. Then his wife takes his signed application and in front of the family announces to her husband: "I'm now going to put your Peace Corps application in the mailbox along with mine. Speak now, or *forever* hold your peace!" He remains glumly silent. She mails the applications, they are both invited to training: they serve successfully abroad as Peace Corps volunteers. Many years later, there is the following exchange with the husband:

> Family Member: Now that you can look backward on having been a Peace Corps volunteer in Peru, what is your advice for other people your age about joining the Peace Corps?
> Husband: Do it!
> Family Member: Knowing now what you know about the Peace Corps, its problems and inefficiencies, would you again join the Peace Corps as a volunteer?
> Husband: Damn right!

THE PEOPLE 77

The couple were my mother and father. The questions were mine.

The writer will conclude his sequel to *The Ugly American* by saying that in his travels in his country, in other industrial nations, and throughout the developing world, he has found a nearly universal affirmative evaluation of the Peace Corps. In answer to his often repeated question "Was the Peace Corps worthwhile?" in a multitude of languages with many variations, he received the same response: *"Damn right!"*

Reminiscence: The Dominican Republic

by Christopher J. Dodd

Dozens of times, in interviews and conversations with friends, I've been asked how my service in the Peace Corps affected me. I'm sometimes reluctant to answer because I know I can never fully explain how profoundly the experience shaped my life and career—the truth sounds too altruistic, even corny.

President Kennedy asked, "How many [of you] are willing to spend two years in Africa or Latin America or Asia working for the U.S. and working for freedom?" When he asked that question, it was like getting a genie out of a bottle.

The original idea hasn't changed all that much. The Peace Corps was meant to help the people of disadvantaged countries learn the skills they need for economic advancement, and at the same time spread the ideals of America and expose some Americans to the culture and outlook of Third World nations.

There is now, perhaps, a greater expectation that the volunteers will create something substantial in their host countries. There is a sense that the standard of success can be measured in the number of water projects or schools that get built.

No doubt the schools and pumping stations and bridges are welcome, but I'm sure the real value of the Peace Corps is more intangible. The communities that have accepted Peace Corps volunteers have been enriched by the vitality of young people who were inspired by the challenge of creating a new and better world. In my case, the experience was pivotal.

The Peace Corps took a nice kid from suburban Connecticut, whose

---

Christopher J. Dodd is United States senator from Connecticut.

THE PEOPLE

father was a United States senator, and sent him to a remote part of the Dominican Republic to "do something good."

I may have done some good, but mostly I learned. I learned about the complexity of a culture that is close to us geographically, but far, far away from our understanding. I learned to speak Spanish, the language of our neighbors. I learned to teach others some of the skills most of us take for granted. I learned to organize people to help themselves. Most important, I learned that one person can make a telling difference in the lives of those around him.

When I arrived in Moncion in 1966, the United States, despite the brewing turmoil of the Vietnam War, was riding the crest of its economic, military, and cultural authority in the world. It is difficult to remember how myopic we Americans were in our relations with the rest of the world.

I was told to expect hard conditions, but I was unprepared for the personal and cultural shock of arriving in a place where people had next to nothing. Nothing of any material value, at least.

I learned more than how to recognize the face of poverty: I learned about the anger and danger that poverty creates. On my first trip into the capital, Santo Domingo, the van I was riding in was pelted with fruit by youngsters yelling *"el Americano feo"* ("Ugly American"). I realized that I had never known blacks or Hispanics or even poor people. I grew up to the world.

The Dominican Republic was a hot blast of reality. Living in a tin-roofed shack without running water was not especially romantic. It was, however, an unforgettable lesson in the results of substandard public sanitation.

Dysentery is not a laughing matter, and it drives home immediately the importance of medicines we Americans take for granted. Living with the threat of diarrhea and dehydration, and watching what it does to tiny children, was a constant reminder of how the basic amenities of society protect us and bind us together. The saddening vision of children needlessly ill with diseases that can be easily treated or avoided prompted me to embark on the central project of my stay in the Dominican Republic. Shortly after settling in, I began organizing an effort to build a hospital for expectant mothers.

The response was so overwhelming that we were able to build the area's first maternity hospital in a matter of months. Almost nothing in life has satisfied me more than working on that hospital.

Our mission in the Peace Corps was not especially well defined, which may have been a fortunate thing. We were there to help, but also to exchange values and to make person-to-person contact. We were there to dispel the image, all too frequently deserved, of *"el Americano feo."*

The Peace Corps was intentionally designed to be the positive expression of the American spirit. It taught me to reject cynicism and embrace idealism. It taught me that our personal choices cannot be separated from the political decisions of nations.

Every day each one of us faces dilemmas and frequent decisions about what to do with his or her life. When we choose to help others, and when we do so as representatives of our country, we make the world a better place and we make our own lives better, too. The Peace Corps provides people with a unique opportunity to help the less fortunate of the world, and in doing so they help America. That they also gain so much for themselves is a blessing for us all.

Reminiscence: Malawi

by Paul Theroux

My record was so bad (they sent the FBI to check up on you then) that I was first rejected by the Peace Corps as a poor risk and possible troublemaker, and was only accepted as a volunteer after a great deal of explaining and arguing. The alternative was Vietnam—this was 1963, and President Kennedy was still muddling dangerously along. I was sent to Nyasaland; soon it became Malawi. And then a month before my two-year stint was over, I was "terminated"—kicked out—fined arbitrarily for three months' "unsatisfactory service," and given hell by the Peace Corps officials in Washington. Of course they believed the truth—that I had been framed in an assassination plot against Doctor Hastings Banda, the President-for-Life ("Messiah," "Conquerer," and "Great Lion" were some of his lesser titles). But the case against me looked bad. I was debriefed. There was a session at the State Department. The Peace Corps deducted my Central Africa-to-Washington air fare from my earnings, and I ended up with $200. Out I went—it was now 1965. I still had the draft to contend with.

It was a mess, and for a long while afterward I hated the Peace Corps and laughed at the posters they put up in the subway. I hated the bureaucracy, the silliness, the patronizing attitudes, the jargon, the sanctimony. I remembered all the official freeloaders who came out from Washington on so-called inspection tours, and how they tried to ingratiate themselves. "You're doing wonderful work here. . . . It's a great little country," they said; but for most of them it was merely an African safari. They hadn't the slightest idea of what we were doing, and our revenge was to take them on long, bumpy rides through the bush. "Sensational," they said. They went away. We stayed. Most Peace Corps volunteers know that feeling: the smug visitor leaving in the jeep and the

---

Paul Theroux is a travel writer and novelist.

dust flying up; and then the dust drifting slowly down and the silence taking hold.

On the subject of Vietnam, these Peace Corps bureaucrats were surprisingly hawkish and belligerent. Most of them, including the reps, believed Vietnam to be a necessary war. The volunteers were divided. This was an important issue to me, because I had joined the Peace Corps specifically to avoid being drafted, and I was dismayed to find so many Peace Corps officials advocating the bombing of Hanoi or the mining of Haiphong harbor. As a meddlesome and contentious twenty-two-year-old, I made a point of asking everyone his views on Vietnam. I believed the war was monstrous from the very beginning, and I have not changed my views. What astonishes me today is how few people remember the ridiculous things they said about Vietnam in the sixties.

But we are a country of revisionists, and the chief quality of the revisionist is a bad memory. No one now remembers how confused Kennedy's Vietnam policy was or how isolated the student movement was. I had been involved in student protests from 1959 until 1963—first against ROTC, then against nuclear testing, and then against our involvement in Vietnam. How could I have been inspired by Kennedy to join the Peace Corps? I had spent years picketing the White House—and in doing so had made myself very unpopular. When I applied to join the Peace Corps, this career as an agitator was held against me. It was all a diabolical plot, I felt. And there was the President with such style—money, power, glamor. He even had culture! I had to fight my feelings of distrust and alienation in order to join. There were many like me—anti-authoritarian, hating the dazzle and the equivocation. And when the President was shot—we learned about it halfway through a lecture in Peace Corps training (something about land tenure in the Nyasaland Protectorate)—we were all properly put in our place. More revisionism, more guilt, and I thought: get me out of here.

Nyasaland—soon to become the independent republic of Malawi—was the perfect country for a Peace Corps volunteer. It was both friendly and destitute; it was small and out-of-the-way. It had all of Africa's problems—poverty, ignorance, and disease. It had only a handful of university graduates. It had lepers, it had Mister Kurtzes, it had Horatio Alger stories by the score. It had a fascinating history that was bound up not only with early African exploration—Livingstone himself—but also one of the first African rebellions, Chilembwe's uprising. It was the setting for Laurence van der Post's *Venture to the Interior*. The people were generous and extremely willing, and as they had not been persecuted or bullied, and had been ignored rather than exploited, they were not prickly and color-conscious like the Kenyans and Zambians. There was a pleas-

THE PEOPLE

ant atmosphere of hope in the country—very little cynicism and plenty of goodwill. The prevailing feeling was that the education we were providing would lead to prosperity, honest government, and good health.

An added thrill was that many settlers were still in residence. Some of these were old-timers—"wog bashers," as they sometimes called themselves—who remembered the place when it was even wilder and more wooded. They had little contact with Africans—the place had never been a colony in the strict sense, only a backwater—and yet they resented us. Most of us hated them and mocked them, and we had a special loathing for the few volunteers who began moving in settler society. These pompous little creeps—so we said—went to gymkhanas and cocktail parties at the local club and dated the settler children when they returned from their Rhodesian boarding schools. We saw them as social climbers and traitors, and feelings were very strong on the issue. It was not uncommon for a Peace Corps volunteer in town for supplies to approach a group of settlers in a bar and say something crudely provocative, such as "The Queen's a whore" (her portrait always hung over the bottles); nearly always a fight would start. To Africans these antagonisms were very exciting.

We had arrived in the country speaking Chinyanja fairly well, and we had plunged in—made friends, taught school, run literacy programs, coached sports, and generally made ourselves useful. We were, as the English say, "at the sharp end"—on our own and exposed, and doing the toughest jobs. The Africans were eager. Afterward it occurred to me that over the years of British rule the Africans had become extremely lonely and curious—always seeing whites at a distance and wondering what the hell they were like. The Peace Corps volunteers were the first foreigners to offer them a drink. They were amazed that we were interested in them, and they repaid our interest with hospitality.

In addition to my teaching, I collaborated with a man at the Ministry of Education on writing two English textbooks to replace the miserable ones that had been standard. *Foundation Secondary English,* Book One and Book Two, is still being used in Malawi twenty years after it appeared, and I am still receiving royalties on it.

We were pestered by Israeli soldiers, who had been taken on to train our students to become single-minded cadets in a goon squad, but apart from them the school ran well. I planted trees, and we put a road through. I was proud of the place; I liked my students, I enjoyed working with my colleagues. And the country affected me as no other country has, before or since. I felt I belonged there, I was happy, I was committed. I was having a good time as well as doing something worthwhile—what could have been better?

Now and then I remembered that I was in the Peace Corps. That gave me an odd feeling. I disliked the idea that I was with an outfit, and I rejected the suggestion that I was an American official working abroad. I had never been easy with the concept of the Peace Corps as an example to spineless Marxists, and the implications of fresh-faced youngsters wooing Third Worlders away from Communism. I was well aware that American officialdom used us to deflect criticism of Vietnam and of more robust and spread-eagled diplomacy.

I wanted the Peace Corps to be something very vague and unorganized, and to a large extent it was. It did not run smoothly. The consequence was that we were left alone. I was glad to be able to call my soul my own. The Peace Corps was only proprietorial when it suited them, and generally speaking, they took an interest in volunteers only when an official visitor arrived in the country. Then we were visited or invited to parties. "You're doing wonderful work. . . . They're saying great things about you." But I didn't want attention. I didn't want help. I wanted to be self-sufficient. Anyway, most of our jobs were too simple to require any backup, and we seldom wrote reports.

We were not trusted by the embassy personnel or the State Department hacks—all those whispering middle-aged aunties who couldn't speak the language. The feeling was mutual. We felt embassy people were overpaid and ignorant, always being fussed over by spoiled African servants. We were, we felt, independent spirits—English teachers, health workers, answerable only to our students and patients. I regarded the Peace Corps as a sort of sponsoring organization and myself as an individual who had only the most tenuous link with it.

I had met many Peace Corps officials, and it seemed that the higher you went in the Peace Corps, the less you knew, the less you accomplished. The officials were ambitious and political, and it often seemed to me that they hardly knew us and had little idea of what we were doing in the country. I think I am typical in believing that the Peace Corps trained us brilliantly and then did little more except send us into the bush. It was not a bad way of running things. After all, we were supposed to use our initiative. And I think we were never more effective as volunteers than when we were convinced that we were operating alone, at the sharp end, putting our own ideas into practice, far away from the bureaucrats.

Because we were on our own, the Peace Corps officials regarded our situation as delicate. The Peace Corps did not want us to be too visible, too friendly, or too involved. "Keep a low profile" was the advice we were always offered; I did not follow it, and so eventually I got the boot. I was insulted when I was sent out of the country. It seemed like the act of an absent parent, someone I hardly knew asserting his authority over me.

THE PEOPLE

That is why I do not associate my years in the Peace Corps with group photographs, horseplay, heart-to-heart talks with the rep, images of President Kennedy showing me the way, softball games with the other volunteers, and the sort of hands-across-the-sea camaraderie that you see on the posters. It was not "the dream—the vision." It was much more interesting.

It was to me most of all the reality of being very far from home and yet feeling completely at home in this distant place. It was a slight sense of danger; the smell of woodsmoke; hearing the Beatles for the first time in a bar in the town of Limbe. In the States there was a sort of revolution in progress, but it had started partly as a result of the first Peace Corps group that had gone to Nepal. Those volunteers returning from Kathmandu had blazed the hippie trail.

In Malawi we had all of that, too—good people, wilderness, music, ganja, dusty roads, hard-working students, and a feeling of liberation. Things were on the move, it seemed. In Malawi I saw my first hyena, smoked my first hashish, witnessed my first murder, caught my first dose of gonorrhea. One of my neighbors, an African teacher, had two wives. My gardener had a gardener. Another neighbor and friend was Sir Martin Roseveare, who liked the bush. He was principal at the nearby teachers' college, and he died only last year, in Malawi, at the age of eighty-six. (He was knighted in 1946 for designing the foolproof and fraud-proof ration book in wartime Britain.) After I lived awhile in a cozy bungalow with two servants, I moved into an African township, where I lived in a semi-slum, in a two-room hut—cold water, cracks in the walls, tin roof, music blasting all day from the other huts, shrieks, dogs, chickens. It was just the thing. The experience greatly shaped my life.

When I think about those years, I don't think much about the Peace Corps, though Malawi is always on my mind. That is surely a tribute to the Peace Corps. I do not believe that Africa is a very different place for having played host to the Peace Corps—in fact, Africa is in a much worse state than it was twenty years ago. But America is quite a different place for having had so many returned Peace Corps volunteers, and when they began joining the State Department and working in the embassies, these institutions were the better for it and had a better-informed and less truculent tone. The experience was an enlightening one for most volunteers. I still do not understand who was running the show, or what they did, or even what the Peace Corps actually was, apart from an enlightened excuse for sending us to poor countries. Those countries are still poor. We were the ones who were enriched, and sometimes I think that we reminded these people—as if they needed such a thing—that they were left out. We stayed awhile, and then we left them. And yet I think I would do it again. At an uncertain time in my life, I joined. And up to a point—they gave me a lot of rope—the Peace Corps allowed me to be myself. I realized that it was much better to be neglected than manipulated, and I learned that you make your own life.

The Veterans

by Roger Landrum

The first 800 veterans of the Peace Corps returned home in 1963. Every year since, several thousand others have come back from service in Africa, Asia, and Latin America. Counting both volunteers and staff, they now number roughly 120,000. They have served in more than ninety Third World countries, under vastly diverse circumstances, having carried out a wide range of different tasks.

Yet a singular image surrounds Peace Corps veterans: the image of a common experience, which they have a mission to share with the nation. And the image holds. In the words of one returned volunteer, "The thing about the Peace Corps is that it doesn't end after two years, it lasts a lifetime." I suppose I am testimony to the truth in the image. Having returned from service in Nigeria in 1963, I have been involved with the Peace Corps—sometimes professionally, nearly always in spirit—ever since.

Addressing departing volunteers in 1961, President Kennedy said, "Come back and educate us." And earlier that year he noted that, "Our own young men and women will return better able to assume the responsibilities of American citizenship and with a greater understanding of our global responsibilities."

Hubert Humphrey, who probably did as much as John Kennedy to make the Peace Corps possible, went even further. "I foresee a new day," he stated, "when hundreds of thousands of Peace Corps alumni will be decision-makers in American industry, our leaders in government, and the teachers of our young." And President Reagan's Peace Corps director, Loret Ruppe, testified at her 1981 confirmation hearings, "Returned Peace Corps volunteers should be exploited in the best sense of the word."

Gerard T. Rice, author of *The Bold Experiment,* reports that between

---

Roger Landrum is a consultant for the Ford Foundation and president of the Returned Peace Corps Volunteers of Washington, D.C.

them, Peace Corps veterans have a "deep knowledge and understanding of a thousand different cultures, a facility to speak nearly 200 languages, and personal bonds with people in 93 countries." And former AID administrator Douglas Bennet said in 1980, "We have an asset that no other country has. Instead of a bunch of retired colonial officers or international businessmen who come home to settle, we've got almost 100,000 people who've been through the Peace Corps experience and who can share their experience with others."

Clearly, Peace Corps veterans are viewed by others as a choice minority. They bring back to this country an intense, grass-roots experience on the frontiers of global development. They are selected for the independence of spirit that initially impelled them beyond conventional careers and wisdom into the Peace Corps. Their separate experiences overseas seem to have hammered and refined an attachment to common Peace Corps ideals.

Peace Corps veterans themselves feel a particular kind of bonding. Former Senator Paul Tsongas, among the most famous of the veterans, cites the Peace Corps as "the formative experience of my life. If I have a meeting with someone and I find he's a former Peace Corps volunteer, there's an instant sort of attachment."

Tsongas has further endeared himself to his fellow veterans by saying, "You can always be a senator, I suppose, by title, but in terms of what made you what you are emotionally and psychologically, clearly the Peace Corps was that experience."

Many former volunteers inevitably ask themselves how seriously to take all this rhetoric. The dictionary defines a corps as a "body of persons acting together or associated under common direction." Perhaps they achieved the cohesion of a corps overseas, despite the fact that they did not serve elbow to elbow, but do they remain in any sense a "corps" back home? What impact are they having on American institutions? Do they remain associated in any organized fashion?

The first organized effort to rally former volunteers came in March 1965. Only 3,000 had returned by this date, but 1,000 came to a conference convened in Washington by Vice President Humphrey at the request of President Lyndon Johnson. Reporting in *The New Yorker,* Richard Rovere called this conference "the most informal as well as the liveliest gathering ever to have taken place in that ungainly pile of concrete [the State Department] in the heart of Foggy Bottom."

The idea was to bring former volunteers together with 250 leaders of American institutions, and to explore the roles that the veterans might play in education, business and labor, community programs, and government. What resulted, however, was more a collision than a conference. Many of the former volunteers reported finding American institutions distressingly rigid and called for sweeping changes, but they had few specific suggestions to offer and detested being called "special people." On the contrary, many declared, they had just had the most humbling experience of their lives.

Bill Moyers chided the former volunteers for their reticence about being called "special." He had helped organize the Peace Corps and was now special assistant to the President. "You are special," Moyers said, "and when you come back from abroad, if you don't think yourself special, you will simply disappear into the bog of affluent living."

The institutional leaders seemed eager to embrace the virtues and talents of the veterans as a tonic for American society, but they were surprised by what seemed to be the volunteers' uncertainty, and even timidity, about how to proceed. Many urged the former volunteers to get proper credentials to make the reforms they desired. Secretary of State Dean Rusk told the veterans, "I can assure you, if you apply for the Foreign Service, that your experience in the Peace Corps will be a plus with respect to others who may be applying for that Service." Yet a report prepared for the conference revealed that 865 former volunteers had already applied for the Foreign Service. Of the 579 who actually took the exam, 110 passed the written exam, 14 passed the oral exam, and only 3 had been appointed.

Chief Justice Earl Warren, Vice President Humphrey, Secretary of State Rusk, and Defense Secretary Robert McNamara all sang the praises of the Peace Corps at the conference. They urged former volunteers to give to America what they had contributed overseas. But even as they spoke, former volunteers were circulating petitions in support of stronger civil rights legislation, action against the Republic of South Africa, and opposition to American policy in Vietnam. State Department guards were given an order to enforce a building regulation against distribution of "outside literature." The Vice President had said: "If you think things are not as they ought to be, right in this State Department, tell us," and higher officials waived the regulation in favor of the right of free speech.

Later, a special session was called to consider proposals by some veterans to form alumni organizations locally and nationally. The large majority opposed the formation of a national organization, as well as any use by returned volunteers of the Peace Corps name. "I didn't join the Peace Corps to have forty-five or twenty-two or any number of people express my views," said one veteran. "If I want to express them, I'd just as soon express them myself." Another veteran echoed this anti-organizational sentiment with the words, "Lord, not another American Legion!"

The worst fears expressed at the conference about abuse of the views of veterans and the name of the Peace Corps were soon realized. A national organization was formed under the name Committee of Returned Volunteers. A radical wing within the group soon drove out all moderating and dissenting voices, moving the organization from support for civil rights and opposition to the war in Vietnam to actions and positions to the left of Mao Tse-tung. At one point, members attempted to blockade the entrances to Peace Corps headquarters. And they threw red paint on the Chinese embassy to protest revisionist tendencies.

The Committee of Returned Volunteers soon burned itself out. It would be many years before efforts were again made to establish a national organization of Peace Corps veterans.

In preparation for the 1965 conference, a questionnaire had been mailed to the 3,000 former volunteers, and, astonishingly, 2,300 were returned. The results showed that more than half were back in school. Forty-one percent were employed, with 14 percent working in government, 14 percent in teaching, and the rest distributed in a wide variety of jobs. Very few were unemployed.

Eighty-eight percent reported they had decided upon lifetime careers, most of them acknowledging that they had changed direction during Peace Corps service. According to the survey, many were planning careers in various types of international work, but only six wanted to enter politics.

The survey also disclosed that many volunteers were troubled by an indifference they perceived in America's attitude toward the Third World, and by the problems of communicating the subtle meanings of the Peace Corps experience to others. Many complained about a lack of sufficient challenge in their present jobs or education.

The pattern of former volunteers has changed dramatically since those days. Recent State Department figures show that at least 10 percent of each new class of Foreign Service officers are former volunteers. A thousand or more are currently employed by the State Department and the Agency for International Development, in Washington and in embassies around the world. By 1980, 15 percent of nearly 100,000 Peace Corps veterans had taken positions with government organizations at home or abroad. At AID, 12.5 percent of its staff were returned volunteers. In Costa Rica, 53 percent of the AID mission were Peace Corps veterans, with 40 percent in Cameroon and 28 percent in Jamaica. Not one of the fifty-five AID country missions was without a former volunteer. Douglas Bennet, then AID administrator, said, "The Peace Corps has changed the face of AID substantially."

By 1985, roughly 540 of AID's 4,000 professional staffers were Peace

THE PEOPLE

Corps veterans. They constituted 40 percent of AID's intern classes and 25 percent of its newest professional staff members.

To take another case, by 1985, half of the Peace Corps' own staff were veterans. For many years they have routinely been appointed directors of country programs, though none has ever been named Peace Corps director. In fact, of the twelve senior positions at the agency, only one is currently filled by a former volunteer.

It is also estimated that over 100 former volunteers currently work on congressional staffs. Two rose all the way to the top: Paul Tsongas, who recently retired from the Senate but remains a leading figure in the Democratic Party, and Christopher Dodd, a Connecticut Democrat who served in the Dominican Republic and has become one of the Senate's experts on Central and South America. Four former volunteers have been elected to the House of Representatives: James Courter of New Jersey (Venezuela), Thomas Petri of Wisconsin (Somalia), Paul Henry of Michigan (Liberia and Ethiopia), and Tony Hall of Ohio (Thailand).

Peace Corps veterans have had enormous impact on private voluntary organizations working with Third World nations. They constitute 50 percent of the staff of the Experiment in International Living, 40 percent of CARE's staff, 25 percent of Catholic Relief Services' staff, 30 percent of staff at Volunteers in Technical Assistance, and 75 percent of staff at International Voluntary Service.

Leonard Robinson, who was among the 5 percent of black volunteers during the 1960s, having worked in poultry-raising in India, was appointed head of the African Development Foundation in 1984. Timothy Carroll, a former Nigeria volunteer, heads Eye Care, Inc. (a private organization that raises money for rural eye services in Haiti). Thomas Scanlon is president of Benchmarks, Inc., a highly successful international development consulting firm. Many others have started innovative private programs and services.

Even at the World Bank, layered with bureaucratic red tape and careful not to hire too many Americans, some 5 percent of the professional staff are Peace Corps veterans. Walter Price, a former Morocco volunteer and an agricultural consultant to the World Bank said, "If I had to choose between the Peace Corps experience and graduate school preparation for a career in international development, I would definitely choose the Peace Corps. I could never have conducted an appraisal of a multimillion-dollar project for the World Bank had I not known how it would affect the grass-roots level." And in the business world, many multinational corporations employ former volunteers on their staffs. It seems likely that these veterans will play a significant role in expanding trade between American businesses and Third World countries into the year 2000 and beyond.

Peace Corps veterans are opening up intellectual horizons as well. Former Malawi volunteer Paul Theroux has written classic travel accounts and, with *The Mosquito Coast,* has become a major American novelist. John Coyne and Richard Lipez, who both served in Ethiopia, are successful novelists. Charles Murray's *Losing Ground* has been called the publishing event of 1985 for the conservative movement. *Impulse to Revolution,* an account of cycles of revolution in South and Central America, was written by former Peru volunteer Jeffrey Barrett. Galen Hall, who served in Malawi, has written *A Small Business Agenda: Trends in a Global Economy.* Several scholarly works have been published by former volunteers, including Kenneth Wylie's *The Political Kingdoms of the Temne.* Large numbers of former volunteers—an estimated 27 percent—have also gone into teaching in American schools and universities. To give a few examples, University of Michigan anthropologist Susan Schaefer Davis has become a leading authority on Moroccan culture. Thomas Gouttiere directs the Center for Afghanistan Studies at the University of Nebraska. One of the country's leading scholars of African art, Yale's Robert Farris Thompson, calls the Peace Corps "a proto-fellowship in African studies." Donna Shalala, who served in Iran, is president of Hunter College; Alan Guskin, who served in Thailand, is president of Antioch University.

There are other signs of impact. A 1979 survey indicated that 75 percent of former volunteers discuss their overseas experiences with community, social, and religious organizations; 16 percent have taught formal classes on the developing nations; and some 66 percent of former volunteers maintain direct contact with their host communities overseas, either by correspondence or by visits.

Gerard Rice argues plausibly that the third goal of the Peace Corps—education at home—has been realized entirely through informal means. No division of the Peace Corps headquarters or senior agency official has ever been given responsibility for implementing this goal. No significant share of the agency budget has ever been devoted to it. There has never really been a plan for carrying it out. What "home education" there has been has come about through the initiative of returned volunteers.

During the late 1970s, the veterans' antipathy to forming alumni organizations gradually dissipated. Local organizations of former volunteers have emerged in at least twenty-five states and cities. Various nongeographical, wild-card groups have also been created.

Paradoxically, this was not a good period for the Peace Corps. Both the organization and its ideals had faded from view during the Nixon

Presidency. Perhaps the obscurity generated a need among Peace Corps veterans to reaffirm their collective sense of identity. Perhaps the fierce individualism abated as large numbers of former volunteers approached middle age. June Gertig, who is a partner in a large Washington law firm, recently said, "I've become middle-aged and well-off, and I want to do something again for the values I worked for in the Peace Corps." She proceeded to become membership chairman of the Returned Peace Corps Volunteers of Washington, D.C.

Many of the local alumni organizations started as social gatherings. The larger, more dynamic groups—in San Francisco, Boston, Atlanta, the Washington area, New York City, and Madison, Wisconsin—prospered with effective fund-raising and educational and social activities. As membership grew and a more formal structure developed, conflicts were resolved between political activists and others who did not want to be pushed into the support of a single political position. Generally, the resolution has been a policy acceptable to both sides: political advocacy is carried out by subgroups under separate names, though often with financial support from the main organization.

In 1979, a core group of former volunteers invited veterans from around the country to attend a conference on the Third World. Over 150 came. They met in a special session and agreed in principle to form a national organization to carry out the "third goal." And in 1981, 46 former volunteers signed a charter establishing a National Council of Returned Peace Corps Volunteers. It operates through a board of 21 members elected by the national membership, and has grown steadily to 1,400 members in early 1986.

Other organizations of Peace Corps veterans include Friends of Togo, Peace Corps Alumni Foundation for Philippine Development, Friends of Ethiopia, Ploughshares (Returned Volunteers Working for Peace), and the Peace Corps Institute. The latter is not a membership organization, but has a board composed primarily of former Peace Corps staff and is headed by William Josephson, a founder of the Corps who was known as its "legal sword." The network of organizations boasts some impressive achievements.

In 1982, attorney Thomas McGrew, a member of the Returned Volunteers organization of Washington, D.C., launched a Committee on the Peace Corps Budget. At that time, the agency was one of the few in the federal government with a budget that had declined in real dollars through the Nixon, Ford, and Carter administrations. During this period, the number of volunteers in service overseas had fallen from a peak of 15,000 in 1966 to less than 5,000 in 1981. If the Peace Corps itself could not lobby for a budget outside White House guidelines, the McGrew Committee could. It identified the level of funding the Peace Corps really needed to be more effective and located allies among congressional staffers (many of them former volunteers). It relayed timely information to the National Council and local groups so that senators and congressmen could be approached and pushed the Peace Corps hearings to the forefront of the congressional appropriations process.

This got results. For the first time in over a decade, Congress in 1983 and 1984 increased the Peace Corps budget beyond White House requests, enabling the agency to reverse its decline. In 1985, the line was held against substantial cuts proposed by the White House.

Feeding on this initial success, the Washington group established a Task Force on Peace Corps Recommendations. Its aim was to identify major policy reforms that could pass Congress and contribute to the Peace Corps' impact. Five consensus reforms were proposed in a widely circulated publication entitled *The Peace Corps in 1985: Meeting the Challenge*. The publication called for (1) an increase in volunteers in service to 10,000, with stronger representation in South America and Asia; (2) removal of political patronage considerations in the hiring of Peace Corps staff, particularly country directors; (3) establishment of a new advisory council of former volunteers; (4) elevation of the third goal to a central mission of the agency with generous funding; and (5) at the end of Loret Ruppe's tenure, appointment of a former volunteer as director.

Senators Cranston, Kassebaum, Lugar, and Dodd skillfully turned the second and third proposed reforms into bills and orchestrated Senate passage. Congressman Jim Leach, who had originated the first 10,000 volunteer goal, got that bill through the House. All three reforms were then passed by both houses and signed into law by President Reagan in 1985.

Meanwhile, local organizations of former volunteers have established a record of fund-raising for selected overseas development programs. Peace Corps Partnership Programs—small-scale village projects identified by volunteers currently in service—have been financed by veterans' groups throughout the United States. Several groups have raised substantial sums for Oxfam America and the Ashoka Society.

Many of the groups have sponsored education activities on Third World topics. A group in Washington conducts bimonthly issue forums. In 1985, the National Council received grants from AID and the Carnegie Corporation totalling $90,000 to plan and implement a national development education program, using Peace Corps veterans. A group in New York City—with support from Mayor Koch and the Board of Education—is sponsoring an essay contest on global development in sixteen high schools. The winners will spend three weeks living with Peace Corps volunteers in Africa and Latin America.

The dilemma currently faced by former volunteers is not only whether some kind of unified national association should be formed, but to what purpose. The National Council and the existing local organizations are only loosely affiliated at this point. They have no paid staff to work on the development of common purposes and programs, or even to keep in touch with each other. They lack a collective agenda. They do not have the means of reaching 120,000 former volunteers and staff—or even as many as can be found—in the absence of good records. In fact, there is not yet a clear commitment on the part of those who have been active in local associations, much less on the part of the many who have not, to shape a wider, unified national association that can reach agreement on strategies and goals. Yet the rapid development in the past few years of an organizational network suggests that such a commitment may be growing nearer.

Through the local organizations, Peace Corps veterans have also demonstrated a willingness to support the kinds of development programs—small-scale, people-to-people projects—on which they themselves worked in the Third World. So far their efforts have been on an *ad hoc* basis, distant from the kind of cohesive undertaking that can mobilize enough funds and energy to have a strong impact on development policy. What seems more imminent is the mobilization of a larger number of Peace Corps veterans to support carefully selected development projects, especially for the countries in which they served. But even this goal requires the establishment of regular communication channels.

Even further from the current agenda of active veterans are larger questions of American foreign policy. Despite their identity as veterans of a *Peace* Corps, former volunteers have not much considered the traditional issues of "peace." Apart from scattered efforts, active veterans have not been inclined to take unified positions on trouble spots in the Third World, on East-West relations, or on disarmament.

Perhaps the fact that volunteers have been drawn from a wide national spectrum precludes their taking collective positions on major foreign policy issues. These are highly divisive matters within that spectrum, and it is no surprise that Peace Corps veterans do not necessarily agree on them. But it is also possible that consensus, or near-consensus, can be reached on a few, carefully selected issues to which Peace Corps veterans have had a virtually unique grass-roots exposure. It is worth noting, however, that even if such consensus is achieved, organizational means will still be needed to bring it to the attention of Congress and the American people.

What is harder to understand than the silence on foreign policy questions is why Peace Corps veterans have said so little in the domestic debate over national service, precisely the kind of issue that touches them.

On the West Coast, for example, Peace Corps veteran Robert Burkhardt directs the San Francisco Conservation Corps. This kind of program—small domestic service corps engaged in community projects—is taking shape in some thirty-five states and localities. It seems to be a growing, and promising, movement. Yet former Peace Corps volunteers have done precious little to build support for it.

One thing by now is clear: if the Peace Corps veterans do not build that kind of support themselves, the Peace Corps headquarters will not do it for them. The Peace Corps, as a federal agency, has obviously decided to keep the organizations of veterans at arm's length. Whatever assistance returned volunteers can give—whether in promoting the Peace Corps' institutional interests or in advancing the "third goal" of educating Americans—it is accompanied by a risk to the agency in making common cause with associations whose purposes and activities it cannot control. The Peace Corps director is, after all, politically appointed and responsible to the President. Similarly, the returned volunteers have made clear an aversion to limiting their freedom for the sake of formal association with the Peace Corps. The consequence is that veterans—beyond some informal help from headquarters—are on their own in developing their organizations and purposes.

Whatever the obstacles, a movement toward some form of collective identification among the veterans has been established, and some 8,000 of them are involved. The form it will take, and its goals and programs, are now being hammered out in debates among groups of Peace Corps veterans all over the country. Together, they represent an enormous potential for translating Peace Corps ideals into a positive force, and they are clearly gathering momentum.

THE JOB

As a Development Agency

by M. Peter McPherson

In 1963, when the blush of early Peace Corps success had subsided a little and the volunteers had begun returning to the United States, several returnees suggested to Peace Corps Director Sargent Shriver that he tone down the ballyhoo and describe a little more realistically what a Peace Corps volunteer could expect to accomplish in two short years.

Shriver and his staff came up with a new series of recruitment ads stressing that change in developing countries is often painfully slow. One ad displayed a single inch of a ruler with the caption, "This is how the Peace Corps measures progress." Another advertised sixteen-hour workdays and hordes of mosquitoes. One poster I remember particularly well showed two identical pictures of a squalid village, side by side. The caption on the left was "Before the Peace Corps"; on the right, "After the Peace Corps." Prospective volunteers were warned that the world couldn't be changed overnight.

It hasn't been overnight, but twenty-five years. The question today is whether the development picture has changed for the better and, if so, how the Peace Corps has contributed to that change.

From the start, it is essential to acknowledge that the Corps has two other purposes besides development: to help promote a better understanding of Americans on the part of the peoples served and to help increase America's knowledge of other cultures.

The explicit, essential tasks Peace Corps volunteers undertake—the development tasks—constitute the vehicle through which the second and third goals are realized. Like Ben Franklin's vision of the thirteen colonies in revolt, the Peace Corps' three goals must stand together—or each will assuredly fall separately.

M. Peter McPherson is administrator of the Agency for International Development in Washington, D.C.

Nonetheless, it is my belief that the Peace Corps has never reached its full potential as a development institution. Each Peace Corps volunteer represents an investment of some $20,000 per year on the part of the American public in the developing world. Though these costs are small when compared with those of other development institutions, they still are real. They are generally justified to the Congress in terms of the impact that the volunteers make in the developing countries. Yet I do not believe the Peace Corps has ever fully committed itself to development as its central, driving mission. The time to do so is now.

The Peace Corps is an important development institution, one of the few that operate at the level where the world's neediest live. It has a record in which it can take pride. And it concerns me when some suggest that its development mission is solely symbolic, or that the Peace Corps can be justified merely on the basis of its role in cross-cultural understanding.

Some point out that it is neither possible nor desirable to describe the Peace Corps' development impact in measurable terms. The journalist Eric Sevareid, in the early years, expected "some spot benefits in a few isolated places," but maintained that "the Peace Corps had little to do with the fundamental investments and reforms on which long-term development of countries depend." Others have charged that the Peace Corps has had virtually no impact on development at all. Recently, one critic said the Peace Corps "survives now largely because its hosts are still too polite to suggest that we may be wasting our energy and their patience." I strongly disagree. I feel that the Peace Corps can be one of the most effective American organizations operating in the Third World.

As a former Peace Corps volunteer in Peru, writing from the vantage point of a quarter-century of experience with the agency, and from my current perspective as administrator of the Agency for International Development, I am convinced that the Peace Corps has contributed to development both directly and indirectly, both concretely and conceptually. I also believe that it can do much more in the years ahead.

The task of measuring the Peace Corps' direct developmental impact is difficult. The very nature of the Peace Corps militates against effective and sustained measurement of progress—two-year volunteer tours, in-country assignments negotiated yearly with host governments, work with institutions that are disorganized, and, most important, the intangibility of the Peace Corps' service to the disenfranchised and the disengaged.

The transfer of skills and knowledge is extraordinarily difficult to quantify. Success is measured by most volunteers at a personal level—the sudden recognition in the eyes of a school child, the pride of a community in its self-built schoolhouse, or the sense of competence of workers who have formed their own cooperative.

The Peace Corps operates at the micro level of development, in one-to-one relationships with individuals or local villages. It would be virtually impossible—and certainly uneconomical—even to attempt to track the impact that an individual volunteer or group of volunteers makes on a country's development. How can one quantify the short-term (let alone long-term) effects on three farmers learning how to raise more crops on their land? Or the development consequence of twelve mothers who understand that they must boil water before giving it to their babies to drink? Or the cost-benefit impact of immunizing twenty children? Yet these tasks are at the very heart of development and, indeed, echo priorities AID has set for itself on a wider scale. Although development is more than simply the sum of these incremental changes, these changes are necessary if development is to take place at all.

The Peace Corps reminds us that peace and development—like war and destruction—are waged in the trenches, even if planned in the staff rooms. One of the great deficiencies of both international and national development efforts, in fact, is that there are so few people with skills and commitment who are willing to carry on the struggle at the village level, where most volunteers are stationed.

Still, there have been some attempts to quantify the impact of the volunteers. In 1966, the Social Research Institute of the University of Hawaii found evidence of a strong positive impact of volunteers on the educational system of the Philippines. A sophisticated statistical analysis by Cornell University concluded that communities in Peru with volunteers made more progress than communities without. Recently, an evaluation of Peace Corps projects to which AID had contributed small cash sums revealed that the projects had met their development objectives in nine out of ten cases.

What is lacking, to the best of my knowledge, are long-term, longitudinal looks at what Peace Corps volunteers did and what effect they have had over the span of years. The ads were right: you cannot change the world overnight. But it is helpful to know, and the Peace Corps needs to determine, whether the cumulative changes made over five or ten or fifteen years have yielded any substantial results at all. Such knowledge will be even more essential in the years ahead, as competition increases for scarce federal budget dollars.

Unfortunately, the institutional obstacles to development may be difficult to resolve. There are several reasons for this.

First, the Peace Corps since its inception has focused on the recruitment, training, and placement of volunteers—a placement bureau rather than a mission-driven agency. Coupled with that has been the enormous logistical task of supporting thousands of volunteers in every part of the world. Measurement has focused on the movement of people—numbers sent out, brought back, trained, debriefed, and so on. These numbers tell us nothing about the achievement of the first goal—helping Third World people to develop their countries.

Second, the Peace Corps has functioned without a vital component: institutional memory. With volunteers leaving after two years, and staff members required to go after five years at most, there is no real mechanism for it. Reinventing the wheel becomes not a popular pastime but a method of operation. And without institutional memory, there is no incentive for evaluation and documentation of achievements over the long term. The early emphasis on evaluation clearly subsided as the volunteer turnover and the "five-year rule" on staff tenure began to take effect.

But perhaps most important, development simply is not at the center of the Peace Corps' agenda. My experience with government management tells me that once the leadership and the institution really adopt an agenda, much can be accomplished, and the required decisions become clear. Accordingly, I feel that if the Peace Corps accepts its development agenda as the primary, driving mission of the organization, certain essential and critical changes in the way it has been been conducting its business over the past twenty-five years will become necessary and, indeed, will be put into place. For example:

- The Peace Corps should change its present method of programming volunteers. Present policies call for volunteer assignments to be based strictly on host country requests. This policy is too reactive, in that it does not allow enough room for creative programming. It results in volunteers being assigned to such a diversity of program sectors that it makes it difficult even to describe the overall program—much less measure its impact.

- The Peace Corps should, in my opinion, consult host countries and adopt a few principal program sectors (such as forestry, child survival, agricultural development, and education), and focus volunteer efforts in these areas. Focused efforts would improve programming, make technical training as well as technical support to volunteers more effective, and help the Peace Corps compete more effectively for federal dollars.

- The current Peace Corps director, Loret Ruppe, has made specific commitments to action on two major development issues: the food problems of Africa and the education needs of Central America. By adopting these problems as Peace Corps goals over the next ten years, Ruppe is pioneering the kind of focused programming that will make

THE JOB

the Peace Corps a more vital development institution in the years ahead.

- The Peace Corps also needs to recruit as overseas staff individuals who are more experienced and better trained in development work. Congress recently prohibited the application of political criteria in the selection of "in-country" staff for the Peace Corps. This is as it should be. The Peace Corps must go beyond this, however, and recruit individuals with extensive experience—hopefully including Peace Corps experience—in development assistance.
- The five-year rule should be reexamined and possibly relaxed, even beyond the recent changes made by Congress. This requirement, which prohibits any staff person from working continuously with the agency for more than five years, has kept the Peace Corps dynamic, energetic, and free of bureaucratic inertia. At the same time, many highly qualified Peace Corps staff members are forced to leave when they are most able to make their best contribution.
- Finally, more focused programming and a stronger commitment by the Peace Corps to its development role will mean that measuring direct impact on developing countries will be more feasible in the future. A focusing of efforts will mean that more is done for poor people, and what better reason could there be to follow that path?

But even in urging change in the Peace Corps' orientation, I should add that I believe the agency is already moving in the right direction. The trend in recent years has been to move toward development as the central focus of the Peace Corps.

It is also true that the Peace Corps has had at least one sure focus almost from the beginning, that of education. In the early days of the Peace Corps, the host countries wanted teachers. Happily, it was precisely teachers—or generalists who could be trained as teachers—who tended to volunteer.

Yet, in spite of its successes, the Peace Corps' role in education has always been controversial. In the early days, critics charged that it was inappropriate to emphasize formal education for young people in developing countries who were for the most part destined to return to subsistence farming. Development economists did not regard education as a form of capital investment.

Fortunately, Sargent Shriver, the first director, was a staunch supporter of a strong Peace Corps role in education. A former chairman of the Chicago Board of Education, he was convinced, whatever the experts maintained, that basic education was crucial for a country's long-term development. And in the long term, development economists and other sages came around to Shriver's view.

The impact of Peace Corps teachers over the past twenty-five years has been astounding. As of 1981, Peace Corps teachers had taught nearly five million students and could take credit for a long list of accomplishments.

In recent years, the emphasis has shifted from expanding school availability and enrollment to improving the quality of education. Fewer Peace Corps volunteers are now being placed as teachers, and more are being asked to develop curricula, write texts, and train teachers. Nevertheless, a need for teachers still exists. In Sierra Leone, for example, colleges still produce only twenty graduates a year in science and math—not nearly enough to fill teacher needs in those important fields.

The same story, year after year, in country after country, is not the sort of thing that attracts the attention of the Congress or the media. It is, however, a story of great importance, when one considers the implications of the numbers and the cumulative effect of the Peace Corps in classrooms throughout the developing world.

One of the most rewarding developments during my tenure as administrator of AID has been the growing cooperation between my agency and the Peace Corps. We have come a long way from the constant bickering that characterized our relationship during the early 1960s.

Much of this animosity, as reported by people familiar with both sides, certainly stemmed from a basic mistrust, or perhaps a misunderstanding, of each other's policies and purposes. At its creation, the Peace Corps was seen as a refutation of traditional foreign aid programs.

In 1960, presidential candidate John Kennedy decried the "lack of compassion" of then-current foreign aid administrators and urged that "Our aid now should be concentrated not on large-scale monuments to American engineering, but on the village and the farm." It is not surprising that AID wanted little to do with the Peace Corps, this neophyte competitor whose very existence seemed to be a reflection of AID's limitations.

Many AID officials of that generation harbored resentment of the Peace Corps' insistence upon independence and its refusal to be taken under AID's bureaucratic wing. Many were skeptical of the ability of the young volunteers, whose role was often overglamorized, to make any meaningful contribution to foreign assistance.

On the other side, the Peace Corps took pains to set itself apart from AID. The Peace Corps set policies to keep the volunteers from being identified with AID money and decreed that "Separateness from other overseas operations of the U.S. is important to achieving the desired image."

Since those days, our agencies have grown closer together in approach and attitudes. We are both mandated by Congress to assist in the end goal of meeting basic human needs. This common goal underpins complementary programs and policies, and provides a common ground for sharing ideas and strategies. Also on the staff of AID there are now five hundred former Peace Corps volunteers, myself included, and their presence clearly promotes mutual understanding.

Over the past five years, we have made a special effort to build upon cooperation between AID and the Peace Corps to achieve a better foreign assistance program. The Peace Corps director and I have attempted to coordinate our development strategies wherever possible, so that the unique resources and strengths of each agency are used to their fullest. Each agency helps the other and gains in the process. And the people we assist reap the benefit.

For AID, cooperation has meant direct access to the communities and people most in need of assistance, important feedback from volunteers on how development projects function in the field, and skilled volunteer assistance with critical programs in fifty-six countries around the globe. For the Peace Corps, cooperation has meant that volunteers and their coworkers in the host countries can benefit from the technical and financial support that AID can provide. The positive results are unmistakable. Cooperation between our two agencies has meant vital joint endeavors, both at headquarters and in the field.

With AID support, the Peace Corps has more than doubled the number of specially trained volunteers working in forestry programs. Our joint child survival programs have trained hundreds of volunteers and local health workers in all regions of the world in oral rehydration therapy to reduce illness and death from diarrhea, and in techniques to assist local governments in improving primary health care for young children. The Small Projects Assistance program, one of our most successful cooperative enterprises, provides modest grants for development projects to communities where volunteers are stationed. The program has overwhelming support from both AID and the Peace Corps because it reaches the really needy in communities that have access to no other resources.

Our efforts have helped the poor of these countries to enjoy a better quality of life by bringing about improvements in food production, health, education, housing, energy, and income. In example after example, AID and the Peace Corps reinforce each other by reaching toward shared development goals. Here are only a few of them:

• We are helping to raise incomes and improve nutrition among the rural population of Cameroon by developing inland fisheries. The Peace Corps has been involved in this effort since 1969; AID assistance in 1980 expanded the project in the northwestern and western provinces.

- AID and the Peace Corps have been working together on a large project to bring safe drinking water to rural communities in Malawi. AID has financed the construction of gravity-fed piped water systems. Peace Corps volunteers organized community residents to help build the systems and taught them how to maintain and protect them. More than thirty-five systems have been constructed, providing water to 800,000 people.
- In Senegal, we have designed a project to save energy by promoting improved, fuel-efficient cookstoves in both rural and urban areas, so that fewer trees will be cut down. AID has provided salaries, equipment, and materials over the four-year life of the project. Six Peace Corps volunteers coordinate Senegalese teams that build stoves (largely from scrap materials) which save 35 to 50 percent of scarce wood and charcoal resources.
- Our two agencies have been cooperating to help small-scale farmers in Paraguay. Approximately thirty-five volunteers complement the efforts of AID and the Paraguayan government by teaching improved production techniques and promoting self-sufficiency among farm families through crop diversification, beekeeping, and other income-generating activities.

One of the most significant contributions of the Peace Corps to development has been its impact, both through its institutional experience and its cadre of former volunteers, on the way in which the United States perceives and practices development in the Third World.

The Peace Corps' approach has remained consistent for twenty-five years—local, low-cost solutions to local problems, direct assistance to the neediest, and direct service in the field. That methodology, through example, has dramatically affected the way in which development has been re-evaluated and development strategy reformulated. It has come to be recognized as having elements of success lacking in earlier development philosophies.

As the Peace Corps moves into its second twenty-five years, I believe it is time for the organization to recognize that it has become an important development agency and that it must focus more attention on achieving specific development objectives. Clearly, the Peace Corps achieves its impact working with and through people. But while mutual understanding is important, it is more a means than an end.

The seriousness of the problems of poverty and underdevelopment demands that volunteers be focused on contributing, in some measurable way, to improving the lives of the people with whom they are working. In many cases, this can best be achieved through an institutional commitment by the Peace Corps to support specific programs and objectives on a multiyear basis.

I believe that the Peace Corps' first twenty-five years have been illustrious ones. And most important, they have provided the experience that will make possible an even greater direct impact on the problems of the poor in the years ahead.

The Experience: Africa

by C. Payne Lucas and Kevin Lowther

In his celebrated Arusha declaration of 1967, Tanzania's president Julius Nyerere articulated a doctrine of rigorous national self-reliance that was to guide the nation's future development. Tanzania would seek foreign assistance, he said, but no more than was absolutely required to advance toward an authentic African socialism. Education, too, was to be directed to this need. It was to foster national identity and encourage mass participation in national development.

If such was the case, Nyerere was asked, how does the role of the Peace Corps fit in with this ideal? By then, more than two hundred Peace Corps volunteers were serving in Tanzania, most of them teaching in the high schools. Nyerere, himself a teacher, appreciated their work. He often remarked that more Peace Corps volunteers than Chinese worked in Tanzania—though China was a Third World brother, a fellow socialist state, and was building an important railroad line into the heart of the country. How does the Peace Corps fit, he was asked, into Tanzania's ideal of self-reliance?

"It doesn't fit in anywhere at all," he replied. "We know our limitations. . . . I will continue recruiting teachers. . . . I can't close the schools in order to prove that we are self-reliant. The schools will have to go on. And I will teach teachers with borrowed teachers, and go on like that.

"But the emphasis all the time is on self-reliance. This is an indication of our limitations. . . . Borrowing must all the time be what it is: not the answer to our problems but a result of our problems."

The esteem in which Nyerere held the Peace Corps teachers was based more on their personal than on their professional qualities. "They come to Tanzania," he once told the local press, "and if you tell them to go

---

C. Payne Lucas is executive director of Africare. Kevin Lowther is Africare's regional development officer for Southern Africa.

THE JOB

anywhere, they go. They do not complain. If you tell them to go to Kogoma, they go; or to Masailand, they go. . . . The volunteers have a spirit I would like to see more of in Tanzania's teachers."

Nyerere recognized that the Peace Corps volunteers, in spreading their democratic values, had infected some Tanzanian students with an impatience toward his own one-party state. Having survived one coup attempt, he was not anxious for more. But he recognized that Peace Corps volunteers were different from the Englishmen who had ruled the country during the colonial era, and he acknowledged that the Peace Corps had an important—albeit transitional—role to play in Tanzania's development.

Indeed, many Africans were suspicious when the Peace Corps arrived. They liked these Americans, who seemed so earnest and sincere, but they wondered why these foreigners, most of them white, tried to speak their languages and live in villages in the bush. Were they spies? But they seemed too naive, too inexperienced to be spies.

They were certainly different from the old colonial administrators. Not only were they learning to communicate in Swahili and Mende and Twi, but they accepted African hospitality instinctively and readily passed over the cultural threshold that few of the old colonials had been willing to cross. On a continent where the spirit of reciprocity anchors human relations, they were prepared to receive as well as to give. Only gradually were the doubts of Africans dissipated and the volunteers accepted, for the service they were willing to perform and for what they actually were.

We first arrived in Africa with the Peace Corps in the early 1960s. Lucas directed volunteer programs in Togo and Niger for several years, then became African regional director. Lowther served as a volunteer teacher in Sierra Leone and, later, in staff positions at Peace Corps headquarters in Washington. We left the Peace Corps in 1971 to found Africare, a private development organization, and have since continued our work in Africa.

As we saw it, the Peace Corps experience in Africa contrasted sharply with that in Asia, Latin America, and the Near East, where early volunteers encountered nations and societies that were far more established, far more self-assured. By chance, the arrival of the first volunteer groups coincided with a changing order not only in Africa but in the United States as well. The American civil rights movement was forging new bonds between blacks and whites, and the Peace Corps was ready to take on the same struggle for equality in Africa. Perhaps sooner than the volunteers themselves, the Africans sensed that something important was happening and appreciated the broader social and political implications of the races' working together as equals.

Having largely achieved their independence by the early 1960s, African governments were responding to their people's next priority: educational opportunity, which not only promoted development but also, as colonial experience had shown, guaranteed the prestige and salary of a white-collar job. The advent of the Peace Corps coincided with this demand and gave many African nations the means to expand their school systems far beyond anything they—or early Peace Corps planners—could have imagined.

In America, unexpected thousands were applying for volunteer service, and the Peace Corps began sending as many of them as possible to teach in African schools. The Africans had very simple expectations of these young and mostly inexperienced American teachers. Their job was to stand in a classroom and teach, and the more of them who were available, the more classrooms would be filled, and the more parents would be satisfied that the government was meeting their needs.

The Peace Corps, however, soon began to suspect that it was encouraging expansion of school systems and curricula that were manifestly inappropriate to African conditions. Peace Corps volunteers and staff became concerned that they were engaged in mere slot-filling. The Peace Corps' own inspectors frequently confirmed these fears and thus stimulated an ongoing debate over the scope and purpose of the volunteers' role in African education, and the Peace Corps' commitment of teachers to individual countries.

There was a conceit among Peace Corps volunteers and staff that they had something special to offer African education, and it took many forms. It was assumed *a priori* that the British and French colonial emphasis on rote learning, Eurocentric textbooks, and irrelevant curricula ought to be reformed. While valid, this did not necessarily require thousands of Americans who, for the most part, were barely trained to teach, much less to help overhaul entire school systems. In fact, the Peace Corps may actually have slowed reform by enabling several African countries to concentrate instead on expanding their flawed educational models.

It was widely believed in Peace Corps circles that the volunteer teachers' major contribution to their students was not in the knowledge imparted, but in new attitudes transmitted, principally the concepts of individual achievement and responsibility, as well as the power of reasoning. The Peace Corps never asked its African hosts if they minded having their children's values changed. It did, however, seek—and find—empirical evidence that volunteer teachers were having a positive impact on student attitudes and presumably preparing them for the development process.

One major study reported in 1968 that Ethiopian secondary school

THE JOB

students who had been taught over several years by Peace Corps teachers had superior skills to those who had not. They were more fluent in English, were better problem-solvers, had stronger achievement motivation, and generally had a more modern outlook on life.

The report asserted that the hundreds of volunteers teaching in Ethiopian schools were equipping their students with motives and attitudes that would promote the country's economic development. It did not, however, comment on the possible effect volunteers were having as "active catalysts in the ferment of Ethiopia's present age of change," to quote a Peace Corps staff member in 1963. In the mid-1970s, student strikes and violence—some directed at volunteer teachers—brought education to a halt for months. Change was fermenting much faster than expected.

Ironically, the Peace Corps had indeed played a critical role in sharpening student awareness of their world and of Emperor Haile Selassie's slow pace of modernization. Deliberately or not, volunteers encouraged student enthusiasm for a less autocratic political system, as well as for a government less dependent on American help. The Ethiopian Ministry of Education had even felt obliged at one point to remind the Peace Corps staff in Addis Ababa that it was not conducting a community development program. It pointed out politely that the government, in asking for volunteer teachers, considered *teaching* to be their most important responsibility.

Also ironically, Haile Selassie emulated the Peace Corps by requiring students at the national university in Addis Ababa to spend a year teaching at schools in the country's rugged interior. The students went, but they resented their enforced rustication. It was this diaspora of restless and articulate university students that began the indoctrination in the secondary schools of the ideas that ultimately toppled the imperial regime. Yet, well before the fall, the Ethiopian government had begun scaling down Peace Corps involvement in the country, aware perhaps that the volunteers had been all too successful as "agents of change."

The Peace Corps liked being a catalyst for orderly social and economic change throughout the Third World. This was a natural instinct for any organization established to improve the quality of people's lives. But the Peace Corps has since learned to appreciate the arrogance of consciously trying to bring about change and to concentrate on doing the job it has been asked to do. It has learned that change, in any event, is a constant process and that volunteers, by their mere presence as alien carriers of different ideas and values, are participants.

Africans soon understood this, too, and by 1966, governments had begun to have second thoughts about the Peace Corps teaching program. At that time, more than two thousand volunteer teachers were serving on the continent, the two largest contingents being in Ethiopia and Nigeria. Nigeria's fondness for the Peace Corps declined sharply at the time of its civil war in 1967, when many volunteers sided openly with breakaway Biafra. Ethiopia's love affair with the Peace Corps ended in the political turmoil that began shortly afterward. By the mid-1970s, there were no Peace Corps teachers at all left in these two countries.

In Tanzania the circumstances were different—though still enmeshed in domestic turmoil—but the results were exactly the same. Nyerere recognized that the large numbers of volunteer teachers presented the danger of subtly undermining the impetus toward self-reliance, and the volunteers did not necessarily disagree. For the most part, they applauded the ring of genuine independence in Nyerere's words, though it meant they might themselves have to leave. In late 1966, Tanzania imposed a moratorium on all new volunteers, forcing reassignment of more than one hundred who were preparing to take up posts in primary schools. Rising anti-American sentiment, provoked largely by the Vietnam War and the unsavory revelations about the CIA, hastened the disaffection, and by late 1969, the Peace Corps program had been phased out. It was clear that for the Africans, huge Peace Corps teaching programs had proved to be too much of a good thing.

The Peace Corps would return to Tanzania in 1979, again at Nyerere's invitation, to work in much smaller numbers and much more specialized pursuits. This was a different Peace Corps and a different time. The volunteers were no longer known in Tanzania as the "followers of Kennedy" (whom millions of Africans idolized). The charisma and novelty of the Peace Corps had long since faded. Instead of the highly visible, often dominant presence of teachers, the Peace Corps in Africa was now maintaining a lower profile and attempting to provide a broader range of skilled volunteers. In retrospect, the shift from an overwhelming emphasis on education to a more balanced portfolio of volunteer assignments, including food production and primary health care, was historically inevitable. In comparison to 1966, there are 1,500 fewer volunteers standing in front of African blackboards.

Just as dramatic is the overall shift in Peace Corps programming worldwide. Whereas Africa accounted twenty years ago for just over a quarter of all volunteers, today 45 percent work in twenty-three African countries. While much attention over the years has been paid to the steady "decline" of the Peace Corps, in Africa it has established a relevance to development that is far more substantial than the massive teacher programs of the 1960s.

Volunteer projects in Asia and Latin America are today a mere 30 percent of their previous numbers, while African programs are holding at 68 percent. The reason for this is that the Peace Corps, more than any international development agency, has overcome the racial legacy of five hundred years of slave trading, colonialism, and apartheid.

It was not the sometimes questionable skills that volunteers brought to the schools and villages of Africa that made them welcome. Africans usually knew more about growing food, finding water, keeping healthy and protecting the environment than most volunteers acknowledged. In fact, the African was often surprised at how little technical knowledge the average volunteer possessed. Had the Peace Corps at first sent mainly highly trained agronomists, engineers, and economists, however, its stay in Africa might have been far less enduring. Instead, the Peace Corps sent—and continues to send—the legendary "BA generalist," or liberal arts graduate.

These generalists have never had high-tech credentials, but they do have the desire to learn the language and comprehend the host culture. Though many volunteers have failed to master the local vernacular, and few have become as sensitive and knowing as a trained social anthropologist, most have managed to say something extremely important to the Africans. After centuries of dealing with merciless exploitation, Africans have found a new and more humane image of the white race in the guise of the Peace Corps volunteer.

Africans assumed initially that American "volunteers" would bring nothing more than variations on entrenched colonial themes. Given their long and bitter association with Europeans, Africans had no reason to believe that young, mostly white volunteers would be any more capable of respecting their traditions, values, and history than the average colonial civil servant or teacher had been.

Instead, one of the great revolutions of the twentieth century occurred the day the first Peace Corps volunteers set foot on African soil—in Accra, Ghana, in September 1961. Soon there were several hundred, then thousands, of volunteers responding to African hospitality. They ate African food. They rode the buses, lorries, and mammy wagons. They greeted passersby in halting Hausa, Wolof, and Swahili. They made the Africans feel that their languages, their food, their ways and culture had meaning and importance in a world that had seemed to exclude that possibility.

In 1961, when one trainee's postcard home—noting but not complaining about the dirty, smelly streets of Lagos—fell into Nigerian hands, it seemed to confirm the worst fears of American diplomats skeptical of the wisdom of sending naive American youth on such a mission. This would not be the last embarrassment for the Peace Corps in Africa, but after a brief venting of Nigerian outrage—and the voluntary departure of the unfortunate young woman—Africans typically forgave the incident. They did not, however, wipe it from history. Five years later, the Nigerian head of state, General Yakubu Gowon, unexpectedly raised the matter with visiting Peace Corps director Jack Vaughn, to reassure him that Nigerians were not bitter over the affair.

Gowon's gesture reflected Africans' desire to make strangers feel welcome, lest they be given reason to misbehave or become enemies. Perhaps more than anything else, it is this strain running through so many African cultures that has created such an enduring bond between Peace Corps volunteers and Africa—the twin traditions of hospitality and reciprocity. Volunteers have generally understood the importance of both. They have felt curiously at home in Africa, having instinctively understood how and why they could show their hosts that they did so. Volunteers' efforts to comprehend the African cultural and spiritual universe have overshadowed all else the Peace Corps may have contributed in terms of skills and concrete monuments to progress.

In the months following the arrival of the first volunteers, it became widely known among African leaders and villagers that President Kennedy had sent "a new white man." Africans had seldom witnessed white people waiting patiently to see a minister, a local doctor, or even a district police officer. They were delighted that volunteers loved to dance to African music. Villagers were impressed that "their" volunteer would drink palm wine with them, share the joy of their births and grief of their deaths, laugh at their jokes, and listen to their oral history.

While stressing the interracial dimension of the Peace Corps' work in Africa, we also have to cite its failure to attract black and other minority volunteers. Estimates vary, but blacks probably have accounted for no more than 2 to 3 percent of all volunteers. A recurring nightmare for Africa regional staff has been all-white groups of trainees and volunteers. It is sadly ironic that, during an era of black cultural and historical renaissance, the Peace Corps has been unable to represent America's multiethnic heritage to the world, and especially to Africa. If there is one item of unfinished business on the Peace Corps' agenda for the next quarter-century, it should be to rectify this imbalance.

In defining the Peace Corps' impact and effectiveness vis-à-vis Africa's enormous needs, it would be simple enough to produce statistics proving that volunteers, in their collective mass and individual genius, have left their mark on African education, food production, and community development. The Peace Corps has helped to improve the quality of African life.

We would argue, however, that its greatest contribution lies in African-American relations. Had the Peace Corps not been established, especially when it was, American interest in Africa and understanding of its problems would have remained abysmally low. Many volunteers and staff who have served in Africa with the Peace Corps have joined a growing cadre of informed Africanists working in academia, business, government, and private development agencies. Increasingly over the years, when Africans have had to relate to an American—whether a diplomat, US/AID official, educator, journalist, or aid worker—they have found themselves dealing with someone who shared experiences, language, and values drawn from years of working in the Peace Corps in Africa.

Although Africans have strongly opposed American policies in Vietnam, South Africa, and elsewhere; although one continues periodically to hear African charges that volunteers are spies; and although some African governments have closed Peace Corps operations for political reasons, Africans have always regarded the volunteer as an individual, to be accepted into their world or not on the basis of personal qualities. When a Tanzanian village chief was instructed in 1965 to make an anti-American speech to his people, he complained that he could not understand the order. "The only Americans I know are the missionary in our village and the two Peace Corps teachers," he said, "and they are nice people. I guess it is the South Americans I am to attack."

Being shrewd judges of human nature, Africans have long concluded that the typical volunteer comes as a good person and therefore may live among them—in peace.

From a Talk with Dr. Siaka Stevens

Things you take for granted in the United States, you don't get here. Some of our boys have gone to school in Russia, married Russian girls, and brought them here. I don't think we have two here now. It's the environment. Take a girl from Kiev and bring her here, and she'll see hell. But Peace Corps volunteers have a sense of dedication. I've met them in very remote areas, where our own people don't want to go. They have this motivating factor in the back of their minds. That is their driving spirit. When the Peace Corps started here, we didn't like them at first. Some said the volunteers were CIA agents. But they mingled with the people and got integrated. Recently, I told a volunteer when he finished his second year, "To watch you work is an education." Peace Corps volunteers have built feeder roads and other things. It is an education for my people to see them. "Hey, this is a white man who is digging the gutter! Maybe work isn't all that bad." I've seen them everywhere in the country. They teach us to be proud of two pigs and ten chickens: build it gradually, see it grow. Now we are doing fish farming. That is something out of this world. I didn't think it was possible. We need the thinking process. Seeing these volunteers work teaches us to decolonize our minds.

Dr. Siaka Stevens is president of Sierra Leone.

Letter from Kenya (1965)

It does not seem at all like Christmas here. The sun is hot, the corn and beans are growing quickly after several weeks of rain. We have not heard any Christmas carols, and no one is counting shopping days. The sounds at this moment are those of children, cows, some sheep, and bird calls. In the morning, we wake up to a rooster, donkeys make their humorous braying noise all day, and at 4:30 P.M., we are able to hear the beep of the intervillage bus.

Thanksgiving was spent at a coffee society working on their accounting books. It does not sound like a Peace Corps-type project, but the audit year ended last September, and the societies are behind, so we helped. We bicycled there with sleeping bags and a safari cooking set. In the evening we talked to the guard on duty and found we were well-protected. Private ownership of a gun is not permitted, so he had the next best thing, a set of bows and arrows. We slept in the cement-block storage room on sacks full of coffee. I only fell out of bed once. The next day we finished our work, and the secretary brought us milk and ten eggs. These are expensive items; the prices are the same here as in the States. We are often given eggs and are embarrassed to receive them. The children need them more than we. But the people want to give something they know we like, and we do not want to offend by refusing them.

On five out of seven days, we visit the coffee cooperatives to talk to general members. We speak in Swahili, and it is translated into Kikuyu. The topics are cooperative principles, characteristics of a good committee member, how a society spends the members' money, and coffee competition on the world market. Our talk lasts about two hours. We spend from two to four hours bicycling. We also visit primary schools and speak to the seventh grade classes. The first time, they are extremely curious because they rarely ever see a white person. So we talk a little in English about cash crops in Kenya and compare it to farming in the U.S. This gives us a chance to assess their understanding of English and general knowledge. Then the second trip, we discuss cooperative principles with them, and the kinds of cooperatives which have been developed in other places in the world.

A problem in working here is a sense of isolation. It is not the lack of news so much as the difficulty in sharing your thoughts and feelings with others. Part of the problem, of course, stems from the language. We have finally finished our Kikuyu-Swahili-English dictionary. I was surprised to discover what you can learn about a people just by studying the words they use. If we could master these words and the changes caused by adding tenses, we would be able to converse in Kikuyu in most situations. Our Swahili has taken a jump in the last couple of weeks, and we can understand most rapid conversation now. But the rest of the problem is one of culture. Man may share a common humanity but not common life experiences. The same simple words do not evoke the same responses in us and in them. The diversity of experiences enriches our life here, but we always feel isolated.

Report from Niger (1965)

"Your volunteers can show our young people that working with their hands is not shameful," President Diori said last fall in welcoming the Peace Corps to his nation.

Dr. Bana of the Ministry of Health said of the volunteers: "Their effect is primarily psychological, on our educated elites who are so alienated from our people."

When I asked him what the function was, Mark R. simply said: "We care."

Hardly anyone thought the first purpose of the Peace Corps was to bring technical skills, and in fact, many of their counterparts have more formal training than the volunteers.

In the short run, the real function of the volunteer is the policeman's role that some of them find distasteful: by their presence, they incite local officials to be more honest and conscientious. In the long run, the volunteers must have an effect on attitudes that are preventing the nation's development. Like all African countries, Niger is deeply divided between elite and masses. Most members of the elite appear interested in show, in imitating Europe, but little concerned with their people. For the masses, progress is a myth that belongs to foreigners; two of the Hausa terms for Europeans are "the lucky ones" and "the victors."

The volunteer finds himself caught between these two classes. All his instincts are to side with the masses, but the elite runs the government and controls the volunteer's job. Nowhere is this conflict clearer than in public health.

Look at the Maradi clinic, for instance: Long after opening time, Mme. B., the director, is sitting at her desk reading a magazine, while outside dozens of women are waiting silently in the hot sun with their sick babies. Two volunteers are also waiting, acutely and guiltily aware of the women outside. Time drags on, but Mme. B. goes on reading her magazine; the women and the volunteers wait. Inside the clinic is a shocking sight: sixteen dusty cases of powdered milk stacked in a corner. The cases are marked "Gift of UNICEF and the Swiss Confederation." After many months, no one has made a move to distribute their contents. A closet contains piles of unused medicines. Many have now expired; some have been in that closet for years. The women need the milk, and the hospital needs the medicine.

Why doesn't Mme. B. open the clinic, distribute the milk, and send the medicine to the hospital? "Lack of training," someone is sure to say, but this is sheer nonsense. With her three years of midwife studies in Germany, Mme. B. is far better trained for her job than the volunteers. But like so many of the women of her district, Mme. B. is all charm and sex appeal and lies. With a dazzling smile, she tells you that the volunteers are great, that their home visits will get rolling soon. But the milk doesn't move, and the clinic opens late, and a boy with a burned stomach is sent away because it is five minutes past closing time.

Mme. B. just doesn't care. It is as simple as that. Those peasant women standing in the sun and sand are not her people; her people are the fashionable women in that magazine she is reading while everyone waits.

In Bouza, a Saharan hill town to the north, two volunteers wanted to start a soccer game for the local kids. But the school kids refused to play with the kids who do not go to school; they called them "barbarians." In Firgoun, another pair of volunteers was in the market at lunchtime with their counterpart, who is with the Ministry of Agriculture. The volunteers wanted to eat in the market. That is "not done," the counterpart explained; members of the elite do not eat with the peasantry. He said they would have to go to a nearby home and send a servant to the market to get the food so they could eat indoors, away from the masses.

The examples are endless. In a dozen details of their daily lives, the volunteers are forced to choose sides for or against the elite. Each time a volunteer picks up a tool, he is commenting on the elite's view that manual labor is beneath an educated man. If he dresses in casual American-style working clothes, he is also choosing sides, for the elite's natty dress is a class uniform. The austerity (or lack of it) of the volunteer's housing and way of life is still another comment on the values of the elite.

What should the volunteers do? At one extreme, they can denounce the school director openly, tell off the school kids, and refuse to eat anyplace but in the market. In their daily lives, they can stake out firm positions against the elite. But this will alienate the local power structure and ultimately make the volunteers' position untenable, for it is the elite, not the volunteers, that holds the power of decision. At the other extreme, they can conform in their dress and manner, contenting themselves with doing their own jobs well without ever challenging the elite's behavior. This is likely to result in the volunteers going home without having had any effect on Niger at all.

The Experience: The Pacific

by Russell G. Davis

My country treated me to two long looks at the East Asia–Pacific region: one as a rifle scout in the Marine Corps, the other as regional director of the Peace Corps. Both times I was with brave young people in their magic years, when it seems possible to win at least one race in life, the run to change a little piece of the world before it changes a big piece of you. And we did some of it, and some people and things grew. The Marine Corps is remembered, but on the long scroll of Asia, is there even a brush stroke that says Peace Corps?

When I started as regional director, the East Asia–Pacific (EAP) was the largest of the four Peace Corps regions, both in area (though most of it was underwater) and in the number of volunteers. The working areas varied immensely in culture, level of development, and needs. But I knew that in contrast to the other regions the Peace Corps served, it contained a pervasive pride of civilization, a hunger for change, and a freedom from the worst hang-ups of religious and social tradition.

On the Pacific rim was Korea, a high and ancient culture, hard and war-tested. Thailand, richer and softer inland but tough at the east frontier, was looking into Vietnam and a war that threw a shadow all across the region. Peninsular Malaysia had squelched most of its insurgency, but rancor and division remained. Insurgency and massacre were just ended in Indonesia, a place still so riven that the Peace Corps had been forced to withdraw; often as I tried, I couldn't get us back in. The Philippines, with its many regions, languages, cultures, religions, and problems, was complex—except by comparison with American Micronesia. American Micronesia was little dots spread out in a continental-size area

---

Russell G. Davis is professor of education and development at Harvard University.

of water. Its island groups could have been separate country domains, and later were, but then it was treated as one, united only by a common lack of resources, bloody battles remembered, and an uncertain future built on political, economic, and strategic ambiguity.

At times, it seemed that EAP led all the other Peace Corps regions in one thing—problems—and chief among them was that there were too many inspired young Americans in too many uninspired jobs, or in no jobs at all. The solution was to reduce the number of volunteers, or to increase the number of real jobs to assign them. Both solutions were against certain Peace Corps traditions.

It baffled traditionalists that anyone would want to think "smaller." Moving on the alternative solution—increase jobs to match volunteer numbers—revealed that very few in the Peace Corps (or elsewhere, and to this day) know how to create jobs.

Many in the Peace Corps made no pretense of being development "pros." "AID types" was a term of scorn. The staff members saw themselves as "generalists," pursuing not so much development as the other Peace Corps goals: to win friends abroad, increase international understanding, and provide a rich intercultural experience for young Americans. Those more development-oriented responded to this by saying, if that's all they do out there, we ought to pay poor countries tuition for the learning experience. But despite the differences in outlook, there was one thing that joined both camps, and that was a common aim to help people who needed it, whatever the immediate cost in personal reward and comfort.

Both were right: the important thing *was* motivation and human concern, because that was what powered and unified all the efforts. But at the same time, to teach others how to do the job, you had first to know how to do it yourself. The problem was not solved either by cutting the number of volunteers or by vastly increasing the number of jobs. Attrition cut some numbers, and new volunteers were not assigned until programs were tested. Meaningful jobs became a major criterion for program approval, but a secret formula for programming good, developmental jobs was not found.

Programming jobs was easier in large development works, such as in the Muda region of Malaysia, which was an irrigation/area-development project with heavy capital investment. In this and similar programs, jobs with high development potential were created.

Nonetheless, the old standby Peace Corps jobs continued to be in education, especially English and secondary-school teaching. The demand for secondary education—above all, training in math, science, and English—was rising throughout East Asia and the Pacific. In Micronesia, the schools could never have expanded as they did without volunteers.

But educational expansion, especially at the secondary level, chiefly met what economists call "social demand," in contrast to "economic demand." General education met the social and cultural needs of people who craved it as a form of consumption, and as a "credentialing" device. It was less well calibrated with economic requirements, in the sense of training people for the enterprises and jobs that could realistically be developed in the island areas of Micronesia. And there was concern as to how it would be supported when the large human resource subsidy was withdrawn and the Peace Corps went home. What do such things matter to a bright, poor kid who has a chance for more schooling, whatever foreign experts think? The answer from my own experience—one of ten kids in a working-class family—is to get any schooling you can.

In education, the Peace Corps could deploy the one form of manpower it had in surplus supply, the generalist, and whatever the economists say, the generalist teachers were as welcome as the most precious of cargoes in the islands and on the mainland. In EAP, more than 60 percent of the volunteers were generalist teachers, and at times the proportion was higher. Another fact should be noted: many young Americans were vastly versatile. The diploma might say "History," but these could still be farm kids who knew gardening and poultry, swine and cattle rearing, beekeeping and fishing, and how to keep the machinery running to produce the food. From hobbies such as radio and electrical and electronic devices, communications experts were born, and some rural areas were linked by Peace Corps radio networks.

Health was another major service area in which AB generalists served well, usually supported by medical professionals but sometimes working with little close support in island areas or rural Korea. Malaria control, sanitation, and other environmental health activity led to strong programs early on. Later, the cutback came in Malaysia and the islands for the happiest of reasons: diminished need.

Korea seemed as hard a place to serve as any in the region, especially in the countryside. The language was hard, the hills were hard, the winter was hard; and I especially remember it was a hard place on marriage for the young couples who were sent there. Country staff caught most of the marriage counseling, but the problem was that male Americans were invited out for very permissive nightlife by male Koreans, while females were expected to stay home and be happy. Once the partnership became strained, young American wives had few family resources, and sometimes little work or cultural satisfaction, to fall back on.

Korea had another unique twist. A Korean official told me bluntly, when I commented on the difficulty of some of the assignments and low performance ratings: "We don't expect or care if the young Americans do a good job out there. The point of the project is that they are out there, and we can point them out to our people who don't want to serve out there, and say 'Look at the Americans! Do they complain?'" Yes, they did, mightily, but they still hung in and served.

Agriculture was the third main area, and it covered everything but large field crops like wheat and corn. Rice cultivation—paddy in the Philippines and hill rice in Asia—was the chief interest. Backed up by mature scientists and teachers, a strong volunteer-manned "rice program" took shape in the Philippines, then spread to Malaysia and Thailand. Apart from extension and production support, strong work was done in curriculum development (extension education) and instructional technology. Some volunteer curriculum work would impress veteran educators.

Pond and pool fish projects were a big Asian activity, and the Peace Corps served in that department, too. In Fiji and Micronesia, this included improving the technology and gear; installing refrigeration systems to preserve and enhance the catch; and helping in communications, boat repair, and maintenance. The Peace Corps was youth in East Asia–Pacific; it was no country for old men. But older volunteers, those great and exceptional few, were outstanding. One older fellow was a legend—the story had it he had been a World War I German machine gunner—who made a mighty contribution by setting up shops, systems, and procedures for repair and maintenance of motors and craft in Palau.

One of the most dramatic programs, though not large, was helping island free-form divers to go deeper and gather more sponges through improved breath-control techniques. The Peace Corps sent several kinds of divers to the Pacific, including professional salvage and deep-sea types who worked at the end of hose lines. But watching free-form divers, many of them volunteers from Hawaii, working with the islanders was dramatic.

In the Peace Corps, as in the Marines, the stories long remembered and often told are shaped by the exceptions. One young man served through several tours, working with the hill tribes in Thailand on such problems as the ravages of slash-and-burn agriculture in the face of a shrinking land base. A tough Thai soldier, who worked on the same problem using different methods, told me, "He not only taught those people up there, he taught me how to teach people." There were volunteers who performed great feats in setting up communications networks in Malaysia and the islands, some just as an adjunct hobby to their regular job assignments. Areas were linked that had never been linked before.

THE JOB

In development work, many pros find that the hardest thing to do is to aid the development of entrepreneurial activity, the kind that promotes small industries to produce goods and services, to make enough profit to survive, to create jobs and earnings for the entrepreneur and his family, his neighbors, and his landsmen. This is called EDP (entrepreneurial development programs), and it requires a combination of market study, technological analysis, marketing and training plans, credit arrangement, and much support and counseling. Entrepreneurial development is not hard to do in rich countries where family traditions and culture encourage it. The challenge was in the poverty-stricken Philippines and Micronesia. It is easy to teach the rich to take a chance that they might get richer, but to teach the poor to play in a lottery where they have never seen a winner, or even an honest drawing, requires entrepreneurs of great faith and missionary zeal.

East Asia–Pacific, as a region, started with 4,400 volunteers and ended with 3,300, less than two years later. We were not very "entrepreneurial," if that quality is measured in live body count, as some did. There were fewer volunteers in non-jobs or bad jobs at the end, but good jobs were always hard to find.

A few peculiar incidents come back to mind, such as trying to give an earnest young volunteer a sound reason why she should not be allowed to work bare-breasted on her island, when all the other women there did. Or trying to explain to an earnest young man that being a patriot did not require him to brief the CIA station chief on rural politics, and that Peace Corps policy was to keep the two apart. Or chasing a brig rat from Da Nang who wore a big .45 and rode a Honda with a girl attached to the saddle, claiming to be a Peace Corps member to get gas money.

But the memory that stands out above all is of watching a girl who ran extra-help sessions every day because the regular teacher caught an early boat home and some of the kids, stranded there until later boats came, were from remote areas with no schools.

The girl was using a cardboard clock face with numerals 1 to 12 and attached hands to teach time. A kid was having difficulty overcoming the illogic of it all, that the small hand indicated the big time period and the big hand the small. But he worked at it, and got it, and twitched with joy as he rattled back correct times to her.

Afterward she said, "They're really not dumb. I just didn't teach it well. They come from big, poor families, but give them a chance and they can learn anything. All they need is the opportunity." Not hearing anything from me, she got defensive: "Don't you believe that?"

I came to and said, "Yeah, sure I believe it. It's just that the kid reminded me of someone."

She said, "Me, too. He reminded me of me." She waited, then, but the only response she got was New England silence.

The young find it so easy to be honest! That's what the Peace Corps was founded on; that and the need to remember where you come from when you go where you have to go.

Remarks on the Decision to Withdraw from Indonesia (1965)

by Alex Shakow

May 30, 1965, would have marked the second anniversary here in Jakarta of our first group of volunteers. These seventeen were followed by an additional fourteen in January 1964, and the final group of fifteen that December. At one point, we had forty-five volunteers on duty in eighteen provinces and twenty cities, teaching and coaching sports and physical education. But we are not going to reach the second anniversary here, for by May 5th I hope to have all the current crop of volunteers out of the country. What happened?

We came here on an "experimental" basis in a flush of goodwill. Peace Corps Director Sargent Shriver and President Sukarno talked in Bogor in September 1962 and exchanged notes seven months later. At the time that our first volunteers arrived, relations with the U.S. were at a high point, for it looked as though the United States and its allies were going to lend Indonesia $400 million. Despite a barrage of Communist press attacks, the Indonesian government held firm to its commitment. In fact, the next six months were quiet politically. Our volunteers had trouble adjusting to the food, to the people, to the absence of scheduled work, to Indonesian family life. But they learned. Meanwhile, the pressure began to mount a bit as Malaysia became a significant issue here. The attacks on the Peace Corps very rarely had anything to do with the coaches' competence, but rather identified our volunteers with "imperialist"

Alex Shakow, who at the time of this essay was Peace Corps director in Indonesia, is now division chief for international economic affairs at the World Bank in Washington, D.C.

American actions, including the CIA. This was not a real problem until some of the Communist youth became violent.

Our most striking case was that of Semarang in Central Java, where a volunteer named Bob was dragged from his home by a mob of Communist youth and taken to the governor's office for expulsion from Indonesia as a spy. The group was received by the governor, who praised their revolutionary spirit and sent them home. The governor then told the volunteer not to be concerned and to continue his work. Two days later, a dozen of the mob were arrested and detained for a week. Although they were never brought to trial, there was no more trouble in Semarang. The mob neglected the fact that the volunteer lived with an army colonel. Nonetheless, the city was covered with anti-Peace Corps signs; one wall even bore the scrawled expression "Beware of Bob's smile."

In certain regions there has never been any trouble to speak of. In others, the trouble has come in spurts. But lately, political trouble has become our stock in trade in almost all regions, and has come in more difficult and significant ways. Whereas before, resolutions came from Communist groups, recently they have been coming from the local and regional governments. Several regional bodies have requested that the central government withdraw the Peace Corps from their region; other local parliaments did the same in response to the demands of Communist groups. In each case, we would scurry around here in Jakarta and have the sports minister or, more frequently, the foreign minister, take action. I began to feel more like a fireman putting out small blazes than anything else. We never had to withdraw a volunteer from an area where he had been placed, but we did some long, hard thinking on several cases.

Our volunteers are not politicians; they are physical education coaches. They are not paid Foreign Service officers hired to fight for the nation's cause at the conference table, nor are they soldiers trained to battle in guerrilla war. Yet the situation that they increasingly faced resembled something like this. Great struggles are going on in this country that are none of our business. The inner conflict has nothing to do with the Peace Corps, but we inevitably became involved. President Sukarno has of late been making clear Indonesia's opposition to many American policies. In the regions, this policy line is particularly clear, for there is little contact there with anything but official government policy.

I knew that President Sukarno had expressed his admiration and appreciation for the volunteers, as had the sports minister in various closed conversations. As I traveled around, I tried to portray the Jakarta feeling to leading regional officials. It felt very strange, to say the least, trying to explain President Sukarno's support for the Peace Corps to these officials, but if I did not, who would? Almost all these leaders were prepared to implement any decision that the central government presented to them. But it was quite clear that some, especially those not interested in sports, were scared at the injection of this essentially alien, international issue into the already troubled climate of their own political situation.

Under these circumstances, we concluded that the useful life of the Peace Corps here was nearing its close, for volunteers who in some places could coach basketball only under the protection of bayonets were not really Peace Corps volunteers. When our many friends in the regions found it dangerous to help us, then it was time to pack up. When work was hampered not only by the expected and usual technical problems, but also by political and security factors, it was time to withdraw, even though such a decision was made with the greatest reluctance.

The door is open to future Peace Corps programs in Indonesia if the Indonesian government should ever want them. The exchange of notes remains in force. Of course, all depends on future political developments. Although I have an obvious prejudice, I think that our experience here has been a positive one. Despite all the trouble they had, two-thirds of the volunteers who served out their terms said on going home that they would choose Indonesia again if they had the chance. Not a single one of our volunteers has gone home early or quit. They pulled their hair out at how disorganized the sports world is here. They complained bitterly because inflation made their rupiahs worthless and I would not raise their allowances. But all our volunteers will leave with regret at the loss of many close friends and disappointment that they could not do the job they wanted.

The Experience: South and West Asia

by John Chromy

The noonday south Indian sun seared down unmercifully as our train slowly carried us through this, the third day of our trans-India journey. It was June of 1963, and ten days before, we sixteen Peace Corps volunteers had left our homes all over America. Already we felt nostalgia for those lush green landscapes. We stared at the dry, eerily empty Indian countryside, which slid by at barely twenty miles an hour. The fixation of our eyes partly reflected our exhaustion, after thirty-three hours in the air and two days on the ground, where the temperature had not fallen below 100 degrees. But what concerned us more was the mission on which we had been sent in this vast subcontinent.

Here we were to assist village people in growing more food to improve their nutrition and bring new hope to their lives. But how were we to work such miracles in a land that, in three days of travel, revealed to us only dry, barren, dun-colored landscape and almost no people, except those gathered in the towns bordering the tracks? Where were those 380 million villagers we had read so much about? Where were the crops that fed them? Where were the sacred cows, the monkeys, the tigers, the elephants? Where had they all gone? How were we to help them?

This initial trip with its unanswered questions was my stunning introduction to the underbelly of Asia, which stretches from the shores of the Mediterranean to the Bay of Bengal. Later, as the Peace Corps' deputy regional director at the end of the 1970s, I saw more, but the lands remained a mystery. A panorama of ancient civilizations, vast numbers of people, dry, barren hills and plains, stunning scenery, exotic wildlife, millennia of brutal political strife, crossroads of world trade and in-

---

John Chromy is director of management and administration, Special Olympics International.

THE JOB

trigue, and to this day lands of stark contrast. These lands confronted us not only with proud and independent cultures, resistant enough to our assigned responsibility as agents of change, but with even more prideful and more stubbornly independent subcultures, like the Kurds of Turkey and Iran, the Pathans of Afghanistan and Pakistan, the Sikhs of India.

Within ten days of the end of our train ride, barely settled into our homes as brand new Peace Corps volunteers, we learned our first secret about this robe of contrasting colors, the saving grace of the lands of South Asia. The surprise was India's famous monsoons, which struck with their first gentle refreshing and life-giving gift. The rains had come, and now out of everywhere flowed people, animals, wildlife—out of homes, out of hiding places. But what also flowed out was hope.

The people rushed to ready the fields, to prepare the seedlings and sow their crops. And rush they must, for the monsoon season is always fickle and sometimes cruelly short. They must place their seeds in the ground quickly, so that they may drink up the monsoon moisture as greedily as possible. For too soon there would be no more. The crops which, in a warm tropical climate, leap toward the sky, will wither and die beneath the harsh skies of South Asia unless man moves quickly. Water feeds and water cools, and without it the crops die, and so does life.

If the seeds are planted promptly and the rains are good and gentle, at least when the crops near ripeness, then each and every village family will reap from its small plot enough food to eat well through the year and, possibly, to have some small amount left over to sell for cloth, meat, or plastics, and to save for a dowry to marry a daughter. But if something fails, if the showers loiter, the rains start falsely and then turn away, or the rains beat a heavy and crushing drumbeat near harvest time, then each of India's 380 million villagers knows that the family will face January, February, and March with only two meals a day. In April, May, and June many will have only one—mothers and daughters first, and then sons, and finally fathers eating only one meal of the rough, tasteless, ground-grain gruel, since those most able to sow and reap must be fed and kept the healthiest. Then the limited supplies will be stretched until the next harvest, and the cycle will start all over again.

And so this explosion of activity, this rush to till and plant, surprised the volunteers, strangers in this vast, unique, and overpowering land. This dependence on short, focused, seasonal rains is a phenomenon that engulfs and governs the life of nearly all of Asia's underbelly, and it had unique effects upon the assignment of volunteers. It demanded that Peace Corps volunteers work with Iranian farmers, for instance, to seek out and even to breed hardy strains of grain and trees, to find millet that could survive on little water, and to learn the ways of macadamia nuts, whose trees bore fruit with no water in sight. These were strange demands, indeed, for farm boys from Wisconsin and Pennsylvania.

For this, we had journeyed at a snail's pace nearly the entire length of the subcontinent, from the shadow of the perpetually snowcapped Himalayas, across the endless Deccan Plateau, nearly to Kanya Kumari, the beautiful land's end where the powerful Arabian Sea swirls into the flowing Indian Ocean. As we made our way across, the land had been in hibernation, waiting for these rains. For three months the heat of the Indian summer is so overpowering that it saps the mind, body, and soul of every creature. Ten thousand years of unrecorded history had taught these people that in this season the only sane response to the overpowering force of nature is to submit, to drink as much water as is available, to move about only from dusk until soon after dawn, to talk quietly to the young, to protect your precious animals, and to pray to the gods that in their goodness and wisdom they will soon send the rains and the life-giving nourishment they produce.

Hibernation and then a rush to plant, cultivate, and harvest was a cycle that most Peace Corps volunteers serving in South Asia came to know, work with, be frustrated by, and ultimately accept. For truly, it was not only the sane response to the environment, it was the rhythm of life's seasons.

Summer in India was what winter was in my native Minnesota. It gave the land, the farmers, and their animals a chance to rest, to replenish the spirit, and, most important, to pause and think—about man, god, animals, and nature, and their relation to each other. Metaphysics we called it when I was in college, but the philosophy and mythology of Buddhism, Hinduism, and Islam all urge man to focus on the questions of his relationship with his god and the use he is making of his time. And I began to realize that here, ten thousand miles from home, literally and figuratively on the other side of the world, East and West had that much in common, except that maybe East had learned it better. I remembered Ecclesiastes 3 speaking of the same phenomenon: "To every thing there is a season," including the season to die.

Though Peace Corps volunteers all across South Asia understood, in varying degrees, the villagers' need to accept the perils of the environment, to take what advantage they could of them, and, most important, not to fight them, nonetheless to the short-termers, the can-do spirited Americans, this was a source of enormous frustration. Peace Corps nurses fought it. They traveled by camel to remote valleys of Afghanistan to administer medicine and inoculations to people who had never seen modern medical care. These young women of Boston and Austin, Texas, would rather travel over vast, arid terrain on the back of a camel than be kept from their duty.

For those who worked in agricultural production, with only two rainy seasons before they had to go home, there was always impatience. They did not easily face the fact that in two growing seasons they had to help the farmers change, and that it took one season to learn about the setting and another to spread the word, and that was about two seasons too short. Adult learning moves more slowly, especially when the learning so deeply concerns each family's source of life. Two growing seasons were not enough, and by 1967, the Peace Corps had learned to place agriculture volunteers only where there was irrigation, or at least where there was enough moisture for two cropping seasons. Americans do not sit and wait for the gods to deliver the rains very well.

Wherever Peace Corps volunteers served in Southwest Asia and South Asia, they entered into ancient cultures, patterns of living that often evoked Biblical times, cities with names that hauntingly recalled tales of Alexander the Great, the Arabian Nights, the British wars of the Northwest Frontier, the travels of Marco Polo, Genghis Khan, and Shah Jahan. They found peoples who firmly believed in new and old gods that resembled more the ancient gods of Greek mythology than the Christian God we thought we knew so well. They found a hundred million people who believed in a god called Allah, for whom Jesus Christ was only a respected prophet.

These men and women of the Peace Corps went forth to change things among peoples who believed that the most noble thing was to die in Allah's service, while others among them were convinced that the most important thing was to live out your current lot in life just as it was, no matter how impoverished or bitter, because only by accepting one's fate in this life would a person be reborn into a better one in the next incarnation, which would surely come. Worse yet, not to accept graciously one's lot in life risked community censure, or the assurance of reincarnation to a lower form in the next life or, perhaps worse still, the possibility of being unable to find a husband for one's daughter.

Think of how enterprising Americans reacted to this enormous burden of history, culture, religion, and climate, as they worked for change. Then add a more formidable, more daunting foe: sheer numbers. In India alone, the more than 400 million people (now 720 million) outnumbered the populations of Africa and South America combined. If the Peace Corps had placed in South Asia the same proportion of volunteers it had in Micronesia, no less than 4 million Peace Corps volunteers would have gone to the subcontinent.

The sheer numbers of people involved in each problem gnawed away at even the best volunteer's will to go on.

Peace Corps nurses in Indian hospitals would treat two hundred people in a day and still find the line of those waiting to be seen as long as the sunset in the West. The wards in their hospitals contained two hundred beds where only seventy fit, and waiting in the hospital gardens were the families of the sick, cooking food for the patient and reinfecting him even before he was cured and able to be sent home.

Volunteers working in agriculture expended enormous effort to help twenty village farmers produce 25 percent more food in two years, and then noted that the families each had 20 percent more mouths to feed, so little ground was gained.

Peace Corps teachers pleaded with a state Ministry of Education to raise the salaries for elementary school teachers by $3 a month, only to be informed that in that Indian state, there were 33,000 schools and 102,000 teachers, and if each of them received a $3 raise, the funds needed would be more than the Ministry's entire nonteaching budget. Yet only 40 percent of the children in the villages of the state had any school to go to at all.

It was in the face of all this—this vast South Asian subcontinent with its seas and deserts and mountains and plains and heat and cold and wildness and ancient civilizations and multifarious religions—that energetic and enthusiastic Americans went to work. They did much. They helped build schools by the hundreds, raise chickens by the millions, teach people in schools and out, inoculate children, dig wells, build bridges, grow and lose and save crops, form cooperatives. Some were also married, and gave birth, and many nurtured and carefully cultivated friendships which were thriving two decades later.

Yet, in the end, as S. K. Dey, the Indian government's minister of planning, told one group of Peace Corps volunteers, "India has withstood and indeed absorbed many invasions over four thousand years. She often took the best of what the invaders had to offer and discarded the rest. I am confident India will do likewise with the American Peace Corps. So we are glad to have invited you to come and we are glad you are here. Please give us all that is good about America and please do not give us what is bad. And be patient with us, for life has been going on for a very long time in this part of the universe, and it will go on for a very long time after you have gone."

Minister Dey was right.

Letter from India (1964)

Six of us in the India program were trained to work in irrigation extension. We were to be stationed together in one district north of Calcutta to help develop the transmission systems and teach the cultivators how to use more efficiently the water pumped from dozens of government tube wells. More or less, we would act on the "county agent" job level in the States, advising cultivators on agriculture and irrigation. Sounds plain enough, doesn't it? Exactly what I thought, but now let me explain what really happened.

On arrival in Delhi, we six learned that only three would be going to the original destination, and one of these was transferred to work in beekeeping. Tom and I were transferred to Purulia, and the third was sent to a state poultry farm as a mechanic. Flexibility! The sooner the volunteers accept this word, the more they will enjoy India. In reality, Purulia district is like the Imperial Valley of California before the Colorado River was brought in . . . desert! Irrigation experts in a desert with no water. Laugh, but that is the way things stand now. On top of this, we had no actual job definition when we arrived, and still don't. Officially we are under the supervision of the district agricultural officer, but he isn't sure just how we are supposed to be used. We have done some work for the office—surveyed and mapped several new seed farms, helped erect the agricultural display at the state exhibition, advised on crops, etc., for private cultivators—but the most satisfying work we have had has just fallen into our laps.

An example: A family here in town had twenty-five chickens which weren't laying any eggs. One day while visiting them, I was asked to take a look at the flock. I had no training and very little practical knowledge of poultry, but I suggested more feed and a higher protein content. He tried it and two weeks later was getting twenty-two eggs per day. From this conversation a five-hundred-bird project has developed, along with some wheat cultivation that I also urged him to try. He plans to double his wheat acreage next year and has even bought himself a tractor.

An orphanage in town had a tomato patch that was dying. We checked it over and, for lack of anything else, suggested some ammonium sulfate. The idea worked, and they had tomatoes to sell. They also gave us all we could eat. We are also toying with the idea of starting a goat herd and selling sterilized, bottled milk. We are awaiting the O.K. signal from P.C. Delhi.

Letter from Iran (1965)

Z., like many small towns, is prone to gossip. In a Moslem society, there is strict separation of men and women, and people are very sensitive about any infringement on this. The schools, for example, are let out at different times so the boys and girls won't be on the street together. For several months I have been having my advanced English class, six girls about twenty, meet at my house, giving us a more informal atmosphere. Sometimes my husband's closest friend in town, an unmarried boy of twenty-three, comes to the house while my class is here, and usually he and my husband go off to the bazaar. But when the weather was bad, they sometimes sat talking in the other room of the house. Imagine my chagrin when the chief of education and several of the English teachers informed me that I had better move my class back to the school building, as it was a bad idea to have boys over when the girls were here. These men, realizing the extent of gossip that goes around town about us, primarily because we're the only foreigners here, wanted to tell us who we could have come to our house and when. They informed us that since my husband's friend was "only a bank clerk," we shouldn't associate with him at all. It was most uncomfortable, especially since he has been one of the kindest and most devoted people we have ever known, and aside from him we really have no close friends here. Now, if he happens to come when my class is meeting, my husband simply meets him at the door and they leave.

Letter from East Pakistan (1963)

I've been assigned as a communications technician to the East Pakistan nutrition survey team. The survey team goes out to a rural site about once a month, and I go along with them. I've made one trip, and it was quite an experience.

I was the big sideshow. In fact, I felt like the Pied Piper as droves of children and assorted adults followed me around. Then delegates from neighboring villages came to see the main attraction. One afternoon I was quietly minding my own business when I saw a long line of women and children coming across the rice paddy. I hid in my room until I got so hot that I had to come out. There were forty-eight women and children, and they just stood there and stared. When they finally left, another group of about twenty-five came over. The next afternoon, I was taking a nap and suddenly awoke to find about twenty women and children standing around my bed looking at me. Needless to say, I jumped up, rather shaken, and shooed them out. Everyone was quite surprised that the women would come out of the villages to see me, because the purdah tradition is very strong in the rural areas.

The Experience: Latin America

by Frank Mankiewicz

To understand what distinguished the Peace Corps program and philosophy in Latin America from those of other regions, I think you have to begin with Sargent Shriver, the first Peace Corps director. Then, as now, Shriver was an intellectually curious man, unwilling to accept any orthodoxy without a thorough testing and, if possible, a robust argument. It was Shriver who best exemplified for me the Peace Corps' emphasis on action and its disregard for bureaucratic formalities.

In late 1961, the Peace Corps already had volunteers in the field, but it was still unsure in what direction either they or the organization itself was going. So one day, Shriver called in John Kenneth Galbraith, then ambassador to India but also one of America's leading development economists, to talk with his senior staff. Galbraith was a man who combined a knowledge of international economics with an urgent sense of the political needs of emerging nations.

For two hours, Galbraith talked about development in the Third World (a new phrase, but a useful one) and the optimum way for American policy to emerge there. But instead of the then-current (and highly ethnocentric) theories of the wisdom of large-scale U.S. projects—dams, highways, infrastructure investment—Galbraith talked in terms of *barriers,* and what the Peace Corps could do to break them down. He spoke of "brakes" on development, continent by continent, region by region, culture by culture.

In India, Galbraith said, the great barrier was a lack of investment. No industrial fortunes had survived independence. The British had taken

---

Frank Mankiewicz, executive vice president of Gray and Company in Washington, D.C., served as the Peace Corps' regional director in Latin America.

their capital with them, and the Indian banks were unable to fill the gap. The United States, he said, could help most with substantial credits.

In Africa, the problem was not a lack of capital or resources but of educated and trained personnel. The colonial administrations had made no effort to leave an educated, trained bureaucracy behind, having preferred to run the countries through expatriates. The Peace Corps' best contribution could be a massive infusion of teachers to take the place of the colonials, without their preferred status.

In sharp contrast, the barriers to economic development in Latin America were neither resources, which the region had in abundance, nor capital, with which the government and governing classes were amply supplied. Nor was it a lack of trained personnel. In theory, at least, independence had come in the nineteenth century, and local bureaucracies were well trained and in place. The great obstacle to development in Latin America, Galbraith said, lay in a feudal social structure. So long as upward social mobility was strictly limited—as it had been since the Spanish arrived—no significant amount of wealth would reach the people. Thus, the goals of economic development would never be achieved.

Galbraith's words reminded us that, in Latin American countries—a difficult concept for many North Americans to grasp—the great majority of people despised and felt remote from the leadership that presumed to speak for them. As *el presidente* or *caudillo,* these leaders were regularly on the front pages of their newspapers in the company of the U.S. ambassador, starting a new "project" or announcing a new offensive against Communist guerrillas. In the eyes of the great majority of Latin Americans, that scarcely spoke well for the U.S.A.

Galbraith's words further reminded us that throughout most of the region, the rich effectively paid no taxes, and tiny fractions of the population owned virtually all of the arable land. In the United States, where homesteading and a progressive tax system was commonplace, land and tax reform may not have seemed a monumental change. But in Central and South America, this was truly a revolutionary doctrine—and was seen as such by the wealthy, land-owning class that began a savage attack on the Kennedy administration. In this effort, alas, they were often joined by the local administrators of U.S. foreign aid, who were unwilling to contemplate changes in traditional economic assistance, as change could mean termination of their programs and their jobs.

Past American failing thus imposed a very heavy responsibility on the Peace Corps in Latin America. We thought the Peace Corps had not just to teach, not just to build water or sewage systems, not just to introduce new methods of agriculture, but to bring enough awareness to an excluded majority so that they might reach for the levers of power. In

American foreign policy, characterized since World War II by resistance to social reform in friendly countries, by support for political dictators, and by a comfortable embrace for the local aristocracies, there were few models for young Peace Corps volunteers.

To put the Peace Corps' work in the context of its times, it is important to recall that in 1961 Latin America was undergoing one of its periodic pulsations of change. In Venezuela, Colombia, Peru, Honduras, Cuba, and the Dominican Republic, brutal military dictatorships had given or were giving way to progressive regimes pledged to a better life for the *campesinos* and the urban poor. These "revolutionaries"—Rómulo Betancourt of Venezuela, Juan Bosch of the Dominican Republic, Fidel Castro of Cuba, Alberto Lleras Camargo of Colombia, among others—talked openly of ending a century of privilege in which a handful of oligarchs owned virtually all the valuable land. In the case of Peru, they even owned the Indians who worked the land.

It is also important to remember that President Kennedy had explicitly put the United States on the side of change. For the first time since Franklin D. Roosevelt took the Marines out of Nicaragua and proclaimed the "Good Neighbor Policy," an American administration had rejected the repressive regimes of Latin America in favor of reform. Kennedy had announced the Alliance for Progress, and it is hard to remember just how revolutionary it appeared. We will give no foreign aid, we said, to countries where democratic governments are overthrown or where militarism reigns. Furthermore, we will tailor our aid precisely to those countries with broad programs of human rights, tax reform, and land redistribution programs, and we will extend technological help to those countries that need assistance in the effort to reform.

It is hard, even now, to measure President Kennedy's extraordinary impact on the ordinary people of Latin America, and even on some of its leaders. To this day, his picture (often on yellowed and fading newsprint) is taped and tacked to millions of adobe, tar-paper, and straw walls in the mountains and the *favelas*.

The memory is enshrined, to be sure, not because of any single tangible achievement. The Alliance for Progress soon dwindled down to just another technical assistance program, in which U.S. bureaucrats spent tours of duty shuffling papers with their local counterparts, reviewing countless feasibility studies and compiling mountains of meaningless statistics. Still, Latin Americans, with the exception of the rich and powerful, loved John Kennedy because they sensed he loved them. "If we cannot help the many who are poor," he told them in his inaugural address, "we cannot save the few who are rich." In that time, in that place, they knew he was talking about them.

At that moment, the Peace Corps arrived on the scene. This "other arm" of U.S. policy strengthened and reinforced the Alliance for Progress. It told the miserable of a continent, abused by their leaders for decades while the United States supported those leaders and reaped the economic benefits, that at last we had changed. Not only were we to alter the habit of a century and actively support reform and policies designed to bring economic and political power to the poor; we were even going to send our young people to live with them and help them change their lives.

Step by step, the peculiarly Latin American version of the Peace Corps emerged. It was not the almost mystic village-style Peace Corps of India, nor the technical-assistance programs of Southeast Asia, and surely not the teacher-dominated program of Africa. It was, as we all freely recognized, a "revolutionary force," and we called it "community development."

In truth, we hardly knew where to start, but our model was in the streets of Chicago. The community development movement began in Chicago's "Back of the Yards," founded by Saul Alinsky and his disciples, who forged an instrument by which the scorned and disenfranchised could reach for a share of power and participation. Alinsky believed in working by building organization, almost for the very sake of organization. He thought the poor should "rub raw the sores of discontent," and if that meant demonstrations, then his people would demonstrate. If it meant picket lines in residential neighborhoods, they would picket. Alinsky's community development groups were highly vocal and highly visible. They brought home to the "haves" the needs and deprivations of the "have-nots."

Any organizational tool would do, just to get people together who had never sensed a feeling of group power before. Sooner or later, the theory held, the establishment would take note, recoil in horror and sometimes in violence, and then, reluctantly, act, often too late and mostly with too little, but act. And then, as time went on, they would act some more. It was a time-honored principle of American governance—"the wheel that squeaks the loudest gets the grease." The trick was to get the poor to squeak at all.

At first formlessly, then with conscious direction, community development became the model for Peace Corps programs in Latin America. Later, under Sargent Shriver, "community action" became the technique adopted for the War on Poverty. The "maximum feasible participation" of the poor mandated by the anti-poverty law was an extension of the principle validated by the Peace Corps of Latin America, the principle which held that organizing the *outsiders* of society could bring them *inside*. Volunteers bound for Latin America were trained, at least for the

THE JOB

first five years and sporadically thereafter, to believe their job was to bring the dispossessed into a society whose leaders did not want them in. That, for better or for worse, was a *revolutionary* mission, and it was not without its opponents. Even within the Peace Corps, a strong conservative tendency soon appeared, manifested in a bland "hands across the sea" missionary instinct, endemic to foreign policy bureaucracies.

To those of us in the day-to-day training and administration of community development, with its emphasis on projects to transform urban slums and remote Andean villages, it was often distracting and even irritating to find scarce Peace Corps resources diverted to soft, easy-to-publicize projects whereby, for example, an American school could build a counterpart school in a developing country, whether it was needed or not. But for the most part, the community development effort proceeded with high-level support and, best of all, some discernible success on the ground. Shriver was never less than wholly supportive and enthusiastic, and often cited communities of the poor who had forced their way, through the techniques of organization, into the mainstream.

The challenge faced by volunteers was aggravated by the remoteness in Latin America of the concept of cooperation that was central to community organization. De Tocqueville, in *Democracy in America,* had made much of the American genius for self-government and voluntary association, a quality scarcely apparent in Central or South America. The notion that people in a neighborhood could pool different skills to help build one another's houses was not to come naturally to Latin American culture.

This was hardly surprising in countries where the suspicion prevailing between insiders and outsiders was so harsh. From Guatemala south to Chile, all along the spine of the Andes, are countries where the Indian majority was regarded as not only inferior but hardly human at all. It was the white and *mestizo* elements that ran and decided everything in those countries.

In Peru, for example, Peace Corps volunteers questioned whether it would do any good to build a new school in an Indian village if the white teachers who would be sent there continued openly to regard the children as animals for speaking their native tongue, rather than Spanish. When a social worker ostentatiously wipes off the chair in the family home on which he or she is about to sit, the interview is not off to a good start. Peace Corps volunteers were appalled when Andean children, asked which animal they would most wish to emulate, offered the ant or a rat as a reply. When they were asked to draw themselves and their families, the figures often appeared without hands or feet—a classic self-portrayal of helplessness.

During the early years, a conscious effort was made to keep volunteers' living standards close to those of the people with whom they were working. That meant, in remote mountain villages and near-jungle settlements along the river, a lack not only of electricity and running water but of any source of reliable medical care. A Peace Corps doctor was on duty in every country, and kept fairly steadily on the road, but it still seems a miracle that more serious illness did not occur.

Such handicaps notwithstanding, conscientiously and imaginatively the volunteers plodded forward to apply the best community development training the Peace Corps knew how to provide. Usually they worked in pairs, to lessen the degree of cultural trauma. Characteristically, they took some time at the start to make an inventory of their community, ask questions, identify potential leaders, and seek organizing possibilities. If it turned out, for example, that one of the "sores of discontent" was a closed and locked playing field, then the appropriate organizing tactic might be to form two community teams and enlist the local priest, perhaps by a collective visit, to join in petitioning the authorities to unlock the field. Or perhaps it was simply a matter of climbing the fence and using the forbidden field for practice. Community development called for experimentation and improvisation. For each success, there were many failures.

Organization around credit unions and co-ops proved to be a useful tool in small towns and villages. The task was harder in the sprawling shantytowns, where agriculture was impossible and the daily gathering of food and water consumed almost all a family's time. These shantytowns—not really slums in the American sense of decaying urban environments—are a phenomenon of Latin development. With the exception of Cuba (where Castro put almost all available development funds into roads, health centers, markets, and schools in the countryside, while starving Havana), every large Latin city is ringed by squatter settlements containing perhaps twice the population of the city itself.

The settlers, classically, seize vacant land, usually under cover of darkness, carrying rudimentary straw or cardboard walls and roofs with them. By morning, a sizable new "suburb" is in place, complete with marked-off streets, a few small "stores" selling soft drinks and cigarettes, and perhaps a defiant flag or two. These invasions are highly organized and include, usually, people from a particular zone or village or of a single political persuasion—sometimes both. If the invasion is successful, and it nearly always is, then the settlement expands. Newcomers arrive, a rudimentary administration is set up, and the residents take their place as an urban interest, embarrassing to the government but a presence to deal with.

In the cities, the Peace Corps volunteers had a harder task than in the villages. Outside the city, the population is identifiable, origins are easily acknowledged, and a need around which a community can be organized is not too hard to locate. In the countryside, an organization formed to get a playing field, protest an inadequate farm-to-market road, or create a co-op can be held together when its members begin to sense their power. But in the city, allegiances shift, populations are far from stable and hard to track, and needs proliferate. Leadership there is very often plain old demagogy. The urban barrio dweller, ripped from familiar surroundings in the country and humbled to the point of scrounging for food, was a far harder target for the Peace Corps volunteer than the villager who came from a stable family structure.

Much has been made, some of it by the very Alliance for Progress bureaucrats who found Latin America's community development projects hard to "quantify," of the "failure" of urban community development volunteers. It is true that the work was difficult, and for a young American in a strange culture-within-a-culture, it was often easier to succumb to boredom and culture shock than to listen, observe, and organize around a community need, however dimly perceived. But for those who succeeded, the rewards were great. For many volunteers, a sense of success would not come until years later, and many have reported returning to their villages or settlements after a decade or more, to find the seeds of early community organization grown to the sturdy young branches of a co-op, credit union, playground league, or burgeoning political center. Nearly all have found stronger communities, which are more willing to speak up and try to influence the traditional sources of power. Community development seems, by and large, to have made an impact.

Since the peak days of the middle and late 1960s, the number of Peace Corps volunteers, as well as countries in which they serve, has declined significantly in Latin America. That may be a statement of the volunteers' effectiveness. Some of the traditional governments asked the volunteers to leave, no doubt, for the very reason that they were *too* successful. It was the same reason that made the mayors of many American cities glad when the War on Poverty ended and the community action organizers went home. As soon as the outcasts of society begin to claim the right to be involved in the process of government, the establishment resists. In many countries of Latin America, I believe it was an index of community development's progress that the Peace Corps was asked to leave.

In reviewing the Latin American experience, I recall that the first of the Peace Corps' objectives is to better people's lives. Cuba and Nicaragua, where no volunteers ever served, also had revolutions, accomplished by force of arms. While the lot of the ordinary citizen is far better than under the old military dictatorships, the immediate future, without strong institutions and under relentless American pressure, is not promising. I would contend that the Peace Corps' work in community development has produced results that, while surely less dramatic, perhaps stand on a sounder foundation.

Centers of power alternative to the traditional oligarchies continue to develop. The social structures today, in most countries, are not so feudal; the number of people excluded from meaningful participation in decision-making has declined. Governments—again, in most countries—seem somewhat more responsive to the ordinary citizen.

Perhaps more important, there is in Latin America today a clear trend back to democratic institutions. In Argentina, Guatemala, and Peru, freely elected presidents have taken over from military and oligarchic strongmen. Other democratic leaders are waiting in the wings, even in such rigid dictatorships as Chile and Paraguay. For the first time, furthermore, these new leaders seem to have behind them strong democratic organizations. It is not farfetched, I think, for the Peace Corps to claim some of the credit for this change. The generation rising to power in Latin America today was introduced to politics in the era of John Kennedy, when the Peace Corps arrived. The idealism the volunteers left behind—along with the concepts of participation and organization—may have had a more powerful impact than we will ever be able to measure.

The Peace Corps' second objective is to make the people of the host countries better acquainted with the United States. In Latin America, the record seems clear. For at least five years and to a remarkable degree thereafter, our "hosts" saw a different breed of American. They were neither rich nor arrogant, and they shared the hardships of the poor they had chosen to help. In a sense, most important of all may have been the independence Peace Corps volunteers showed from their own country's foreign policy, which for nearly two centuries most Latins have considered misguided, if not actually oppressive.

A dramatic example came in the Dominican Republic in 1965. A government proclaiming its commitment to constitutional rule was under attack by generals anxious to return to the military dominance of Trujillos' time. President Johnson, citing "Communist atrocities," airlifted American troops to "preserve neutrality," which meant to safeguard the military junta. When the U.S. troops arrived, the one hundred members of the Peace Corps in the country were unanimously on the other side. Indeed, when a U.N. observer team visited Santo Domingo, it was only Peace Corps volunteers and staff who could pass through the lines and enter the territory controlled by the constitutionalists. As power in the Dominican Republic continues to shift back and forth, the lesson of the Americans who cast their lot with the people has not been forgotten.

THE JOB

The impression in Latin America of the volunteer as being from a truly democratic society has persisted. The volunteer is a role model in a continent of societies by no means all committed to freedom. It is perhaps significant that the new reformist regimes in Latin America, while extremely jealous of their independence, seem to be less reflexively anti-American than the reformers in the past. The notion carried by the Peace Corps—that the United States can be on the side of democratic change—remains alive and well.

Finally, the Peace Corps experiment was intended to create in the United States a better understanding of life in the underdeveloped countries where volunteers had served. In this respect, the Peace Corps in Latin America has been an unqualified success. More than 37,000 volunteers—about a third of all who have enlisted in the Peace Corps—have served or are now serving in Latin America, and they will carry with them permanently a sense of what life is truly like for the underclass of a continent.

It makes them, in the majority, more skeptical of easy theories, and of the automatic fear of reform and freedom that has so often characterized U.S. policy in Latin America. As those volunteers come increasingly to assume the central places of leadership in our country, they will undoubtedly continue to work a change in our views and our policies. Then the Peace Corps will have proved to be, as Sargent Shriver once exuberantly called it, "the point of the lance," the instrument by which Americans will have come to understand the best part of our natures and to act, as a nation, on our best impulses. For so small an investment, that will have been a major return.

Peace Corps Bulletin #5, Guatemala (1965)

Last week, the government of Guatemala decreed a "State of Siege" condition throughout the entire country as a measure on behalf of public safety and against terrorism and sabotage. Because of this situation, we urge you to observe the following instructions:

1. In case of demonstration, riots, disturbances, or street disorders, stay in your household. These things don't last long. You are safer among the people who know you than anywhere else. If you are not at home when trouble of this nature arises, get away from the scene of disturbance and head for home or a well-known safe spot (church, prominent hotels, etc.).

2. During "State of Siege" periods, do not travel at night, except for emergencies that merit risking your life. Curfew restrictions might be imposed suddenly. If you do not hear about curfews, it then becomes dangerous to you in that roadblocks may legitimately try to stop you. You will have no way of knowing whether to stop or not. Both can be dangerous.

3. During a "State of Siege" or trouble times, listen to a radio frequently in order to keep abreast of news, announcements, or developments.

4. Stay away from areas that present dangers (example: Do not travel in zones of rumored or known guerrilla activity).

5. Touch base with the local authorities frequently. Let them know where you are and how you can be located. In case of emergencies, we usually must resort to calls to the police, military, and *alcaldias* in order to reach you.

6. Carry adequate identification at all times.

7. Do not carry or possess firearms or dynamite or anything that might subject you to suspicion of violation of Guatemalan laws. Furthermore, during troubled times, be wary of doing irregular favors. You may unwittingly be storing weapons, hiding wanted people, carrying unlawful messages, etc.

THE JOB

8. Refrain from voicing opinions relative to delicate local issues of the day. (If pressed to do so, merely state that you are not aware of all the facts on which to base an opinion.)

9. Contact some Peace Corps staff as expeditiously as possible whenever you or your property are threatened or whenever you are in any danger. If you can't reach us, try to contact U.S. consul or duty officer at embassy. Always contact local authorities (military, police, *alcaldia*) for immediate needs for protection.

Letter from Bolivia (1965)

The area in which I work with two other volunteers is an ambitious colonization project, to bring Bolivians down from the Alti Plano to the Alto Beni, where, hopefully, they can build a better life. When you first see the jungle that is presented to the new colonist, armed with only his machete and hatchet, you can't help thinking that his task is impossible. Yet in a few months he will have cleared 2½ acres, enough for 500 cocoa plants and space for his house. It has been a great feeling to see these houses go up—a sign the project may succeed. I became pretty discouraged at first, but now things are shaping up.

My life here is so different from what I had grown up in that perhaps this change will be the greatest one I will ever experience. Living in a small, dirt-floored room and eating low-quality food are things that anyone can adjust to. The big problem comes with the psychological adjustments necessary to let you do a good job.

Every volunteer shares the problem of the lack of privacy. Physically, my room affords no corner in which I can shut myself from the rest of the world. People always want to know what the volunteer is doing, where he is going, etc. As a result, my life is open to inspection at all times. This has been especially hard for me, for I treasure quiet and meditative periods. Even when I'm alone, the noisy sounds of the battery record player penetrates, so there is little chance for complete quiet.

Another problem which I had to overcome was the recollection of the things that we North Americans have in abundance. The thoughts of good food, opportunities to go places and do things, and other material joys must be put out of mind. This becomes easier to do as one becomes more involved in the life around him.

Due to isolation and lack of diversion, fiestas are popular. These people have a fiesta that could last a few hours or all night, and the day of the week doesn't matter, since work can always be put off. Birthday fiestas are perhaps the most grueling, because they commence at midnight. As a Peace Corps volunteer, I feel I must put in an appearance at these events, but I am one of the earliest quitters and lightest drinkers. We

THE JOB

average two fiestas a week, but so far I have kept to my work schedule regardless of fiesta activities.

We have no church, and the nearest priest is fifteen miles away, downriver. There is no sign of religion here, either through symbols or religious observances. I had the opportunity to say the first table grace at Thanksgiving time, when the Peace Corps volunteers took over the dinner.

So you are wondering, no doubt, what I am doing here. Let me tell you about my work. The first month was difficult, but the one thing I did do was help put in an irrigation system for a nursery. I'm sorry to say that this project has not been completed and may never be. Basic tools are lacking, but in three or four days of searching, things like pipe wrenches can usually be found. The whole job ground to a halt when the pipe thread cutter broke. We have had pipe fittings on order in La Paz for two months now, and I don't know when the parts will arrive.

I spent the next six weeks after I was foiled on the irrigation project surveying farmers' property lines. This work was needed before the cocoa could be planted, and it should avoid disputes later on. The work allowed me to have a fixed program, but, most important, I got to know the colonists better as I worked on their land. I had a crew of three Bolivians with me every day, and one of the fellows was able to learn enough about simple surveying that he could probably do the next surveying job in the area. He still cannot lay out the work on paper, but once that is done, he can follow plans and construct the appropriate lines in the field. The surveying work allowed me to get exercise, since we estimate that we have walked seventy-five miles each week.

Now I am working with individual farmers and their cocoa, trying to be with each of them when he first plants. Most of the farmers have attended demonstrations on proper planting, but I have not encountered one who remembers the correct way. In the course of the work, many questions are raised about other crops which colonists want to plant. Through these questions and my study, I am learning about tropical agriculture.

Two months ago a naturalist passed through, and I had the good fortune to take a couple of hikes through the jungle with him. In the course of about four hours, I learned more about the jungle than I would have in two years on my own. He showed me a wild vanilla plant and mentioned that it might make a good food crop for the area. With the thought of a second cash crop for the farmers in mind, I initiated a study project on vanilla. The U.S. Department of Agriculture supplied some good material, but, considering the soils and the planning involved, I had to rule the vanilla plant out.

Now that I have become better acquainted with the farmers and their problems, projects pop up right and left. Though my time is so occupied with the cocoa, I have attempted a few side projects. Some problems have quick and easy solutions. For example, farmers in one particular area have to make a four-mile round trip to get water. I suggested that they make simple water catchments, using their roofs as a start. They did, and this alleviated the problem to some extent.

The Vocation

by Francis A. Luzzatto

The early days of the Peace Corps are still remembered for how they inspired a generation of Americans. It was a legendary burst of energy and creativity that carried the Peace Corps forward for its first twenty-five years and will likely carry it forward for many years to come. Few government programs began with such promise; even fewer have managed to retain such a spirit of idealism and success. Those of us who came later were conscious that we were guardians of a precious legacy.

The Peace Corps' mission was and remains "to promote world peace and friendship." How this rather lofty mission is to be pursued has been discussed continuously since the beginning. The development of Third World countries was an afterthought. As far as I know, none of the founders originally saw development as central to the Peace Corps' role. The shift was based largely upon early volunteers' experiences and the need to attract support from Congress and the executive branch. By 1963, the Peace Corps' leaders had begun to present the program, at least in part, as contributing to Third World development.

From the very beginning, the Peace Corps' three goals have been: (1) "to assign volunteers to interested countries to help them meet their needs for trained personnel"; (2) "to promote a better understanding of Americans among the people served"; and (3) "to promote better understanding of people of other countries among the American people."

With these three goals, the founders indicated that technical assistance was not the Peace Corps' *raison d'être.* They insisted that in order to make significant contributions to world peace, the Peace Corps would have to go beyond the more traditional, impersonal modes of "trickle down" development assistance. Likewise, they committed the Peace Corps to reaching beyond the scope of existing international educational and cul-

---

Francis A. Luzzatto is a consultant with NDPL and Associates in Washington, D.C.

tural exchange programs. What motivated them was a recognition of the intrinsic value of having people from diverse cultures living and, above all, working together for extended periods of time.

Thus the Peace Corps was to be an investment in the future, to be paid off by creating a cadre of Americans who would come to understand the beauty and strength of other cultures, while contributing to the development of Third World nations. The founders firmly believed that it was in this country's long-term interest to learn more about the rest of the world, just as it was in the interest of other nations to learn more about us. It was expected that the volunteers would share their insights with America and would ultimately help shape national policy. The founders understood, then, an idea that is only now beginning to be accepted and that is still not fully understood by most, namely, that we—rich nations and poor—truly live in an increasingly interdependent world.

From the outset, the emphasis was on structuring field assignments so that the volunteers would be living and working with their "counterparts" at the village level. Recruitment, selection, training, and field support were all designed to create an entirely new brand of international worker. It is now, perhaps, difficult to appreciate the extent to which new ground was being broken. Until then, no one really knew whether large numbers of predominantly young Americans could function effectively for extended periods of time in physical and cultural circumstances so alien to their own. No one knew whether the volunteers would be accepted by the people with whom they lived, much less be taken seriously by host government officials.

Reports on the success of the early volunteers came quickly. The first volunteers not only functioned effectively, they seemed to thrive. The personal rewards of working directly with people and becoming part of their community were incomparable. Physical difficulties appeared to be inconsequential and even lent mystique to the Peace Corps. In the public arena the Peace Corps was declared a success.

Within the development community, however, the volunteers were regarded as well-meaning amateurs, at best. The experts argued that serious development work could not be performed by "unskilled" volunteers, ignoring that our own country, not to mention every other industrialized country in the world, had been developed by its own ordinary citizens. It has been said that among the tragic legacies of colonialism is the attitude that advanced degrees are essential to all forms of development work. To some, one of the Peace Corps' greatest contributions has been to demonstrate through its volunteers that effective programming, intensive short-term technical training, and, above all,

THE JOB

motivation can make ordinary people into effective development workers. This is a view, however, that is not universally held. Most development professionals, particularly in the early 1960s, argued that specialists alone were capable of having a substantive impact in development.

My own father, who by the early 1960s had spent many years of his career directing foreign assistance programs, had grave reservations about the Peace Corps on just those grounds. Having succeeded in Europe with the Marshall Plan, he and his fellow "development experts" turned their attention to the Third World, initially equating development with reconstruction. They did not then fully appreciate that while the process of *reconstruction* can be accelerated by massive amounts of external assistance, *development* is a far slower, more evolutionary undertaking, particularly in predominantly rural societies. Those early criticisms of the Peace Corps' approach to grass-roots development were taken seriously enough so that the stage was set for periodic examination of the Peace Corps' role in development.

Every Peace Corps director has, in fact, attempted to clarify the Peace Corps' contribution to development. There were those who used their tenure to make the Peace Corps into what they felt was a more serious development agency. Inevitably, their successors would try to reestablish a balance between the Peace Corps' three rather elusive goals, reemphasizing the experience of the individual volunteers and their relationships with the people with whom they lived and worked. No matter how important the Peace Corps' role in development was to become, goals two and three continued to be seen as essential to overall success.

Over the years, attempts have been made to reinterpret or otherwise alter the Peace Corps. And, while some of these attempts have left their mark, few substantive initiatives have survived. The Peace Corps remains essentially unchanged. It still sees itself almost exclusively as a "volunteer-sending" organization. Volunteers still serve two-year terms, are still assigned to work on development projects at the community level, and are still supported by a Peace Corps "in-country" staff. The Peace Corps' second and third goals, which stress mutual understanding, remain the Peace Corps' soul.

And yet, while these "bottom-line" tenets represent the Peace Corps' rather unique sense of purpose, they have served to isolate it from change. New ideas and challenges have all too often been treated as threats rather than seen as opportunities to expand the scope of the agency or to make it more effective. I say this as a strong believer in the program's success, but also as someone with strong convictions about what the Peace Corps could and *should* become.

Perhaps inevitably, and with few exceptions, Peace Corps directors have spent the bulk of their time administering the program as it was turned over to them. They spent their first six months learning about the program and the remainder trying to keep the program on track. The imperatives of day-to-day operations have dominated their tenures. I am in no way denigrating the past or present leaders of the Peace Corps. To the contrary, each of them has worked hard to sustain the program, at times against great odds. Yet, any review of how the Peace Corps has evolved must question whether over the years, the Peace Corps has become a little too self-satisfied, and too resistant to change.

In the late 1960s, battles were fought over the effectiveness of community development projects. Peace Corps volunteers were trained to spark development by first identifying and then addressing problems once they had been assigned to a specific village. In reality, and by necessity, programs were so loosely structured that training could not predict what technical skills would be needed. These programs served to strengthen the view that the Peace Corps was populated and run by well-meaning amateurs. Peace Corps loyalists responded that traditional foreign assistance strategies were bypassing the vast majority of the people at the community level and that the Peace Corps approach was on target.

Perhaps the most aggressive effort to redirect the Peace Corps began in 1969. Joseph Blatchford, appointed director by President Nixon, responded to the increasing criticism of unstructured programs by propelling the Peace Corps into what he called his "new directions." At the heart of these "new directions" was a commitment to professionalize the Peace Corps. He called upon the overseas staff to program for more highly skilled volunteers. He revamped the recruitment, selection, and placement systems to accommodate this new agenda. Countries began to see the Peace Corps in a different light. They now looked to it as a means of acquiring additional skilled technicians without having to expend scarce resources.

To the proponents of these "new directions," the Peace Corps was finally responding to what the Third World needed and wanted. But to many, Blatchford's approach upset the delicate balance between the agency's three goals. No longer were an applicant's personal qualities and motivation considered as important in the selection process as professional skills.

And whereas great emphasis had been placed on having volunteers become involved in community activities and in initiating projects on their own, more volunteers were now placed in ministries or research institutions in an effort to increase their impact. By necessity, many of these volunteers were assigned to urban areas, where the sustenance derived from becoming part of a community stopped being an inherent part of the experience. More and more volunteers viewed their assignments as a nine-to-five job, rather than as a twenty-four-hour-a-day commitment.

Trainee and volunteer attrition climbed, and within a short time requests for highly skilled recruits outstripped the agency's ability to deliver. But most of all, by sanctifying "higher skills," the Peace Corps demeaned the integrity of other volunteers. The term "generalist," which had been part of the Peace Corps' lexicon from the very beginning, took on a pejorative connotation. More people began to see the Peace Corps purely in development terms.

By 1974, the "new directions" approach had begun to give way, as the Peace Corps staff shifted back to making constructive use of its natural constituency, the recent liberal arts graduate. Only this time, greater emphasis was given to developing programs with more carefully defined goals and objectives, and to designing more comprehensive technical training. And while there was an attempt to rehabilitate the "generalists," the more self-conscious term "skill-trained volunteer" formally took its place. This was an indication that the Peace Corps could not go back. The theme emerged that, through more sophisticated programming and better training, "ordinary" volunteers can in fact become effective development workers. There is no doubt that the Peace Corps of today is in many ways stronger for having had to resolve some of the issues raised during Blatchford's time.

In 1971, Blatchford was appointed to head ACTION, a new federal volunteer agency that incorporated both the Peace Corps and VISTA, its domestic counterpart. VISTA (Volunteers in Service to America) was started by Shriver in 1965 as part of President Johnson's War on Poverty. In its early days, VISTA was virtually a carbon copy of the Peace Corps, recruiting predominantly middle-class Americans and assigning them to inner cities, Indian reservations, and rural pockets of poverty. By 1968, VISTA had made a radical departure from the Peace Corps by recruiting some of its volunteers from the "target populations" for service in their own communities.

Those of us who had worked with VISTA and who had been advocates of VISTA's move to enlist "locally recruited volunteers" first viewed the merger with the Peace Corps as an opportunity to conduct "joint programming." We even saw the potential for working with some of the emerging domestic volunteer programs in the Third World. From an administrative point of view, it was hoped that the two agencies could operate more efficiently by performing such functions as volunteer recruitment in common. From the start, however, the merger with AC-

TION did not work well. Both VISTA and the Peace Corps immediately felt under siege. The staff in both agencies, rankled by no longer being able to control their own destinies, worked hard to preserve as much independence as they could. Eventually, both the Peace Corps and VISTA went their separate ways.

Despite the failure, a number of initiatives taken during the first six years of the Peace Corps' uneasy relationship with ACTION should be noted as having had an impact. In making a departure from what had been done in the past, at least three innovations should be considered major factors in the Peace Corps' evolution.

One innovation focused on training: heretofore, volunteers had been trained either in the United States or at "regional" training centers in Puerto Rico, the Virgin Islands, and Hawaii. By 1973, most pre-service training had been transferred to "in-country" locations. This move had a positive effect on the entire Peace Corps: training was brought closer to programming, it incorporated more actual experience; language and cross-cultural training were redesigned to take advantage of new opportunities provided at the new sites. The decentralization of training contributed to the further decentralization of many administrative and programming decisions.

A second major innovation was the establishment of the Peace Corps' Information Collection and Exchange (ICE). ICE was begun on the premise that, in addition to providing volunteers to development projects, the Peace Corps could become a *source* of technical information about how development works at the micro level.

The theory behind ICE held that volunteers living and working at the local level learn to function within constraints as tangible as the lack of resources and as difficult to define as cultural attitudes. Volunteers are sent to their assignments with only limited access to the capital and materials associated with development programs. By necessity, they often have no choice but to approach problems in the field by making use of locally available materials. Furthermore, they are in a position to understand and take into account whatever inhibitions to development affect the people they live with. As individuals, they discover some of the most precious lessons in development, namely, what works, what doesn't work, why, and under what circumstances.

In 1973, Ernst Schumacher popularized an approach to development now known as "appropriate technology." Schumacher argued that all too frequently the more sophisticated technologies introduced by Western development agencies were not relevant, at least in the poorer areas of the Third World, where a vast majority of the population lives. Furthermore, the principles he promoted recognized the role culture plays in the acceptance of technology. He stressed the importance of putting

THE JOB

people to work, instead of replacing them with a machine for the sake of modernity. He placed high priority on the use of local resources, so that development projects would not inadvertently cause communities to become even more dependent on outside sources of material and capital. But most of all, he underlined that appropriateness can only be judged in local terms. In a very real sense, the Peace Corps had become a unique primary source of field-tested "appropriate technologies."

By 1975, over 60,000 Peace Corps volunteers had served, covering a wide spectrum of community-level development programs. They had accepted, rejected, modified, and even invented countless tools, methods, and technologies. They had not only adapted technologies to a particular set of circumstances; in many cases they had even written or translated technical material into a local language. The possibilities of harnessing these experiences seemed limitless. But despite scores of reports, files, and even numerous technical papers and manuals written by volunteers on their own, there had never been a systematic search through the records in Washington and in field offices for descriptions of practical techniques and strategies that could be used by volunteers, not to mention by other development workers.

ICE set out to identify and collect these by-products, then gathering dust in closets and filing cabinets in Peace Corps offices throughout the world. The "take" was impressive, and in short order ICE had catalogued materials covering nearly the entire range of Peace Corps activities in the field.

ICE became a great success. For the first time, staff and volunteers alike could write to an office in Washington, asking for technical information. Inquiries were answered by sending a manual published by the Peace Corps, a technical publication purchased by the Peace Corps, or a copy of an unpublished technical paper selected from ICE's extensive files. In the years following its inception, ICE has continued to grow. It has published well over one hundred technical manuals and has greatly increased its collection of field-generated information, making it available as a technical information base.

Those of us who started ICE had also theorized that the information produced by the Peace Corps could be of use to development workers outside the agency, thus greatly multiplying the Peace Corps' overall impact. Almost immediately, individuals and organizations concerned with micro-level development projects, such as private voluntary organizations and international donor agencies, began asking for ICE publications. In some cases these requests came from ministry officials and other organizations in the Third World that had little or no association with the Peace Corps.

It is unfortunate that the Peace Corps does not present itself as an agency whose impact could go well beyond the direct work of its volunteers. There are just too many villages and too few effective development workers of any kind to be satisfied with the work several thousand volunteers perform each year. To put it bluntly, in terms of actual development, its five thousand or so volunteers each year are hardly making a dent. However, the systematic dissemination of technical information derived from the work of the volunteers could greatly enhance the Peace Corps' effectiveness, but it would take a major step, which thus far has been resisted. It has been argued that such a move would detract from the public's perception of the Peace Corps and would be rejected out of hand by the Congress as not being within the purview of the Peace Corps. I am not convinced. Presenting the dissemination of field-generated technical information as a natural function *co-equal* with the assignment of volunteers in no way diminishes the volunteers. On the contrary, it lends greater dignity to their work. What I have just described is a familiar concept to the business community, where the marketing of by-products often becomes as important and as profitable as the primary product itself.

A third innovation of this period actually had roots back in the early sixties, when the Peace Corps was instrumental in organizing an international conference on voluntarism, held in Puerto Rico. The purpose of this conference was to determine whether the Peace Corps and the other bilateral volunteer-sending programs should band together to help other nations start their own international and domestic programs. The result was the formation of the Peace Corps Secretariat (later the International Secretariat for Voluntary Service).

Yet within a few years, in part due to tighter budgets, the Peace Corps' interest in promoting domestic voluntarism in the Third World had waned. In retrospect, I would attribute this lack of interest, once again, to the Peace Corps' single-minded concern with its "main-line" function of deploying volunteers in the field.

In the late 1970s, the Peace Corps negotiated its first interagency agreement with the U.S. Agency for International Development (AID). Heretofore, there had been little or no collaboration at the agency level, although in many countries, informal arrangements were made locally. It had taken more than fifteen years for the two agencies to recognize that each had something to offer the other. AID, under pressure to support more programs at the local level, sought to take advantage of the Peace Corps' special ability to sustain small projects in rural areas. Meanwhile, the Peace Corps saw AID as a source of money to support additional volunteer technical training, short-term technical consultants, and programming and training conferences, particularly for its staff.

THE JOB

The marriage of convenience worked. Several additional interagency agreements have been negotiated under directors Richard Celeste and Loret Ruppe. In each case the interagency agreement allowed the Peace Corps to expand its technical support to its field staff and volunteers in specific program areas such as agriculture, energy, forestry, and health. One of the most recent agreements with AID created the Small Projects Assistance fund (SPA). SPA allows Peace Corps country directors to fund small community projects identified by volunteers, while providing AID with the administrative ability to support a wide range of small community projects. For the first time, volunteers had direct access to project funds specifically set aside for their use by the agency. And while reserving money for volunteer use may appear to violate one of the Peace Corps' original principles, in practice, ambassadors in several countries had for some time been setting aside portions of their self-help funds for the volunteers. They, too, had concluded that volunteers were in the best possible position to identify worthwhile projects at the community level. The SPA program has met with the almost unanimous approval of volunteers and staff alike.

The Peace Corps' relationship with AID has come so far that, today, there is a standing AID/Peace Corps Coordinating Committee chaired by the director, Loret Ruppe, and Peter McPherson, the AID head, who is himself a former Peace Corps volunteer.

To many, the Carter election of 1976 seemed to herald the "restoration," after the Nixon/Ford years, when "new directions" were foisted upon the Peace Corps and the agency was administratively subsumed under ACTION. And yet the Carter years would prove to be among the Peace Corps' most trying.

The reasons for the antagonism between the ACTION and the Peace Corps directors were complex. Part of the problem can be attributed to the continued resentment on the part of the new Peace Corps leadership of ACTION's role in determining its policies. After all, didn't restoration imply independence? In retrospect, other disagreements can be attributed to stylistic differences between the leaders. But the most significant disagreements between Sam Brown, the ACTION director, and Carolyn Payton, the newly appointed director of the Peace Corps, stemmed from a rather fundamental disparity in the vision of what the Peace Corps had become and what it could be.

The first such disagreement erupted over the role of the "education" volunteer. Prior to this time, it had always been assumed that assigning volunteers to teaching was one of Peace Corps' strongest programs. From the very beginning teachers were assigned to primary schools, secondary schools, universities, and teacher training institutions. Also from the beginning, a significant number of education volunteers taught English, primarily at the secondary school level. Education volunteers were relatively easy to recruit, train, and support, and by all accounts derived great job satisfaction from their work. Most of all, some host governments had made it clear that their highest priority was to have the Peace Corps teach English.

But shortly after his arrival at ACTION, Sam Brown began to ask some difficult questions. Should the Peace Corps expend its scarce resources on teaching English when so many in the Third World did not have such bare essentials as food, potable water, or adequate medical care? Why were Peace Corps volunteers teaching English to the elite of a country, giving them an even greater advantage? Why, after so many years of teaching English, were volunteers still needed in some countries, and didn't this indicate a lack of effectiveness? At the very least, did it not suggest an unhealthy dependency? Maybe the Peace Corps had gone on too long on its own momentum without rethinking some of its program assumptions. Maybe there were other roles in education that volunteers could perform.

The leadership of ACTION charged ideological impurity, contending that the Peace Corps was out of touch with progressive forces in the Third World. ACTION wanted the Peace Corps to perform as a "true" anti-poverty effort or, in development jargon, as technical assistance to the poorest of the Third World's poor. The Peace Corps, on the other hand, charged the leadership of ACTION with failing to understand the realities of programming in the Third World and of trying to impose its own American anti-poverty rhetoric on host countries. It argued that legitimacy lay in pursuing all three of its goals and that it took seriously its commitment to be responsive to the requests of host governments.

Earlier, a group of experienced programming and training specialists had been hired to analyze the Peace Corps' work, from recruitment to impact, and to recommend improved models. A later group developed additional models, published a comprehensive set of "core curriculum" training manuals, redesigned the programming system, and upgraded the skills of the field staff through a series of workshops. They also responded to a series of questions now raised as to whether Peace Corps projects were designed to meet "basic human needs." By and large they found that much of what the volunteers were doing met this standard. Nevertheless, the questions posed during this process did force the Peace Corps staff to engage in a rather tough self-evaluation. Policies were rewritten, and priority was given in the allocation of resources to projects that appeared to meet the "basic human needs" strategy. In some

THE JOB

cases new projects were developed that might not otherwise have been considered.

ACTION's leadership also tried to get the Peace Corps to update its vision of how the program would operate in the future. From ACTION's point of view, while the world had significantly changed since the 1960s, the Peace Corps was relying on a watered-down version of how it had operated in the past. From ACTION's perspective, the Peace Corps gave an unacceptable response: to a large degree, the Peace Corps is defined by its host countries; what the Peace Corps is, and what the Peace Corps will be, is the sum of what our host countries ask of us; we will tell you where the Peace Corps is going when we add up the sixty-odd country management plans at the end of the year. It was not long before relations between the two agencies broke down. When the dust settled, ACTION was forced to give the Peace Corps a greater degree of autonomy, and the Peace Corps had a new director.

The new director was Richard Celeste, whose first goal was to ensure that the Peace Corps had the authority to set its own policies. Having accomplished this, he took a step that set him apart from most of his predecessors. To educate Americans about the development needs of the Third World, Celeste appointed an associate director for development education. Of the Peace Corps' three goals, development education aims at the third. In the past, implementation of the third goal, by and large, had been seen solely as the responsibility of returned volunteers. The only effort to explore an institutional response had been taken under the leadership of Blatchford. Under his direction, the Peace Corps experimented with "transition centers" for returning volunteers, but the program was soon discontinued for failing to meet the test of contributing to the Peace Corps' overseas operations. Celeste's effort was to be more comprehensive, stressing the responsibility of the Peace Corps as an institution to assist its former volunteers in sharing with the American people what they had learned.

In 1981, Celeste's replacement, Loret Ruppe, endorsed his proposal, but more important, she presided over the restoration of the Peace Corps' full statutory independence. Henceforth, the agency would report directly to the President. Universally, Peace Corps supporters are grateful to Ruppe for providing the agency with stable leadership and strong public advocacy. The African Food Systems Initiative recently established under her direction is a case in point. The enthusiastic response to her public appeal by individuals willing to work on agricultural projects in Africa once again proved that the Peace Corps can excite the imagination and idealism of the American people.

During her five years as director, Ruppe has taken a number of other initiatives that should be noted. The first, and possibly the most significant, is the rapprochement with AID. Under her leadership and Peter McPherson's, the two agencies have encouraged efforts to collaborate at all levels. Among a series of other steps they have taken was the decision to develop a joint strategy for how the Peace Corps and AID will support the work of the many private voluntary organizations that have become an integral part of this country's foreign assistance program.

This effort on the Peace Corps' part has a precedent. In the early 1960s, the Peace Corps relied heavily on the expertise of the major organizations that had preceded it in the Third World. A separate division of Peace Corps headquarters coordinated agency relations with private voluntary agencies, universities, and other non-governmental organizations. But rather quickly, two camps formed. There were those who favored assigning volunteers to private agencies because they were relatively less bureaucratic, and those who favored assigning the volunteers directly to host country ministries as a way of instilling confidence and gaining support from the leaders of these countries. The latter position prevailed, and the Peace Corps' formal relationships with the private agencies gradually diminished. Only recently, in fact, has the Peace Corps reestablished formal ties with the private community.

In the past several years, at least three countries have let it be known that they are interested in hosting a group of Peace Corps volunteers, but not if it means accepting a Peace Corps *staff* responsible to the U.S. embassy. A departure from the Peace Corps' standard approach is a recent program that places a group of volunteers in the Sudan without staff. Its support is furnished by AID, and its program is conducted under an agreement between Transcentury, a private development organization, and Georgia Tech. This model eliminates the need for a government-to-government agreement, as well as the need for an "in-country" Peace Corps office. While this approach has been applied to only one country and for a limited number of volunteers, it is one of the very few times the Peace Corps has experimented with an alternative model for fielding volunteers.

Over the past several years, the Peace Corps has left, among other countries, Korea, Malaysia, Colombia, the Ivory Coast, Venezuela, and Brazil. In all these cases, the departures were amicable. In each case, the point was made, either by the country itself or by the Peace Corps, that the country had "graduated," that it did not *need* the Peace Corps anymore. Objectively, this argument may be correct. Such "middle-income" countries often do not require the type of technical assistance the Peace Corps usually provides. But such a narrow interpretation of the word "need" misses two points: no country, including our own, is ever so developed that there is no work left to be done; and the world we live in is so interdependent that we do *need* each other.

If these assertions are correct, technical assistance cannot be the primary justification for the Peace Corps. No matter how difficult it is to accept, and no matter how much we believe our own mythology, we must face the fact that over the years we have come to rely more and more on technical assistance arguments to sell ourselves to our host countries and to justify ourselves to the Congress. We must also take into account that most countries see us principally as a source of technical assistance. But inevitably, fewer and fewer nations will find it acceptable to host a Peace Corps that has come to symbolize their dependence on external assistance. Unless we begin developing an alternative rationale for placing our volunteers in someone else's country, and unless we design new program models that embody that rationale, we may wake up someday to discover that the Peace Corps has been bypassed by history.

The seeds for such a rejuvenation already exist. Those of us who worked in VISTA know firsthand that no country ever graduates from developing itself. We may have thought otherwise in the early 1960s, but by the mid-1970s we knew better. If there will always be a need for development work in our own country, it is likely that this will be true in every other country as well. The issue, then, is whether other nations will accept having Peace Corps volunteers working side by side with their own citizens, only this time *not* in a "giver-receiver" relationship. The standards we should apply for providing our volunteers are not so dissimilar from the past: the volunteers must be productive, but they must also have a positive "volunteer experience."

Depending on the country, this may mean not insisting on having an "in-country" Peace Corps office with American staff members, but assigning the volunteers directly to a host-country institution or domestic development service. With some other countries, particularly those now referred to as "middle-income," we may well have to work toward a reciprocal Peace Corps as the price of admission. Not only would we benefit, but it is a price we should pay willingly. No single step would more convincingly change how the Peace Corps is perceived than to be able to bring host country "volunteers" to work on "development" problems in our own country. Ironically, such a pilot program existed in the late 1960s but was eliminated after two years because a senior congressman stated that "we don't *need* them"—the very argument now being used to exclude the Peace Corps from numerous countries.

The problems the Peace Corps will face are real. And while the solutions are more elusive, I am convinced that the Peace Corps should experiment with alternative models, particularly models involving cooperation with private agencies and those better suited to "middle-income" countries and countries with strong volunteer programs of their own. The models should emphasize "equal" rather than the "giver-receiver" relationships that the Peace Corps has adopted over the years. While there is no question that the present model for how the Peace Corps supports its volunteers is effective, and is likely to be so for many countries for the foreseeable future, it is also evident that it is no longer relevant to a growing number of others. Unless we solve this problem by developing a variety of program models, the Peace Corps is destined to become increasingly marginal.

For the Peace Corps to survive for another twenty-five years and to continue to excite future generations of Americans, it may well have to make some rather fundamental changes. It must, first of all, recognize that we do *not* want to "work ourselves out of a job," as one of the Peace Corps' most popular slogans asserts. This and other similar phrases may make eminent sense at the volunteer level, or even at the project level. They most certainly do not, however, make sense at the country level, where they are a direct contradiction of the second and third goals. Without volunteers, there are no opportunities to learn about one another. The challenge ahead is to make sure that the Peace Corps is as relevant and important to the United States and to the Third World as it has been in years past. Our children and grandchildren who may want to serve deserve nothing less.

Reminiscence: the Philippines and Mali

by Parker W. Borg

The traditional "naming" ceremony was one of the first contacts I had as ambassador to Mali with the new group of Peace Corps trainees. This is the occasion when all the trainees are given an African name by the Malian families with whom they have been living for the "in-country" training.

We had no trouble finding the site: an open area, brightly lit with a string of bulbs connected to a whirring generator and surrounded by a large circle of chairs. The trainees bubbled with excitement as they spoke of how their families had arrived at the names they would receive. Without any announcement, groups of women began dancing to the beat of drums in a circle in front of us. The beat moved from one frenzied tempo to another while women of all ages entered and left the circle, sometimes waving their scarves, but always stomping their feet and stirring up a fog of dust. Occasionally, one or two of the men, usually older ones, would enter and execute a few fancy steps. On invitation, the trainees and some of the guests joined the group. The dancing continued until, finally, a notable went to the microphone to announce solemnly the names of the new members of the village community.

Through the din, dust, and excitement, I thought back twenty years to my own initiation into the Peace Corps. It was the spring of 1961; the Peace Corps had just been announced. When I visited the new headquarters in Washington, I was told the organization was not looking for liberal arts graduates like me, but people with experience, or graduates

---

Parker W. Borg is deputy director of the Department of State's Office for Counter-Terrorism and a former United States ambassador to Mali.

from agricultural and technical schools. This negative reaction plus the opposition of my parents to such an outrageous post-graduate plan made me even more determined to join. I looked over the first programs, directed at Ghana, Tanganyika (now Tanzania), Colombia, and the Philippines. I made out my application to look as if I would be a good prospective English teacher in the Philippines, and I was selected for training.

Our training at Penn State was intense but jumbled. Psychological testing was an important part of the process. Of the 150 of us who arrived, only 128 would be selected, and we were never sure of the criteria. I was not "selected out," a fate which all of us were convinced would blacken the rest of our lives. We finished our six weeks at Penn State about the same day Congress made the Peace Corps official.

"In-country" training in the Philippines consisted of six additional weeks of living in a Boy Scout dormitory on the campus of the University of the Philippines. We studied the national language, Tagalog (though not more than a dozen of us went to Tagalog communities), heard lectures about Philippine culture and institutions, got to know some Filipino students and faculty members, and observed Filipino life from our pleasant mountaintop. Although we studied something called "culture shock," few of us were prepared for the realities of the rural Third World, where we found ourselves a few weeks later.

A hand from a Malian woman beckoning me into the dusty dancing circle brought me back to the present. I thought to myself, how much better prepared volunteers are now, at least in Mali. This cultural introduction was less artificial. From the beginning, the Malian Peace Corps volunteers had learned to live among people like those they would find in their villages. Whenever they returned to the capital, they would look upon their village, rather than some academic dormitory, as their home. If the training program in Mali was the norm, the Peace Corps had come a long way in twenty years.

Like all the volunteers in the Philippines, I was supposed to work as a teacher's aide in the elementary schools in the fields of English, math, and science. Since the Philippines already had a surplus of teachers, we were not permitted to displace Filipino teachers. I was told we might assist teachers in classes, offer special courses, or run seminars for them. Since the Filipino school officials had no idea what a teacher's aide might do, the project was seriously flawed. We were each left to work out whatever role we liked. As long as we did not cause any problems, the Peace Corps staff did not seem to care what we did. The priority of the Peace Corps at that time was to get as many volunteers placed as quickly as possible in this, the biggest of its early efforts. By June 30, 1962, nine months after we went to our villages, there were already 272 volunteers working in the Philippines and another 282 in training. If we did not

THE JOB

like the school, we were encouraged to build toilets or piggeries or take on any project we wanted as long as we seemed busy and did not complain.

I chose to stick with the school. During the first months, I wandered between classrooms as an observer, and it was agreed I would substitute for certain teachers on a regular basis to give them time for administrative activities. Soon I had four days a week at a local elementary school, teaching English to first graders, math to third graders, and science to sixth graders. On Fridays, I taught American literature and current events at a high school. As rote memorization was the standard, I attempted to find special techniques to make learning enjoyable: games to learn multiplication tables, science experiments, and dramatic presentations. I also coached the elementary school soccer team, emphasizing drills, passing the ball, and not drinking or smoking. Largely because there were so many overaged sixth graders, we won the provincial championship. I never learned whether the Peace Corps considered me a success, but I kept myself productively occupied.

I did not think too highly of the Peace Corps' efforts to encourage frustrated teachers to become organizers of community development projects. The Philippines already had plenty of trained cadres working throughout the country. If Americans built sanitation projects or promoted piggeries, it not only undermined existing development programs, but, more important, it seemed to reinforce the Filipinio rural mentality that Americans, by their very nature alone, could accomplish things that were beyond their own capacities.

Several years later, my previous Southeast Asian experience made me a natural candidate to fill the State Department's Vietnam quota, and after one year of language training, I found myself doing rural development work with a thirty-man army unit in a small Vietnamese town. My counterpart was a Vietnamese lieutenant who was responsible for all civil operations in this district of about one hundred hamlets. A development skeptic, I was transformed suddenly into a community development officer. Our job was to help restore the government's civilian presence through the construction of roads, bridges, schools, or whatever seemed necessary. We asked village officials to select priority projects for their communities—and if the villagers agreed to provide the labor, AID would supply the funds to buy materials.

The program proved that the initiative of the villagers could be harnessed if the resources were available, but the funds necessary from the United States for the effort were staggering. It was war relief on the cheap through self-help, and we never learned whether the principles of community organization could make a difference in the absence of seemingly unlimited money.

When I arrived in Mali in 1981, I found that community development projects had been a central part of the Peace Corps program for several years. I attempted to travel outside the capital as often as possible, setting for myself a goal of one trip per month to a different part of the country. I liked escaping the unending rounds of official ceremonies and diplomatic receptions I was otherwise forced by protocol to attend. After selecting the place I wanted to visit, I would assemble a list of local development projects, and the names of volunteers in the area.

I never worried about knowing where a volunteer lived. Upon pulling into any community, I could ask in the market area and find somebody willing to guide me to the American's house. At first I was appalled by the living conditions. Most volunteers lived in quarters made of mud with thatched roofs and an adjacent outside toilet area. I remember one volunteer living on the ground in an eight-by-ten foot mud hut—just room enough for his mattress and mosquito net—with a solitary window opening on the pen where the owner kept a flock of bleating goats. Inevitably, I would be asked to compare these conditions with my own experiences twenty years earlier, when the Peace Corps was just beginning. With some embarrassment I talked about our large house with electricity and running water.

The differences between Mali and the Philippines—and all other countries where I have lived—are striking. I avoided comparisons whenever possible, explaining that geographic, climatic, cultural, and historical conditions made every development situation unique. Each country was different, I would explain, but common to all Third World communities was the ongoing process of change which twentieth-century technology and communications had forced upon the traditional societies. I recalled arguments we had as volunteers about the merits of the development process. Rather than act as agents for change, wouldn't it be better to let traditional societies decide for themselves whether they wanted change? One volunteer in our Philippines group resigned over this question. Even at the time I argued that such change was inevitable and that the outsider's role should be to introduce the many beneficial elements of technology appropriate to the problem.

Peace Corps projects in Mali were varied, and demonstrated that the Peace Corps had come a long way from the early days when we were dumped in villages. There were teachers running the English department of Mali's teacher training institute, math volunteers in secondary schools, health workers at dispensaries and maternity clinics. There were also community development projects, some related to water and others devoted to building more fuel-efficient earthen stoves.

Some of the projects were better than others, but the Peace Corps staff was regularly evaluating the effectiveness of each program. For example, the staff abandoned a program to monitor the weight of babies with a view to reducing infant mortality through nutrition awareness, largely because mothers considered it a foolish exercise and instantly questioned the qualifications of the volunteers.

Fortunately for everyone, the Peace Corps had a strong staff, and the management formula was a good one: establish well-defined projects, but permit each volunteer flexibility in the implementation; bring problems promptly to the attention of responsible officials; provide staff support that is technically competent and sympathetic but capable of firm action. On my part, I met frequently with the Peace Corps staff to discuss plans and difficulties, participated in special events, invited volunteers to the house on occasion, and attempted to visit as many of them as possible in their villages.

Americans are known around the world for always being in a hurry. In the United States, our technology, communications, and system of government provide quick fixes for situations and quick solutions to problems. As Americans working overseas, we think about what we might accomplish in terms of the length of our assignment. We are willing to devote two or three years to a particular activity, but we expect to see concrete results.

While working as head of the U.S. consulate in Lubumbashi, Zaire, in 1976–78, I asked a Belgian Jesuit who ran one of the country's teacher training institutes how he could put up with the corruption all around him. He responded by noting that there had not been much change since he arrived fifteen years earlier, but he always tried to set a good example for the students and teachers. "We have to look ahead," he added, "not five or ten years, but to the difference our collective effort will make in a hundred years."

The American effort to provide development assistance to countries around the world is full of half-completed, canceled, and forgotten projects. Not only do we as individuals want to see rapid progress, but our institutions also frequently demand it. When traveling around West Africa in 1979 and hearing AID officials talk about current and future projects, I often asked about the past. If Congress required you to prepare a report about projects completed here through the American assistance effort since it began, what projects would you list? It was surprising, in country after country, how few specific past projects they could name.

Too many projects are canceled because there is a change in available funds, the transfer of the project's promoter, the arrival of a new project officer with a different perspective, or a change in priorities directed from Washington. Sometimes corruption is also a factor, but rather than recognize the inevitability of this type of problem and take steps to minimize it, we are too quick to halt U.S. participation. We prefer to plan new projects, rather than sort out the problems of the past. For too many of us, by the time we move our projects from the approval process into implementation, our tours have ended and our replacement has arrived, only to start the cycle again.

One such failed project, in a desert community of Mali, started with a promising cooperation program between AID and the Peace Corps. AID had supplied the villagers with motorized pumps to permit the cultivation of three times more wheat than could be grown by the traditional system of irrigation. But the project floundered because the villagers could not maintain the pumps, while corrupt officials lined their pockets with project funds. Unfortunately, such scandals attract more publicity for development efforts, including the Peace Corps, than dramatic successes in food production or in the adoption of other changes.

In this case, however, the AID mission agreed to fund a Peace Corps program to repair the pumps. Since there were no mechanics in Mali, volunteers were recruited for three months of temporary duty from Peace Corps programs in neighboring countries. About eighteen volunteers spent the planting season traveling between villages putting the pumps back in order. The experiment, on the second go-around, was more productive, and motorized irrigation based on this project may yet become a part of the landscape in Mali. Only time will tell. If the project had been dropped at the initial setback, which many in Washington urged, the villagers would have been even more resistant the next time outsiders brought in proposals for change.

When the history of the development effort is finally written, there are two ways that the Peace Corps should be remembered. First, there is the direct legacy: the thousands of volunteers and their projects, which have brought education and technology, and perhaps some self-sustaining activities, to hundreds of Third World communities. The second Peace Corps legacy is even less tangible. Each year since 1963, hundreds of volunteers who have finished their Peace Corps tours have found ways to continue participating in the process of economic development. Some stay on to work on specific projects, others find similar jobs in neighboring countries, join government organizations, or go to graduate school to develop special technical skills that will permit them to pursue careers in the Third World. This is true throughout Africa, Asia, and Latin America, where the Peace Corps doggedly has made important contributions to the long-term development effort during the past twenty-five years.

Reminiscence: Thailand

by Judith Guskin

When my husband, Alan, and I arrived in Bangkok in January 1962 with the first group of Peace Corps volunteers, we were met at the airport by Thai officials, who seemed pleased to have us respond in our hesitant but accurate Thai to their speeches of welcome. The picture in the Bangkok *World* the next day showed a newly arrived volunteer properly making a *waj*, the traditional Thai greeting with the palms of the hands placed together, while one of the Thais held out his hand for a handshake. We were all a bit embarrassed, as we would frequently be over the next two and a half years. But when Alan and I said good-bye in 1964, we were genuinely sad at leaving so many close friends.

From time to time we have looked at the pictures of our farewell at the airport. I look young in my bright blue Thai silk suit (which I later gave to Sharon, our daughter). Al was gracefully returning a respectful *waj* when the camera snapped him. We kept in touch with a few of them, but in the ensuing years, we wondered often what had happened to all our former students, colleagues, and friends.

Like most volunteers, we kept in our lives something of the country in which we had served. We cooked Thai food and displayed our friend Chumpon's wedding picture and the silver bowl our faculty colleagues gave us. We shared stories about our experiences with friends and other Peace Corps volunteers. A few of our Thai students and colleagues visited us in the United States, bringing us much joy.

Finally, sixteen years later, we returned, and as we approached for the landing, we searched for the once familiar emerald green rice fields, thumbed one last time through the torn and stained copy of the Thai language text we had saved, and wondered if anyone would remember

---

Judith Guskin is an independent television producer in Yellow Springs, Ohio, and is on the staff of Antioch University.

us. In a way, we wanted to see things unchanged, but we also wanted to see positive change. Like many former Peace Corps volunteers, we had considerable anxiety about this return visit.

Once we were out of the plane, the airport seemed big and unfamiliar. We gathered our suitcases and made our way to customs. Suddenly, we saw a sign with our name. Someone had come to meet us. Our Thai friend Sippanon Ketudat, who had married Emily, a Peace Corps volunteer in our group, had sent a car to get us. He was then minister of education, and as we were whisked through customs, we smiled to ourselves at the strange feeling of being (as Thais would say) *phu jaj*, or "big shots," in Thailand, rather than volunteers.

Then, through the window, outside the customs area, we saw a familiar smiling face. Dirake! He had received a message from us. A student who had lived with us for two and a half years, Dirake had helped see me through the ordeal of Al's serious illness and Kennedy's assassination. We had shared meals and dreams together. Dirake had taken vacation days to be with us during the visit and wanted to take us to the hotel. After a moment of embarrassed negotiation with the ministry official, we were off with Dirake to a fancy new hotel, a place we would not have felt comfortable entering as volunteers sixteen years before.

As volunteers, we had been university teachers, teachers of teachers. We were not community development volunteers. We did not dig wells, breed chickens, or create fish ponds. We did not live in a thatched-roof hut in a small, rural village. We lived in Bangkok, a major city. We taught at Chulalongkorn, then as now Thailand's most prestigious university and one of the best in Southeast Asia. In the early days, we struggled with our assignment. Were we really Peace Corps volunteers, as many people had come to imagine the volunteer to be? In a moment of humor, we thought that to be effective volunteers at the university, we should dig a ditch through the center of the campus. This would be a real Peace Corps assignment!

One of my sharpest memories is of a field visit by Sargent Shriver, for whom all the Peace Corps volunteers we knew had love-hate feelings. We liked him because in spirit he was one of us. Yet we were determined to criticize what we regarded as his tendency to oversell us. On his first visit, the Thailand volunteers met him at the American embassy. Many had traveled considerable distances to see him, no doubt complaining about him all the way. We met in the large living room in the ambassador's residence. The volunteers sat on the floor and on couches; some stood. For hours we grilled him as to why he didn't stop telling all those glamorous stories about us. He pretended to be shocked, but he was unrelenting in his enthusiasm for our work, and he berated us for being too self-effacing. He said we had trouble looking beyond our work to the large picture. Shriver understood the Peace Corps as a social movement, and, in retrospect, after twenty-five years, I think maybe he was right.

While we were in Thailand, we struggled with the image of the volunteer created by the Peace Corps staff and supported by an adoring press. We thought the reality of our role as teachers was quite different. Like other volunteers, we were involved in a people-to-people program. Our success, like theirs, could not be judged by major economic and social changes, but by small increments, through the individuals we taught and befriended. Al and I resolved our personal concern only when we saw our students develop and grow. Finally, we took heart in thinking that some day they would be teaching the courses we taught, doing the research we did, and preparing their own students to teach teachers.

We even recognized our potential to have a long-term impact, but we did not like to indulge ourselves with it. While some of our students were from wealthy families, others were children of working people. Some were poor. But all had been admitted to Thailand's best university, and all were intelligent. We reasoned that we might be exercising an influence on a generation that one day would be running the country. An early evaluation report of the Peace Corps in Thailand seemed to emphasize this point when it recommended expansion of university teaching assignments. But on a day-to-day basis, we did not have such grand ideas. Our real work was with relatively few people.

It was to them—a circle of former students and friends—that we returned. Like us, they had grown to maturity. We knew from correspondence that many had become successful in their professions and had children. How did they remember us? Had we made a difference? Was it important to them that there had been Peace Corps volunteers teaching at the university?

The first evening, we had dinner with a group of our most intimate old friends. The restaurant, which we remembered as a modest place in the shabby neighborhood where we once lived, was now large and elegant. Sippanon, the minister of education, greeted us warmly at the door, and when Al and I sat down, we all began exchanging news. Somsak had married Nisa and they had a child, and Nitya had married Emily's colleague at the Institute of Asian Technology and had two children. The former Peace Corps volunteers who had remained in Bangkok were doing very well. The biggest surprise was that half the people invited had recently been appointed to high government positions and had just come from their first cabinet meetings. Two were ministers, one was a deputy minister, another an assistant to a minister, but they were still the same warm, bright, funny, wonderful men and women we remembered. As the conversation switched from English to Thai and back again, we found ourselves rapidly picking up words we had not heard for so long. We felt at home with our friends.

The next day we returned to the university to visit the Faculty of Education, where Al and I had taught. We loved seeing familiar faces and receiving the warm greetings that accompanied them. The tree under which my students and I had read *The New York Times*—I remember our talking together about the civil rights movement in Alabama and Mississippi—had grown larger. Al's glass-topped desk was being used by a former student, who was teaching some of the same psychology courses he had taught, and the two of them discussed Al's ongoing influence in legitimizing research at the Faculty. I was thrilled to see Sumitra, who had been one of my brightest and most intense students and who, having gone on to obtain a Ph.D., now headed the graduate program. That evening, we had dinner with a former student of Al's, now a well-known author, and as we parted, she gave him a very low and respectful *waj*. When Al returned the gesture, she placed her head on his outstretched hands. Tears welled up in his eyes. To have placed her head on Al's hands was the highest form of respect a Thai can show.

I should note that we did not like everything we saw in Bangkok, like the huge building downtown with a sign in English and Thai that said "Central Plaza." It was a large shopping mall, not different from those at home, where Thai families shop in clean, air-conditioned comfort. I went to the food section and tried to remember the names of the strange and wonderful fruits with prickly skins that I had not seen in so many years. In the mall, Thais have a wide selection not just of food and clothing, and books in all languages, but snacks at Mr. Donut and Kentucky Fried Chicken. I couldn't help but compare it with the dark, damp, fly-infected markets I remembered. This was economic development, central to the Peace Corps' mission, and Thais were now able to afford the items that were for sale. But I was nostalgic for an earlier day and regretted that Thai boys and girls now meet each other at fast-food stands rather than at temple fairs.

Our visits with our friends were intimate and intense, and full of the laughter and teasing that we remembered from our Peace Corps days. We talked about the pains of development, and of the transformation that had taken place in Bangkok as it grew from two to five million people. We understood the tension, and the personal struggle, as they pursued their careers and raised their children while trying to change Thailand and at the same time preserve its essential culture and traditions.

In some ways, our conversation was more candid than it had been in our Peace Corps days, when Thailand was under a military dictatorship. Students and faculty avoided talking about politics then, out of fear. There was very little sense of the importance of freedom of speech. Al and I took some satisfaction in learning how the people at the university had played a major role in the revolution that led in 1973 to Thailand's adoption of democracy, with free speech and political parties. Unfortunately, there was a painful regression shortly afterward, which our friends called the "dark ages," when people were shot and books were burned. But then another change took place. A new and democratic prime minister was appointed, and it was he who asked our friends to serve in the government.

Our return to Thailand and our visits with old students and friends filled both of us with a sense of pride. It is possible to count the number of wells dug or acres sown by Peace Corps volunteers, but how do you measure the results of teaching? It's hard to measure the impact of a teacher anywhere, and Peace Corps teachers are no exception. What matters for teachers is not only that students learn, but that they learn to love learning, to have faith in their own abilities, to want to give themselves fully to whatever they do. A teacher feels a sense of accomplishment through the achievement of his or her students. I think Al and I can say, like most Peace Corps volunteers, that we affected the lives of a few individuals. For them, we thought, we had somehow made a difference. Our Thai students, colleagues, and friends are different as a result of our being in Thailand.

But then, so are we.

In the Developing World

by Abdou Diouf

On the occasion of the celebration of the twenty-fifth anniversary of the creation of the American Peace Corps, I want to pay tribute to an organization which, in my judgment, is among the most exciting experiments of the latter part of the twentieth century.

In 1963, three years after the resounding appeal of President John Kennedy and the attainment of our own national independence, Senegal received its first contingent of Peace Corps volunteers. They were fifteen teachers, and they came to teach English in secondary schools throughout our country. Then others arrived to train our athletes for the first International Friendship Games, and our teams comported themselves brilliantly. Since then, nearly 1,500 volunteers have served in our country, working chiefly in the fields of rural development, public health, and education.

Today, twenty-five years after the Peace Corps' founding, there are more than one hundred volunteers in service in Senegal, contributing to a wide diversity of programs, such as rural development, fish farming, appropriate technology, health education, teacher training, and assistance to young farmers. These are the sectors that enlarge the capacity of our people to take the initiative for self-help. They are the foundation stones of our economic, social, and cultural development. They are the stages on which Peace Corps volunteers have played and are still playing a key role in building our society.

The results produced by the Peace Corps between 1979 and 1981 prove—as if proof were needed—just how diverse and how important its work has been. They are evident in "grass-roots" projects responding to the needs and hopes of our population, of a value totaling nearly $90 million. Specific projects have included the boring and repairing of wells;

Abdou Diouf is president of Senegal and of the Organization of African Unity.

THE JOB

the construction of classrooms, day-care centers, and health clinics; the erection of individual and family latrines; the raising of livestock; the organization of a motor repair center; and the assembly of flour mills.

Even this list, however, reveals only a fraction of the human impact, felt by Americans and Senegalese alike, as they worked together as real partners in the Peace Corps mission.

Each Peace Corps volunteer lives and works in a Senegalese village, with an adopted family, and before long considers himself, and is considered, a true member of that family, a son among other sons of the village, doing his share of the work of the community. Day by day, he conveys to the village what Americans already know so well: that a man can achieve almost anything by calculating his needs wisely and managing realistically the means at his disposal.

To reach the goals established in the Peace Corps Act of September 22, 1961, the volunteer's first task is to assimilate the culture of Senegal. He learns and talks one of our local languages. The ways and customs of the community in which he lives become his own, and each day he works shoulder to shoulder with his hosts. The personal determination, discipline in organization, and modern methodology that he demonstrates are the richest elements of his culture, which the culture of the village in time absorbs.

Another benefit emerging from the Peace Corps presence comes from the experience acquired by the agencies of the Senegalese government that supervise the work of the volunteers. This experience emerges from the intimate collaboration between these agencies and the Peace Corps. Allow me to attest here that this collaboration has become progressively closer over the years, particularly the relationship between the Peace Corps staff in Senegal and the Ministry of Social Development, which is directly responsible for utilizing the services of 60 percent of the volunteers stationed in the country.

This collaboration is most dramatic in two types of programs, separate but largely overlapping.

They are, first, the Peace Corps programs directed at the recruitment and preparation of volunteers for specific tasks proposed by Senegal; the maintenance of these volunteers during their stay in our country; the collection of useful information to improve their training, including the evaluation of the Peace Corps program and of the volunteer's effectiveness; and the assistance to the volunteers, within the framework of the agreed rules, in the exercise of their tasks.

And second, our own programs directed at organization and selection of programs, and the priorities attached to them; the definition of the projects and conditions of work; the support of the volunteer at all times in the accomplishment of his tasks, including the improvement of his selection, welcome, and integration in Senegalese society. In the accomplishment of these tasks, I point with pride to the important training center situated in the city of Thiès. This center, built at a cost of several million francs, has been donated for Peace Corps use by the Ministry of Social Development and is operated efficiently by the Peace Corps staff.

Thus the integration into village life, as well as into useful work, provides the volunteer with an opportunity to be a bridge between two cultures, engaged in a dialogue in the interest of peace.

For Senegal's part, in the interest of furthering even more the cooperation between our two peoples, the government, working directly with the leadership of the Peace Corps, has committed itself to specific responsibilities in long- and short-term planning. They include the selection of sites for the deployment of volunteers, based on geographic, socioeconomic, and work criteria, and the readying of living and working conditions through programs of training to promote understanding at the level of the Senegalese village and family. At the same time, the government provides Peace Corps volunteers during the in-country preparation period with a village to serve as a training site, as well as a place in which to study the life they will be living for the ensuing two years. Thus, before being taken to "their own" village, the volunteers will be exposed to the real rural life of our country.

After this preparation, the last but essential preparatory phase is to provide each volunteer with a base of operations. At that moment, national, local, and village authorities combine to prepare an annual work plan to permit efficient and cooperative administration of the Peace Corps program. To achieve this objective, management committees are created to supervise and evaluate designated projects in agriculture, the development of water resources, and health and nutrition programs to improve the condition of women, and others.

On the national level, a committee under the direction of the Ministry of Planning and Cooperation provides the guidelines for the activities of the Peace Corps in Senegal. Each year, all of the government agencies that use volunteer services meet with the Peace Corps staff to determine logistical needs and provide for their being met. The committee has been in existence, doing this work, for more than ten years.

We are delighted that the volunteer, having selflessly and devotedly served the needy population of a developing country like our own, does not forget us. The volunteer will bring a vital mission home with him, a readiness to explain to his own compatriots the economic, social, and cultural realities of a nation that he will know from the inside out. From the time that he leaves us, his role will be to clarify the vision; to combat

THE JOB

the prejudice and confusion he encounters; to permit two peoples so distant from each other in their character to come closer together, to respect each other, to grow fond and confident of each other. Can we ask for more in the hope that peace will reign?

The Peace Corps represents a special moment, coming none too soon, which permits committed young Americans to work for the cause of world peace and human understanding. What I am saying would be no more than a pious wish if, in spite of all kinds of obstacles, the Peace Corps did not confirm it with hard evidence.

In making volunteers welcome in their land, many African countries send the message that they share the same peaceful ideal as the United States. We are today nearly twenty-six countries, all members of the Organization of African Unity, having established relations of cooperation among ourselves. Nearly 120,000 volunteers have followed the first Peace Corps pioneers in performing service in eighty-eight countries of the world, each volunteer mobilized for the same noble cause. I salute these young men and women, and their willingness to make personal sacrifices for peace.

We commemorate this year the twenty-fifth anniversary of the Peace Corps, at the same time we celebrate the Year of Peace, which the United Nations has declared 1986 to be. We pray that God will in 1986 bring to the combatants in this army of peace the satisfaction and energy needed to continue their work, and to win new and dramatic victories.

Excerpts from Interviews with Foreign Leaders (1981)

From the very beginning, I had direct contact with the volunteers who arrived in Costa Rica, and during the past twenty years I've seen really extraordinary things. To donate a piece of machinery or to provide financial resources is to give something away, but the period which a young person of the Peace Corps gives to our country is a synonym of giving of himself. It is the closest possible joining together in human relationships. I could tell you I've seen a volunteer putting together a fishing net. I've seen a volunteer driving a jeep he helped a farmer repair. But what he really brought was understanding, and that is fundamental. We're establishing the basis of a relationship that is different from that which we've had before. I'm sure that in a country like the Dominican Republic, the Peace Corps volunteer helps present another face of the American people from the Marine who also arrived there. Almost all of the members of the Peace Corps that I have known are Anglo-Saxons, but they're learning to live with Latins. We're cultivating mutual understanding.

—PRESIDENT RODRIGO CARAZO ODIO OF COSTA RICA

When we obtained our independence, there was an exodus of Europeans, technicians, and teachers. Among those who came to help us were the Peace Corps volunteers. This was important to West Cameroon, because it is an English-speaking area, so we had volunteers in our schools. I was prime minister of West Cameroon then, and was always in touch with Peace Corps leaders and with the volunteers when I made my tours. Right in my village there is the fish farm which is being run by the Peace Corps volunteer. Not only that, I have a personal fish pond which is a demonstration project. Apart from these activities, they took part in cooperative societies, getting people to work together. Sometimes we would see a single young lady in a village, alone, in a small house, spending her

THE JOB

time with people. Or a young man on a motorbike going through very rugged roads. I think they have done a great deal to contribute to our development, particularly among the peasant families.

—SOLOMON MUNA, PRESIDENT OF THE
NATIONAL ASSEMBLY OF CAMEROON

As a student here in the 1960s, when President Kennedy announced the Peace Corps program, I was aware of the charisma and appeal it had. As a young man at that time, I shared that dream and vision. Soon thereafter, I went back to Nepal and was instrumental in signing the Peace Corps agreement. My first role in the government was as a central planner. I was chief coordinator for all foreign technical cooperation. I visited Peace Corps people in the field, including in the village where I was born.

The overall effect of the Peace Corps begins with a dialogue at the people's level, independent of both our governments. Both governments facilitated the Peace Corps' work, but once the volunteers were there, they were with the Nepalese people. One of the first groups that went to Nepal was a group of English teachers. We were short of manpower. There were not enough Nepalese who knew English or who could teach English, so the Peace Corps volunteers filled an important gap. But on another level, in the community, Peace Corps volunteers were winning friends, really winning friends. They came from afar to live within the community as one of our people, not beyond the means of the local community, sharing the level of poverty of the Nepalese village people.

What the Peace Corps volunteer did was extraordinary. For the average Nepalese, Americans were cut down to human size. Such a rich country, with GIs throwing dollars all over, a country which can afford almost everything, competing with the Russians to go to the moon—you know all the euphoric and highfalutin things. The impact the Peace Corps volunteers left was not only on children who learned English, but on others at the local level who witnessed their lives and behavior.

One volunteer who I went to visit, for example, was living in a hut with two Nepalese school teachers. Inside the hut he had changed the living arrangement, the living environment. He had used essentially the same things that Nepalese use but had created more hygienic living conditions. The teachers picked up these habits and, in turn, taught them to the rest of the village. If we were to take the same problem to the World Health Organization or another interested agency, the first thing they would do is send a $40,000 consultant to look at village sanitation.

By the time they write the reports, thousands of dollars flow into documents, and then bureaucrats at both ends go and organize a health team. They take months to prepare a report. But the Peace Corps is different. Things like these may be very small, but how profound an impact they make. They cannot be measured in economic terms.

—BHEKH BAHADUR THAPA, AMBASSADOR TO THE UNITED STATES AND FORMER FINANCE MINISTER, NEPAL

In a Changing World
by John W. Sewell

Development progress throughout much of the Third World is threatened in the 1980s and 1990s by a combination of natural disasters, slow growth, rising protectionist pressures in the industrialized countries, and poor policy choices by donor and recipient countries alike. The critical issue for those concerned with development is how social and economic progress can be resumed in the remainder of this century.

The Peace Corps has a special role to play in meeting this challenge. For the past twenty-five years, Peace Corps volunteers have been a symbol to Third World peoples that America does care—and cares deeply—about development. The role that Peace Corps volunteers have played in American public diplomacy may be their single greatest and most enduring contribution to American policy toward the Third World. The organization has much more than a symbolic function, however. It is a well-managed, innovative, and effective organization that can have a significant positive impact on the lives of those it touches.

In the period ahead, the Peace Corps' effectiveness will be strongly challenged by adverse trends in the international economy. To an extent, this is nothing new. The organization has always had to work within boundaries set by host countries and the U.S. government, and by cultural, economic, and technical limitations. But as the problems of the 1980s persist, the context within which Peace Corps volunteers operate will become increasingly difficult and complex. For the organization, and for the development community as a whole, the central challenge will be how to use its always limited resources most effectively throughout the remainder of the century to pursue both economic growth and poverty alleviation.

John W. Sewell is president of the Overseas Development Council in Washington, D.C.

The relationship between the United States and developing countries, and the role these countries play in the international system, has changed radically since the idea of a Peace Corps was first proposed in 1960. In that year, there were 67 independent developing countries. Foreign aid comprised two-thirds of total financial flows from the North to the South. Today, the 141 independent developing countries of the world are of far greater importance to the U.S. economy. Developing countries purchase over one-third of all U.S. exports and comprise half of the top U.S. trading partners. Developing-country debt to U.S. commercial banks totaled over $125 billion in 1985. U.S. direct foreign investment in the Third World was $54 billion in 1984, 23 percent of total U.S. foreign investment worldwide.

The growing importance of Third World economies to our economic health is clearly illustrated by the impact of debt and recession in developing countries on the United States. Between 1980 and 1984, the United States lost 560,000 jobs as a result of the decline in exports to the Third World. In addition, 800,000 new jobs would have been created if the developing countries' growth rate of the 1970s had been maintained after 1980. The U.S. trade deficit with the Third World reached $53 billion in 1984, roughly 43 percent of the total U.S. trade deficit.

These changes in the economic relationship between the United States and the Third World mean that the success of the Peace Corps' efforts has become even more crucial. Development is not a purely altruistic endeavor; growth and progress in the Third World have considerable implications for America's own economic well-being.

Over the past twenty-five years, the number of volunteers has fluctuated from a high of 15,500 to a low of 5,200 in 1982. Happily, it is now being reinvigorated. Volunteers have increased steadily over the past four years, and the agency hopes to raise the number back to 10,000. But its small budget makes this difficult. Last winter, when the tragic impact of the drought and famine in Africa penetrated American awareness, Loret Ruppe made a public appeal for volunteers to fill six hundred posts in Africa. Ten thousand Americans responded to her call. Routinely, the organization can accept only one in four qualified applicants for volunteer positions. At a time when there seems to be much "aid fatigue" among policymakers, it is heartening to know that so many Americans are still willing to contribute their skills and their time to the development effort.

The Peace Corps' popularity is not restricted to potential volunteers. At their own invitation, sixty countries now host volunteers, and they request at least 50 percent more volunteers than can be provided. In addition, several countries are on a "waiting list" to receive volunteers. The success of the Peace Corps is also illustrated by the fact that several other countries, such as France, Germany, and Britain, have initiated similar programs.

Despite the Peace Corps' special strengths and the talents at its disposal, the fact remains that it is a very small actor on a very large and complex stage. The organization has proved time and again that a single talented volunteer and a little bit of money can successfully mobilize indigenous resources for significant local impact. But, over the long term, the success or failure of many if not most Peace Corps projects is determined by forces beyond the control of the agency, the volunteers, and the project participants. These forces include:

The slow growth rate of developing countries. The world is slowly emerging from one of the most serious global recessions of this century, and most Third World economies remain sluggish. The International Monetary Fund estimates that GNP growth in Latin America in 1985 was only around 2.5 percent. The record of the last eighteen months indicates that resumed growth in developed countries—even with sharp reductions in the price of oil—will not automatically trickle down. The economic prospects for low-income countries are poor.

The foreign debt crisis. Total developing country debt was $686 billion in 1984. In an effort to meet debt obligations, developing countries have adopted radical policy responses, cutting government spending and slashing import levels to save scarce foreign exchange for debt service. While adjustment policies have been intended to eliminate waste or correct structural economic problems, the impact on development progress has been severe. Import limits have affected not only consumption but production, as access to imported spare parts, fuel, and machinery has become limited. Development projects have been halted due to a lack of local counterpart funding. Per capita income levels have clearly declined in many countries. While empirical evidence is lacking, it seems clear that poorer, disadvantaged groups have borne a large share of the adjustment burden.

Poor trade performance. Growth in the volume of world trade slowed from about 8.5 percent in 1984 to around 3.5 percent in 1985, as demand weakened and protectionist measures increased. The International Monetary Fund estimates that the exports of developing countries—oil exporters aside—grew by only 4 percent in volume in 1985, a third of the 1984 rise. Prices for commodity products, which comprise approximately 70 percent of total developing country exports, have been generally falling for the past three decades. While international interest rates fell in 1985, for most developing countries the loss in export earnings has been greater than the benefits of lower interest rates.

Uneven pattern of development. The past two and a half decades have been a period of tremendous growth and progress for most of the developing world. Perhaps the recent global recession and the tragedy of African drought and famine have contributed to a now-popular perception in the United States that development has failed. Placed in the perspective of development history, however, this conclusion is not persuasive. From 1960 to 1982, the low- and middle-income countries grew at an average annual real rate of 4.8 percent, a growth rate well in excess of any sizable group of countries over any equally long period prior to World War II. Their share of gross world product increased from 15 percent in 1960 to 20 percent in 1979. Even in the poorest countries, indicators of quality of life—health, life expectancy, literacy, infant mortality—have improved.

While the development experiment has been a success in general, the pattern of development has been uneven. There is a growing differentiation within the Third World. The newly industrialized countries are now not only major markets for American products, but are also new competitors, providing the United States with relatively sophisticated goods. Brazilian commuter airplanes are shuttling passengers between American cities, and Korean passenger cars have recently entered the U.S. market. The middle-income countries have also done well, taking advantage of a relatively open trading system and expanding capital markets. The low-income countries, however, particularly those in sub-Saharan Africa, have lagged far behind in development progress.

Africa's development crisis. Nowhere are the failures of the development experience more clear than in sub-Saharan Africa. With limited access to commercial capital, these countries continue to rely heavily on foreign aid for investment. Average per capita incomes in the region are actually lower than they were fifteen years ago and will continue to decline for the next decade. Increases in African food production continue to be outpaced by population growth rates. Because many African countries remain largely exporters of commodities, low commodity prices have severely cut into export earnings. While the region's debt of $100 billion receives little attention from the international community, since it represents only about 10 percent of the total developing country debt, it places a staggering burden on African countries.

Poor policy choices. Many developing country governments have pursued unwise policies that have stalled or reversed development progress. These policies differ in each country, but among them are inadequate investment in agriculture, poor incentives for small-scale farmers, concentration of resources in large, inefficient public projects, overvalued exchange rates that prevent exports from competing on the world market, and inflationary fiscal and monetary policies.

Aid donors have also pursued ill-conceived policies. Changes in donors' preferred strategies—from large-scale infrastructure projects, to an emphasis on providing basic human needs, to the current private-sector focus—have provided little continuity to the development effort. In a similar vein, fluctuating aid levels and uncoordinated efforts have occasionally distorted priorities as recipients are encouraged to take advantage of whatever funding is currently available.

Inadequate resources for development. In the immediate future, scarce resources will be a significant constraint to development efforts. Alarmed at the deteriorating quality of their assets in the Third World, commercial banks have cut back on lending. U.S. direct foreign investment in most developing countries is unlikely to expand significantly, as long as these countries continue to be plagued with slow growth, debt, and general economic uncertainty. Lower demand and rising protectionist sentiment in the United States and other industrial countries threaten the efforts of developing countries to boost export earnings needed for debt repayments and for investments for growth.

Since development resources are not likely to expand commensurate with need, new strategies and approaches are required to improve development progress. How can the Peace Corps respond to the harsh international economic conditions of the 1980s and 1990s?

Concentration of resources. Resources must be concentrated in those regions and countries most in need of assistance, and most likely to profit from development cooperation.

Africa must be given high priority. The Peace Corps currently has programs in twenty-five African states. Of the 2,700 volunteers in the region, 1,200 are involved in agricultural efforts. The Peace Corps has also launched the Africa Food Systems Initiative, a ten-year campaign to help up to twelve African countries reverse their decline in food production. Under the initiative, volunteer teams, in collaboration with other agencies, will work with small-scale farmers on activities such as irrigation, local fertilizer production, and preservation of food crops. These efforts deserve further support so they can be continued and expanded.

The Peace Corps could also play a significant role in assisting African states to meet their short-term need for skilled personnel as training for Africans expands. Peace Corps volunteers with specialized skills could be recruited selectively from American management schools and from the pool of retired Americans to help fill the gap in areas such as economic planning and forecasting, program evaluation, and computer programming, while local personnel are trained to assume these responsibilities.

Increased coordination for maximum impact. There are dozens of official aid agencies and hundreds of private agencies operating in developing countries today. In order to maximize the impact of resources, better coordination among agencies and between agencies and host countries is essential. The Peace Corps has already made significant progress in this direction. Under the Small Projects Assistance program established in 1983, the Peace Corps works with the Agency for International Development in community-level projects. And volunteers often work with private voluntary organizations, such as CARE, Catholic Relief Services, Africare, and others. In 1985, the Peace Corps had over 250 ongoing projects with private voluntary organizations worldwide. These efforts must be sustained and expanded.

Growth. Short-term budgetary constraints are severe, and the likely possibility is for cutbacks in all programs, including the Peace Corps. But over the longer term, expansion of the Peace Corps should be a prime goal for those concerned with U.S. development policy. It is hard to claim that six thousand volunteers are adequate for the challenging task ahead. The current level of volunteers is less than half that of the mid-1960s, while the need for volunteers is greater. Further, the cost per volunteer—roughly $40,000 for the two years—is not high when measured against the impact a single volunteer can have. In Botswana, for example, one volunteer working with host-country nationals constructed fifty dams, which benefited sixty-five villages, bringing potable water to thousands of people. This is not an isolated example. Peace Corps projects have a high payoff at minimal cost. In the long term, the number of volunteers should be constrained only by the number of qualified applicants, the requests received for volunteers, and by issues of volunteer safety.

In a recent statement before Congress, the Peace Corps director said, "Only at the village level, where incentive and technology must fuse with social, cultural, and economic realities, will the final battle against hunger be won." But in order for progress against hunger, poverty, and disease to be achieved and sustained, even on the village level, both national and international economic and political conditions must be conducive to growth. The Peace Corps can change one life at a time—no small task. But the challenge of creating open, progressive, and equitable national and international systems is a global responsibility.

THE PLACE

In a Changing America
by Loret Miller Ruppe

Like most twenty-five-year-olds, the Peace Corps strides toward the next quarter-century with the boundless energy for which it is famous and with a heart full of hopes for an ever more influential future, armed with the confidence that it makes an everlasting contribution to both the United States and the world. Peace will come through development, through partnerships, and the Peace Corps has set free the American spirit of voluntarism in pursuit of it.

Reaching this point has required fortitude and character. While we had an easy birth, our childhood was difficult, and I think it's fair to say our adolescence was troubled. Observers look at our history, at the current conservative bent in the country's political profile, at a strife-torn world in nuclear jeopardy, and wonder how we've been able to survive. I tell them it's because we have a strong, absolutely bipartisan family that has sustained us throughout, has been an unending source of ideas and counsel, and is united in its motivation to pursue world peace and friendship.

Like most families, we have had disagreements from time to time, but we have managed to remain focused on our mission and its universal importance. The family comprises all who have played a role in the evolving Peace Corps story, from the first director, Sargent Shriver; through the nine directors who have followed, the thousands of returned volunteers, and the members of Congress who have supported us; to leaders and villagers in countries where we've served. All of them are still an integral part of the Peace Corps.

The Peace Corps' maturation has relied on flexible, rather than rigid, nurturing. Each person who has assumed the agency's helm has brought to it a particular vision and has applied whatever special skills he or she

---

Loret Miller Ruppe is currently director of the Peace Corps.

could muster to the challenge of the moment. Sometimes the conditions were extraordinarily difficult. But the deep conviction that what the Peace Corps does is valuable has kept us all on track.

In 1961, Sargent Shriver sent the first group of volunteers off from the Rose Garden with the willing assistance of the President. Part of America's first foray into grass-roots development, these young men and women left with much fanfare and the abiding hope of all concerned that they would do well. Products of an idealistic era in our national history, each volunteer had signed on in response to President Kennedy's challenge to find out what they could do for their country. It was a long time before another group of volunteers got a Rose Garden send-off.

During the Vietnam War, Peace Corps directors had to grapple with volunteers' protests against American foreign policy. A mirror of domestic ferment over national values and policies, the Peace Corps as an official government agency had to balance its concerns over bad publicity against the volunteers' rights of free speech as Americans. They were, after all, volunteers, and they were carrying the flag of American ideals—free speech among them—to foreign lands. Some at home worried that Third World citizens, unaccustomed to protests and generally inexperienced in the ways of democracy, would be unable to understand the volunteers' behavior as a legitimate exercise of their citizenship. Looking back on it, we can celebrate the fact that we have such a society and that it has survived transitory periods of painful and dramatic polarization. Such challenges were all part of our growing up.

Then there was the period when the Peace Corps, combined with all the voluntary agencies under an umbrella called ACTION, had to struggle to keep its unique focus and identity. Though appreciated by the public and supported by the Congress, it had to spend precious energy advancing its case within a sometimes inflexible bureaucratic structure. This hurdle and others notwithstanding, volunteers continued to work at their posts, and requests continued to come in from one foreign capital after another for technical assistance. This period also saw the Peace Corps refine its capacity to deliver increasingly specialized services, particularly in agriculture.

The product of what was forged during all those trials and tribulations has now begun to emerge. We make our contribution to bettering the lives of Third World people without *imposing* American values on them. We do not hold ourselves out as their saviors or even as wise men, nor do we stand on soapboxes. Instead, we place our values in the hearts of villages, in schools and fisheries and forests, and let our example speak for itself. American values, for many people in the Third World, *are* the volunteer they get to know and live with for two years. On this, our silver anniversary, we can take pride in the worldwide recognition we have earned as a genuine grass-roots development organization.

When my own term as Peace Corps director was launched in 1981, some harbored doubts that a housewife from Houghton, Michigan, could master the Peace Corps' administrative intricacies or keep it safely distant from the mire of partisan politics. The Peace Corps at that time was still struggling to overcome its 1970s image as a haven for hippies, and like so many valuable programs, was so busy doing its job that it didn't have time to stop to talk with the very people on whom its continuation depended—from members of Congress to key people in the executive branch. There were growing misperceptions about what we did or did not do, and how we went about it. Frequent changes in leadership had led many people to think there wasn't either a program worth leading or a leader capable of handling it. Morale was low. Somehow, the Peace Corps machine chugged ahead, but with an extremely low profile and an aloofness from the political process on which it was dependent. There were those who had concluded that the Peace Corps wasn't or shouldn't be functioning.

I was convinced that I was equal to the challenge. I possessed political connections through years of Republican organizing and had sharpened my political skills during the years my husband served in Congress. People whose judgment I respected most, including my husband, Phil, encouraged me. What an honor to be appointed to such an important post by President Reagan, and what hopes I carried to the consuming task before me! As a deep believer in the necessity of the Peace Corps, I was determined to meet the challenge vociferously.

It was during my initial visit to the White House that my hopes hit the first snag of political reality. I had been told that a certain man would be my contact there, and I was eager to discuss the Peace Corps with him. I sat in his office for nearly an hour while he rearranged furniture and even took a few phone calls. Finally he sat down long enough to tell me that he believed in candor, and candidly, he thought the Peace Corps ought to be abolished. He went on to report that he'd recommended as much during the campaign. In his mind, the Peace Corps was an anomaly in the Reagan administration, falling into the category of a "mushrooming federal agency" that was breaking the national treasury. He did allow, however, that "The President must not agree with me, since he appointed you." For my part, I promised to change his mind, and to find another White House contact.

I refused to agree that the Peace Corps was an anomaly. When the whole land is swept with conservatism, what could be more conservative than thousands of Americans willing to sacrifice two years of their lives for the betterment of people in the remotest areas of the world? Could there be a more conservative call to action than Kennedy's "Ask not . . ."? And if liberal Senator Hubert Humphrey was the Peace Corps' founder and congressional mainstay at the outset, it was his pairing with the conservatives' own Senator Barry Goldwater that sealed passage of the Peace Corps legislation. The Peace Corps, I told my White House contact, had actually shrunk in size over the years, so it didn't even qualify as one of those "mushrooming federal agencies." I vowed to stand in the way of its extinction.

Everyone in the Washington power structure needed an update on the Peace Corps. It has a mission of self-help that American volunteers perform with an almost religious fervor. Day in and day out, for the past twenty-five years, anywhere from 6,000 to 15,000 volunteers have been at work making valuable contributions to other countries, all of which are important to us. The Peace Corps illuminates the tenets of democracy for all who participate, whether they're doers or receivers. It is pro-American and pro-world. It is anti-poverty and anti-hunger. It is humanitarian. It is educational, for both the developing world and the United States.

It also responds to changes in America, and not just political ones. Over the years, the United States has moved from being a youth-oriented society to one that is older and more conservative, and the Peace Corps has had to adjust accordingly. Volunteers are older now, which is not surprising in a nation slated to grow "grayer" as we near the turn of the century. As the volunteer corps has grown more mature, our approaches to training and placement have had to change. We are learning to prepare older volunteers, to look for creative ways to maximize their skills, to open programs for them to be contributors in host countries. We're already discovering that the Peace Corps is now a second and third career, rather than the first step it has been for so many years.

Women, furthermore, are growing to be a greater part of the Peace Corps, which parallels another change in our society. We've gone from 32 percent women in 1962 to nearly 50 percent in 1985. Women are also emerging in nontraditional professions—as foresters, agricultural workers, engineers. My own daughter is presently an engineer helping to design rural bridges in Nepal, certainly neither the place nor the occupation I would have imagined for her twenty years ago. But how proud I am of her and each of our six thousand volunteers!

At the same time, a decrease in America's stock of certain skills has forced the Peace Corps to make adjustments accordingly. In 1961, the fifteen million family farms across the country fed us a supply of agricultural workers. With only one-third or so of those farms still in existence today, we have to look harder for our agricultural volunteers. Fewer young Americans are majoring in math and science these days, robbing us of prepared teachers still much in demand in Peace Corps countries. All of these changes, and more, have required adjustments—and the Peace Corps has responded.

As the new director, I knew that if we were going to flourish, we must take the success story of the Peace Corps in the 1980s to Congress, the executive branch, the diplomatic corps. We made it a policy to keep track of congressional and executive delegations planning trips to sections of the world where there were Peace Corps sites. We provided briefing papers on the region and followed up with personal visits whenever we could.

Once, I went with some trepidation to see conservative Republican Representative Gerald Solomon just after he had returned from a much-publicized trip to Africa. During the trip, he and his Democratic counterpart had had public disagreements over the role American aid could play, and I was apprehensive about his opinions of Peace Corps volunteers. But I was barely inside his office when he declared, "I've seen them. They've convinced me. Any time you want me to speak on their behalf, let me know."

Former House Foreign Affairs Committee member Representative Edwin Derwinsky admitted to me in a talk that he had not been a Peace Corps supporter—"You probably think I'm a Neanderthal . . ."—but once he had had a chance to see it firsthand on a visit, he was converted. He has been helping the Peace Corps ever since.

When I first came aboard, the Peace Corps budget was so undernourished that it was hardly noticed by anyone. By sheer chance, I discovered this budget had been sent over to the State Department and then to the Office of Management and Budget without my ever being invited to defend it, much less to try to get some of the drastic $10 million cut reinstated. A $10 million reduction without a day in court! I insisted on a review, and I marched on the White House armed with facts enough to smite any cuts, drown any dissent. I discovered opponents who could not comprehend why we needed staff in each country where we had volunteers. I don't think the people in charge of cuts had ever traveled to a developing country, or even heard of the Peace Corps prior to meeting me, so my persuasive tactics were sorely tested. I did return with a small triumph, though; I managed to get $2 million restored.

That the Peace Corps has *not* mushroomed into a massive federal agency has, in a sense, been our undoing. In terms of purchasing power after inflation, our current year's budget is far below earlier levels. We're so small that we are in constant danger of being traded away in budget negotiations, despite any of our arguments to the contrary. Our volunteer commitments run on a two-year cycle, but our budget allocations are on an annual basis. Thus, to grow, we must have an assured commitment that lasts for *at least* a two-year congressional term.

Meanwhile, the Peace Corps has received an increasing number of requests for volunteers, from countries of every size and description. I advise each country to make a formal request through diplomatic and executive channels, and I have worked with their embassies here to assist when possible. I also encourage their leaders to visit Peace Corps headquarters when they come to Washington. It often takes years now, and plenty of bureaucratic effort, before we can finally open a new program.

Not long ago, we received a boost from Prime Minister Ratu Sir Kamisese Mara of Fiji. Since he was the first head of state from the Pacific Islands to be invited to Washington for a state visit, a Cabinet meeting was called to welcome him. I had had the honor of visiting with him on a Peace Corps inspection trip earlier in the year. At the oval table in the Cabinet Room, I positioned myself near the Fijian delegation. After a discussion of nuclear-free zones and sugar quotas, there was suddenly a moment of silence. The prime minister, speaking with great intensity, then said, "Mr. President, I want to bring my people's appreciation for the men and women of the United States Peace Corps, who for so many years have served the needs of Fijians throughout the countryside." Every eye in the room turned to me.

Few could imagine the weight of this endorsement, however, until several weeks later, when I learned about a meeting that the budget review team had had with the President. The conservative Heritage Foundation had just issued a highly critical report about us, and many feared that this session would mean the end of the Peace Corps. The Peace Corps' turn on the agenda came, and whose voice rose to speak first? The President's! "We can't cut the Peace Corps," he reportedly said. "The prime minister of Fiji was just here saying how important their work is."

Sensing that the greater our constituency the more compelling our recognition, the Peace Corps has enlisted, in addition to the President, legions of others in our extended family. Families of Peace Corps volunteers themselves are now included in preparations for their children's missions. Promoting small business development throughout the world, chambers of commerce have become partners with us. Universities are offering attractive graduate packages, some subsidized by major corporations, to returning volunteers, in recognition of the valuable contributions they make to campuses. When the Reagan administration launched the Caribbean Basin Initiative, they turned to the Peace Corps as a natural partner, since we have had volunteers in that region since 1961 and could provide the necessary linkage to farmers and small businessmen targeted by the Initiative's programs.

Our crusade to put the Peace Corps on the registry of permanent American institutions, I believe, has left few stones unturned. Friends of the Peace Corps testified before both the Democratic and Republican platform committees in 1984, ensuring an endorsement in both platforms. White House speechwriters are provided with material about relevant Peace Corps programs in advance of every major speech the President gives, and in the 1985 State of the Union address, President Reagan mentioned the Peace Corps' unrelenting efforts to relieve famine in Africa.

Whenever we get a chance, we call attention to the fact that Peace Corps volunteers don't stop serving their country when they come home. They return to the United States and serve fellow Americans on development issues and community activities, and in a wide range of other ways. We hear back from congressmen that when they hold town meetings in their home districts, they often encounter returned volunteers and find them extremely knowledgeable and increasingly active constituents.

I think we have overcome the skepticism of a few years ago. Most of our leaders now recognize that the Peace Corps is important in providing plenty of bang for the foreign aid dollar. So I say it's time to turn to all of our "stockholders"—the citizens of this changing America—and suggest a doubling of their investment. We've proved ourselves to be cost-effective, prudent, and popular, and now we're ready for the next step. We need to be too big to trade away. The Peace Corps has enabled America to see what a few people can accomplish. I now propose that we enable the Peace Corps to show what an *army* of volunteers could do.

Recently we sent another group of volunteers off to their posts, with President Reagan present. It was my pleasure to say to them, "The Peace Corps is back in the Rose Garden, where it has always belonged."

The President had these words for the volunteers that day:

> When Loret Ruppe announced a recruitment drive for agricultural volunteers for Africa, the Peace Corps was besieged by responses from people rushing to volunteer, willing to interrupt their lives and devote two years to meeting the emergency. You are a cross section of America. Some of you are first-generation Americans; some of you are naturalized citizens. You come from all across the country, and you represent a wide variety of people. Soon you will be in Africa, where you'll be a vital part of the relief aid to help millions suffering from malnutrition and starvation. You'll be living in some of the most impoverished nations of the world, working for

food production, soil conservation, fisheries production, forest preservation, and water supply development.

By bringing your training and skills to bear on the underlying problems of agricultural and economic development, you can help your host nations make the difficult but vital journey from dependence on short-term aid to self-sufficiency. Last month, when Vice President Bush returned from his trip to the famine-struck regions of Africa, he gave me a personal account of the heartbreaking conditions in the land, and he told me of the outstanding work of the Peace Corps volunteers."

In a period when we are dedicating so much of our national might and wealth to building up security systems, I cannot help making a comparison with the few dollars it takes to do the current Peace Corps job. Look at the mammoth pie left to defense, and the relatively small slice it would take to reach our potential. When I look at the endless parade of missiles, tanks, and warships being procured, I have to ask myself, where are the battalions of teachers, agricultural workers, and health personnel who can personally deliver assaults for peace in the world? I look at the debt we continue to incur and wonder if this is a fair legacy for the generations we hope will follow us. I read that the most gifted and talented young Americans graduating from our universities are being attracted to jobs in the defense industry, and I wonder what they might be able to wreak should they be handed the challenge of developing interdependence on this planet.

What really is the true measure of America as a world leader? We don't want to be the only rich ones in a sea of raging discontent. Wouldn't it be the most magnificent boast of all if we were able to field tens of thousands of our youth, our mid-level technicians, our newly retired, and our elderly, around the world, a mobile Pentagon of ploughshares? Our example would be the mightiest of deterrents, a powerful sight to behold. I am mindful of the tribal chief in Sierra Leone who said he'd heard of America before the Peace Corps volunteers came, but "Now we know what it means."

In a belt-tightening, more conservative, older America, the Peace Corps must rekindle its torch, lighting the way to a reordering of our priorities in the pursuit of peace. That is the challenge before us. We must continue to raise the flag of an interdependent world and let it wave over us. We have a covenant with the people of the world's developing countries to help them help themselves, so we all might live in peace together.

A Conservative Institution

by James A. McClure

It's been twelve years since my daughter, Marilyn, six months after graduating from William and Mary College, told my wife, Louise, and me that she was going to join the Peace Corps after she graduated.

Like many of her fellow volunteers, she was motivated in large part by a "What-can-I-do-to-make-the-world-better?" idealism.

Although Louise and I didn't relish the thought of our only daughter—born and raised in our small hometown of Payette, Idaho—living in a mud hut in the jungles of Africa, Asia, or South America, we supported Marilyn's decision wholeheartedly. The call to serve is admirable and necessary if hunger, disease, and squalor are to be wiped out.

As a strong believer in traditional American values, I was much in sympathy with the Peace Corps notion of having the individual give a hand to other individuals to create a better life. I was attached to the pioneer spirit, in which folks did things for themselves and helped others, without waiting for government to step in. People did not call that "conservative" when I was growing up; it wasn't even political. We just did it. And I was proud that my daughter, following in that tradition, wanted to do it, too.

Several months later, we saw her off as she began a 3,500-mile trek to the Ivory Coast.

In retrospect, what stands out most in my mind is the irony of it all. For years I had considered the Peace Corps a good idea gone awry. Much happened in those years to change my opinion of the Corps, but I still considered Marilyn's decision an interesting twist of fate.

The Corps' stated purpose, at its inception, was to help the uneducated, malnourished, and impoverished people of the Third World help themselves to a better life. Nonpartisan, philanthropic, relatively inex-

---

James A. McClure, a Republican, is a United States senator from Idaho.

pensive, and largely independent of government influence, it had the makings of greatness.

But during the 1960s—particularly the middle and latter part of the decade—there were many instances in which that lofty goal was cast aside. Altruism, unfortunately, was sometimes supplanted by politics.

In Latin America, for example, Peace Corps volunteers engaged in public demonstrations against the regimes of several nations. As a former volunteer put it, "The Peace Corps was selling America," and not imparting skills to the poor people it was supposed to be helping. Not surprisingly, some countries asked the Corps to leave.

Other problems beset the Corps as well. During the Vietnam War, the Corps was an easy escape for young men who didn't want to serve in the military. Others joined because—to use the vernacular of the day—they wanted to "find themselves." That's not what the Corps, its founders, or the people it was intended to aid needed. Some volunteers who protested U.S. involvement in Vietnam made their views known in anti-war demonstrations abroad.

The Corps, it appeared, was a noble experiment on the brink of failure—a victim of the political and social turmoil of the era.

Fortunately, the pending demise didn't come to pass. Public outrage and internal criticisms pinpointed the problems, and the program was put back on its intended course.

Ultimately, this catharsis transformed the Peace Corps into a thriving agency. To look at it now, at age twenty-five, is to look at a different organization from the one I cast a critical eye upon twenty years ago.

Programs have been streamlined to focus on problems unique to a particular country or village. There are no longer stories like the one about Peace Corps-built grain silos in Ghana being used as bedrooms because they weren't needed.

Foresters, engineers, agronomists, accountants, nurses, and nutritionists are sent to regions where there's a need for their services and where they'll do the most good.

The volunteer selection process is more stringent, with increased emphasis on skills and language, and greater participation among people over forty. Idealism is no less prevalent now than it was during the sixties, but it's more refined, aimed at community assistance instead of political reform, career development instead of career postponement.

The beauty of the Corps is seen in the void it fills between the military and economic aid the United States provides to other countries.

Military aid, while important, is difficult to keep in balance. Too much can exhaust a country's economic resources. Too little can mean the difference between freedom and oppression.

Economic aid often comes in the form of a gift, such as money to build a school. Unfortunately, there is no guarantee that those most in need will benefit. The haves get richer in some countries, while the have-nots continue to suffer.

The Peace Corps can often transcend these kinds of problems. It gives people on the bottom rung of society the kind of instruction and information they can use to improve themselves and their environment.

It's a people-to-people fight for improved economic and living conditions. Stable nations are based on a large, stable middle class—people who have a stake in society. They have something they want to protect and improve. The Peace Corps is a means to that end, helping the poor, sick, and uneducated to become active participants in their countries. What's more, it's not coercive in nature. The Peace Corps goes only where it is invited.

"By and large, volunteers are received warmly. People are anxious to get projects under way," Marilyn said recently. "They want schools and clinics, and the Corps is there to lead the way. That kind of acceptance fosters teamwork—and teamwork fosters success, which they hopefully will continue after the Corps is gone."

Some triumphs are big—eliminating tuberculosis in Bolivia or helping alleviate famine in Ethiopia. Most are small, like digging a well in Niger so villagers can drink fresh water, or planting cash crops for the first time in Botswana.

The impact of some efforts lasts forever. Others die the day a particular volunteer goes home. But it all contributes, in one way or another, to a more peaceful, neighborly world.

When Marilyn returned from the Ivory Coast, she said that if nothing else was gained, she and the villagers she lived with had had the chance to meet.

Being immersed in another culture, having the opportunity to partake of unfamiliar customs are rewards that can't be measured in dollars or any other form of commerce.

Marilyn said she was one of the few white women the villagers had ever seen. They wanted to braid her hair and touch her skin because the textures were so different from theirs. She learned much about herself, her country, and the world from her Corps experiences. Similarly, the Corps has learned much about itself in the last twenty-five years.

I liken the development of the Corps to the natural maturing process of a human being. There are the uncertain early days of living in an unfamiliar world. There are the preteen and teenage years of growth, sometimes rebellion, and, inescapably, mistakes. But we learn from it all. By the time we're in our late twenties, we have a clear focus of where we've been, where we're going, and how we're going to get there.

The Corps has matured nicely. Its future is bright. With emphasis on cost-conscious voluntarism and minimal government interference, it is one of the few programs embraced by politicians of every persuasion. It puts charity where it belongs—in the hands of individuals. The Corps knows where it's going and how it's going to get there.

Henry David Thoreau once wrote, "To affect the quality of the day is the highest of the arts." Twenty years ago, I wouldn't have drawn the parallel between those words and the Peace Corps. But his words do justice today to the Corps' mission and direction.

A Liberal Institution
by Hubert H. Humphrey III

"Peace is not passive, it is active. Peace is not appeasement, it is strength. Peace does not 'happen,' it requires work."

These words, spoken by my father, summarize the overarching premise of the Peace Corps. Whether by planting in the fields of a distant country or teaching in a classroom in Africa, Hubert Humphrey's dream was to work at peace by working with the citizens of our world. The Peace Corps idea was truly a "people helping people" program.

I can remember hearing about the idea from my father in the late fifties. He told me how he had talked to some missionaries who mentioned an idea roughly the same as the Peace Corps. Although their concept was smaller and contained within the church, my father understood the great benefit a national Peace Corps program would bring to our country's foreign relations. The United States could supply developing countries with the knowledge, ideas, techniques, and teachers to help maintain their people. From increased agricultural productivity to increased literacy, a Peace Corps would be the model to supply the resources. My father once said, "Critics ask what visible, lasting effects there are, as if care, concern, love, and help can be measured in concrete and steel or dollars or ergs. Education, whether in mathematics, language, health, nutrition, farm techniques, or peaceful coexistence, may not always be visible, but the effects endure."

It was no small endeavor to promote and pass into law this plan whose idea was enigmatic and whose benefits were so intangible to decision-makers, more accustomed as they were to facts and figures, dollars and cents.

My father's other objective was to provide our young people with options to their education and work plans. He hoped to appeal to the al-

---

Hubert H. Humphrey III, a Democrat, is attorney general of Minnesota.

truistic vision of thousands of young people. When my father started to examine this issue seriously, he found more and more that young adults did not want to travel the traditional "four years and out into the world of work with a college education" route. The Peace Corps would be an attractive alternative to those not ready to don a suit and tie.

There was no political ideology in the Peace Corps notion of allowing young people to learn through experience. It took just good common sense to see that Peace Corps volunteers would gain as much, or more, from their experience as the countries in which they served. I doubt if anyone would dispute that this has happened. We can all point to a situation where we've said, "I had to work hard, but I learned a lot, too." This attracted many volunteers to the Peace Corps. They knew they would be sent to foreign surroundings, and they knew up front they wouldn't be paid for their service. Yet many volunteered because of their commitment to their country and also, I believe, because they thought they were making a significant and valuable contribution to world peace.

My father had an especially keen interest in agriculture. He said, "A hungry man knows no reason. Democracy or totalitarianism, peace or violence—they make little difference to starving men with nothing to lose." What Dad most wanted was to feed people. He thought that if a person had a full stomach, he had little need to ponder revolution. With our surplus of food and our great knowledge of optimum production, our nation, he felt, could export our ideas and experience to developing countries of the world. Although much work needs to be done, our programs to communicate our own farm technology have been a success—almost to the point of our losing abundant agricultural markets because countries have become more self-sufficient in food production.

My father had a great deal of respect for and confidence in young people. I am sad that this respect wasn't always reciprocated. He surrounded himself with young people who either worked on his staff or advised him on policy considerations. Hubert Humphrey admired their youthful spirit. The Peace Corps was one program intended to enrich the experience of young Americans. Like his confidence in the judgment of young people, Dad believed no one person had a monopoly on the concept of peace. If thousands of young Americans could scatter to all ends of the earth, we might find a thousand unique experiments in peace. This is why he lobbied hard for flexibility in the Peace Corps. He did not want the countries to fit into the Peace Corps model; he wanted the Peace Corps to adapt to the countries and their cultures.

Many fine people collaborated with my father to promote and refine the concept of a Peace Corps. One person was U.S. Representative Henry Reuss, from Wisconsin. He put a great deal of time and effort into convincing his colleagues in the House to support the Peace Corps. As hard as it was for some to accept, Hubert Humphrey and Henry Reuss demonstrated that even folks from the Midwest know a thing or two about the peacemaking process. You can see the Midwestern flavor in the Peace Corps in many aspects, not the least of them being its strong emphasis on agriculture and public education.

Although the word "liberal" has become a dirty word used to label anyone advocating government intervention, the traditional and practical elements of liberalism espoused by my father are still as relevant today as they were during Franklin Roosevelt's Presidency. My father said that the true liberal "looks upon the state as an instrument of society and servant of its members. The responsible state is held strictly to account for serving the common end of its citizens by means which are freely chosen and which may be freely changed." In this sense, the Peace Corps, instrument of a society serving the common needs of all people, is a liberal institution.

The opportunity to obtain a useful education, work, live in a decent home, and have access to health care and adequate public protection is a basic need of all citizens. These are the implicit concerns in our ideology. In the clearest definition, we, as liberals, feel government can help solve certain ills of society. We don't view government as the problem.

I have always been committed to the idea of providing service to a community. In this, I am an attentive student of my father. In Minnesota, I have been a strong proponent of a Youth Service Corps, which contains many attributes of the Peace Corps. A Governor's Task Force is now examining the issue and will decide how to implement such a program. Many young people today have to wait too long before they can do anything that we adults feel has any importance to society. A Peace Corps and a domestic Youth Service Corps are two ways our young people can move beyond the often rigid line between childhood and adulthood.

It is hard to measure the progress and achievements of an operation like the Peace Corps. But one would have to conduct an extensive search to find an individual who believes it has been a failure. I believe its acceptance among both liberals and conservatives serves as the testimonial to its continued relevance in our global relations.

I can remember the difficulty Dad had in the infancy stage of the Peace Corps. When he first introduced the idea in 1957, it did not meet with much enthusiasm. Traditional diplomats quaked at the thought of thousands of young Americans scattered across their world. Many thought it a silly and unworkable idea. It really wasn't until after the 1960 presidential primaries that the Peace Corps received serious discussion. John

F. Kennedy had recognized the merits of this idea and began advocating a Peace Corps during his campaign. With Kennedy in the White house, the Peace Corps was almost surely going to be implemented in some form. Dad felt that if the idea could ever be implemented, the Peace Corps would take on a life and character of its own. What is unique about the Peace Corps twenty-five years later is that it is not an idea, a law, a legal structure, or a bureaucracy that has outlived its useful purpose. Instead, just as Dad envisioned it would be, the Peace Corps today is action-filled, and flexible enough to meet the most practical needs of the diverse people it serves, bringing to them the real tools of life and peace.

I think if my father had a chance to speak out on this anniversary of the Peace Corps, he would say it is the best example of what the peace process must really be. Peace is not a passive condition. It is not just an intellectual concept. Rather, it is an active and practical application of constructive works by people dealing with real problems affecting individuals at the most essential level.

As our nation and others consider how to bring peace to the world, I hope our leaders remember that beyond political, military, and economic considerations, the action of peacemaking must take place with the people, in the villages, on the farms, in the factories, and at home. The Peace Corps is one of only a few programs to endure the recent budgetary retrenchment. I suspect the reason for this lies within its mission. No one can debate the issue of providing American aid to the less fortunate—not in the form of massive economic expenditures, but, rather, in personal training and education. The Peace Corps credo is simple yet enigmatic; its greatest benefits are not concrete but are certainly visible.

The Future

by John R. Dellenback

At twenty-five, the Peace Corps stands on the brink of a bright future, born of a distinguished past, bred with constant care, deep relationships, and commitment to service. Will the next twenty-five years be the same as the last? Does the Peace Corps have an expanded role to play in the world? Should the Peace Corps be cutting back or surging ahead? Can the Peace Corps maintain its reliance on the human factor in a world grown increasingly dependent on technology?

Tens of thousands of Peace Corps volunteers have done much good in assisting the people of developing countries to learn technical skills and acquire capacities that help raise the physical standards of living. But even more important in the long run have been the hopes and visions that have come alive in individuals, the relationships created, the exciting symbols and catalysts that have influenced so many. It's been estimated that in any given month, Peace Corps volunteers have an impact on more than one million people.

Indeed, the Peace Corps can lay solid claim to fitting within the old dictum of letting actions speak louder than words, for the volunteers have done much of their work without benefit of fanfare, financial reward, or fancy support structures. They have changed the definition of development in the Third World from one that is *thing*-centered to one that is *people*-centered. The bold mission which, initially, many doubted could even last a year has forged friendships between haves and have-nots in the world that I believe have led and will continue to lead to fundamental changes. The Peace Corps created a ripple that has developed the power of a still-rising wave.

A wise man in Thailand saw this clearly. A Buddhist priest, he kept an

---

John R. Dellenback is chairman of the Peace Corps' 25th Anniversary Foundation, Inc., and president of the Christian College Coalition.

eye on a Peace Corps volunteer's work teaching English to the village children. When asked if he thought the children had learned much English, he replied that he was sure they had. But he added that the most important part of the process was how much he and the volunteer were learning about each other, their new understanding of each other's cultures, and the commitment they had to each other's work. All of that, he said, would far outlast the volunteer's tour.

The Peace Corps' influence does reach far beyond the confines of the villages or countries where we've worked. The deeds of our volunteers, their spirit and commitment, have established a worldwide reputation. The Peace Corps is recognized as a voluntary agency that is an effective, well-managed motor in the complex machinery of development. It has taken its legislative mandate literally to foster world peace and friendship.

The legacy of the Peace Corps volunteers continues to grow even after they return home. In their jobs, their communities, their places of worship, and their families, they remain an important part of our nation's capacity to behave responsibly in a world grown increasingly interdependent. Just as they *became* the United States for the villagers with whom they worked side by side, so they now *are* Ethiopia, Korea, or Ecuador for the legions of Americans with whom they interact and whom they influence on a daily basis.

My own association with the Peace Corps began during my years in Congress, when, as a member of the House Committee on Education and Labor, I helped write the legislation that created ACTION, our supervolunteer agency, of which the Peace Corps was to be one part. With all the volunteer opportunities we offer as a government, it seemed logical that ACTION would be an effective way to consolidate some of the housekeeping machinery in activities common to voluntary agencies, such as recruitment and training.

In 1975, when I became Peace Corps director, I changed my mind and concluded that we of the Congress had made a legislative mistake, which we of the Peace Corps were forced to live with. I saw that the Peace Corps was aimed at promoting international relationships and world peace, using volunteers as a brilliant instrument to achieve that purpose, while the domestic programs in ACTION were aimed at involving volunteers, using whatever worthwhile domestic programs could be identified. Because the kinds of volunteers needed for the two types of programs differed considerably, recruiting for both suffered. During my two years as director, I became absolutely convinced of the uniqueness of the Peace Corps mission and the impossibility of getting the best out of either the international or the domestic volunteer efforts by lumping them together. Not long after I left the Peace Corps in 1977, I worked with former colleagues in the Congress and many others to undo what we had originally seen as a fine idea. Out of that effort, the Peace Corps reemerged as an independent entity.

The result is that the Peace Corps has regained its flexibility and openness, an American hallmark that has enabled it to shift and change its worldwide programs in much the same way that Congress goes about mending flawed legislation. In the beginning, many feared that we were setting out to Americanize the world—that we felt we knew what needed to be done and were sending forth a corps of do-gooders to save the world from itself. To the contrary, one of the Peace Corps' underlying strengths has been the commitment to working with each country in response to its own perceived needs rather than dictating an American agenda. Thus, if it is teachers the Indian government wants, that is what we send them. If it is planning assistance in Togo, that is what we try to deliver there. The Peace Corps is in some sense a broker for voluntary assistance, and as such it must constantly be aware of changing needs in each country.

The Peace Corps must also keep its eye on change in the world. Cliché or not, the world is much smaller today than it was twenty-five years ago. Technology has reduced the time it takes to communicate or to travel. Most of the remote corners of the world are now within satellite reach, which reduces the sense of isolation felt by individual volunteers. Fifty new nations have emerged during the first generation of the Peace Corps, nearly all of them struggling to survive in increasingly complex circumstances. Positioned in the midst of older and more established countries, involved with them in international trade, bombarded by their television, and rubbing elbows with their tourists, citizens of these countries see the contrast between haves and have-nots more sharply than ever before. Misunderstandings abound on both sides. A sense of interdependence with the rest of the world abides in the countries of the Third World, but their frail and underdeveloped economic systems create barriers and estrangement.

Seeking ways in which we can play an effective helping role in this changed and changing world is a priority of many Americans. With our energy, determination, and creativity; our nation's great blessings; and our demonstrated concern for others, we have solid credentials as agents of change. As seekers of goodwill, we do, however, have to face the fact that in the minds of people in many sections of this world, we are lumped together with the U.S.S.R. in a vat of distrust. However extraordinary the aid given by the United States to a defeated Germany and Japan after World War II, and however considerable our worldwide assistance since then, it is too often correctly perceived that much of our recent foreign aid is military. It does not go unnoticed that, measured by gross national product, more than a dozen countries poorer than we are giving away a larger percentage abroad. It is also widely perceived that much of what America does in the way of assisting developing nations is not out of international goodwill as much as it is to serve our own interests. Against such a backdrop, the Peace Corps stands out sharp and clear as a very special and genuine effort to give and to serve.

So what of the Peace Corps in the next five, ten, twenty-five years? With institutions, as with individuals, there is no point in change for the sake of change. At the same time, unless we remain ready and willing to make indicated, forward-looking transformations, we run the risk of the buggy-whip manufacturer in an age of automobiles and airplanes. However efficiently run and ably staffed his operation may be, the buggy-whip maker should hang it up and quit. The great impact of the Peace Corps has been and will continue to be based on its combining committed volunteers with identified areas of need. Initially the physical needs of underdeveloped nations were the targets upon which the Peace Corps was brought to bear. But its real magic was not in the physical things accomplished, however welcome and helpful they were. The real magic was in the influence of the service itself—both upon the served and the servers.

The served saw volunteers who were willing to perform hard, often unpleasant tasks that needed to be done, tasks from which they did not gain personally. The servers grew as people in what they did and learned much, obtaining great inner rewards from giving help to others. Relationships flourished, attitudes changed, and walls of distrust were leveled. The servers returned home changed people, ready and equipped to make a difference in America.

The deft knitting of volunteers into areas and pockets of need all over the world that has characterized the Peace Corps must continue. In one sense, the Peace Corps is a single organization headquartered in Washington with arms reaching around the globe. But in another, deeper sense, the Peace Corps is some sixty organizations, situated in separate countries and involving some six thousand individuals with different sets of mind, heart, and hands. Naturally, there should always be similarities throughout these organizations and those individuals, but let's be sure that they will never be expected to be identical, or all performing the same service. If something works well in one country, build on it and strengthen it; but if the same thing doesn't work well in another, we must be prepared to try another tack. The Peace Corps experience has

THE PLACE

proved so successful at its root that I believe, whatever else is changed, that we must hold firmly to those aspects which constitute the Peace Corps' uniqueness. We must also stand ready to welcome any new challenges brought about by our experience or the march of time.

I include the following in this:

1. The Peace Corps must continue to be essentially an organization of volunteers, organized and coordinated by professional staff who are servant leaders rather than masters. In this structure, with the idealism and commitment it demands and produces, lies much of the essential genius of the Peace Corps. To remain a credible advocate for the grass roots of the developing world, we must remain fundamentally a grass-roots organization.

2. The Peace Corps must resist all the logical, understandable arguments to shift its emphasis to highly skilled and eventually highly paid technicians in the field. The latter alternative runs the risk that the skill itself—provided free—will be more in demand than the presence of volunteers with their special capacity to motivate and build relationships.

3. The Peace Corps must also resist arguments for making it into a desirable haven for those who would have its service be a lifetime career. The current mandate for most of the staff limits employment to five years. This mandate is meant to ensure a continuous supply of new ideas, fresh approaches, and the limitless energy that is the trademark of the Peace Corps. It should not be changed.

4. The Peace Corps must resist the subtle, steady encroachment of the concept of turning the volunteer's readjustment allowance into a fair and reasonable salary. The message of the willingness of thousands of Americans to give two years of their lives to assist in the world's development will lose tremendous weight if the job of the volunteer becomes just that—a job. "Adequate remuneration" will threaten to corrupt one of the Peace Corps' most basic tenets, our willingness to give of ourselves voluntarily, out of a spirit of idealism.

5. The Peace Corps must continue to look for ways to cooperate with other agencies, both governmental and voluntary, and continue to promote cooperative interrelationships. Over the last five years, the Agency for International Development and the Peace Corps have expanded their ties, and this bodes well for the future. The Peace Corps should expand its Partnership Program, which directs funds from private American sources to specific projects in the Third World. The Peace Corps has also worked side by side with its counterparts from other countries in the "developed" world, adding another dimension to the enrichment of worldwide relationships. This type of partnership can be expanded to produce team approaches, with valuable results for all.

6. Within the United States, the Peace Corps has left returned Peace Corps volunteers and former staff members largely on their own. Until recently, little effort has been made to know where returned volunteers live, or what they are doing, what their special needs may be, or how effectively they could be strengthened in their role as ambassadors. While they are largely individualistic, and though they abhor the idea of being "used," we should not waste this solid core of expertise and wisdom as an important form of ongoing assistance in our joint mission.

7. Over the full twenty-five years of its life, the Peace Corps has had the great benefit of including in its ranks many older volunteers. Some of the very finest volunteers have, in fact, been older men and women, often at retirement age and well beyond, who have combined maturity and experience with commitment and idealism, and have been extraordinarily effective. The years ahead are going to bring into our society an increasing number of older Americans, many of whom could well serve as Peace Corps volunteers. They collectively represent a great resource for the nation. The Peace Corps should make renewed efforts to recruit from this growing supply for use in fields where their expertise can prove particularly valuable.

Beyond these administrative concerns, the Peace Corps of the future should expand its vision to encompass more and more countries. It has established a record of serving as a bridge between the United States and sixty developing nations. We are already profiting from our investment as leaders emerge, from among both the served and server, committed to a world at peace. Now we should move on to serve in every developing nation in the world.

We have been in many countries and left. We must find out why—and show our willingness to return. The needs in those developing countries are endless, and we cannot possibly meet them all. But there is a great reservoir of willing talent here, and we must reach more deeply into it. We know the benefit to ourselves. We must make a persuasive case to potential new countries.

Political ideology and differences may block our entry into some, but if so, let it be a blockade the other country erects, not one of our own. China, for example, the home of one-fifth of the world's population, is a prime candidate for Peace Corps involvement, regardless of its Communist orientation. I am convinced that our efforts in this realm will serve both America and world peace.

A final goal for the Peace Corps should be to establish a presence in every developed country in the world as well. The objective of the Peace Corps is to promote relationships that encourage peace, and rich nations

THE PLACE

need such bonds as much as poor ones. Every so-called developed nation—France, Japan, Australia, and all the others—has its own set of deep and acute needs. Whether it is in the area of health care, or urban problems such as race relations and street crime, the United States has developed capacities that could prove useful to those now experiencing them. Or, we could provide English teachers in areas where there is a need to build fluency in what is nearly a universal language.

At the heart of this new thrust will be the typical Peace Corps volunteer, whose presence and work will help dispel any fears of spying or hidden agendas. With the addition to our program of opportunities for reciprocal activities, in some countries our new linkages may shift from the concept of donor-donee to one of partnership. This new thrust will not come with the explosiveness that marked the beginning of the Peace Corps. Rather, it may come slowly, country by country. It will demand vision, leadership, top-level support from Congress and the executive branch, and large amounts of patience. But the contribution to world peace will be infectious and highly significant.

The world's capacity to feed, clothe, and house its rapidly increasing population can still be expanded. The human potential is limitless, though our supply of raw materials is finite. Strains between rich and poor are sharpening. To a substantial degree, those strains coincide with national and racial divisions. Avoiding an eventual violent confrontation between large blocs of the world's haves and have-nots demands thorough international understanding and demonstrated reciprocal concern.

From my perspective, the Peace Corps comes as close as a government agency can to living out genuine concern for others. It conducts the United States' most effective foreign relations. It is our nation's best instrument for giving to some of our brightest and best the opportunity to put their lives on the line in meaningful service to others.

As Americans, we can be grateful to the more than 120,000 volunteers and staff who have served the cause of world peace and friendship through the Peace Corps during its first twenty-five years. I am personally persuaded, however, that Shakespeare was correct when he said, "The past is prologue." Indeed, the best is yet to come.

Afterword

Making a Difference was commissioned as part of the commemoration of the Peace Corps' twenty-fifth anniversary. Only after I was invited to become its editor was I reminded that I had actually started working on it twenty-five years earlier.

One day last year, while visiting with James Mayer, head of the office in charge of the commemoration, I ran into Judy Guskin, who had been a member of the first group of volunteers in Thailand. Our recognition of each other was almost instantaneous. Judy and her husband, Alan, had led a group from the University of Michigan to Washington in January 1961 to lobby for the establishment of the Peace Corps. Then a city reporter for *The Washington Post*, I was assigned to cover their activities. I have a warm recollection of following them around town, sharing with them the euphoria that, for many of our generation, accompanied those early days of the Kennedy administration. This early involvement did not qualify me as a member of the band of brothers that clustered around Sargent Shriver to found the Peace Corps—a band I have long envied and admired—but perhaps it gave me a claim, as a distant relative, to edit this book.

I recruited Judy Guskin on the spot to write an article on the sowing of the seeds of the Peace Corps at Michigan while she and Alan were students. I then proposed they do another on the meaning of their experience in Thailand. Without even asking Alan, she said they would. I did not know it yet, but that was the kind of response I would receive from almost everyone whom I asked to contribute. Some howled that they were too busy. Many insisted their memories were too dim. All screamed about the deadline. But nearly everyone came through—sometimes with two, three, or even four drafts. All, in a sense, wrote autobiographically, but more than a few did prodigious amounts of research. I could not believe how willingly—nay, enthusiastically—they gave of their time and their services to this book. As an editor, I could not have asked for, I could not even have imagined, a more wonderful body of writers. They made my work a pleasure.

There were a few obstacles, however, not the least of which was that over the years, a very substantial portion of the Peace Corps' records has vanished. Some day they may turn up in an obscure archive. Meanwhile, instead of having twenty-five years' worth of letters, diaries, evaluations, and other documents on which to draw, I had only a seemingly random collection that had somehow survived.

As it turns out, it probably made little difference that I did not have more. When, for example, I examined letters from the early 1960s, I found they possessed nearly the same tone and content as the letters I obtained from the 1980s. Much as young Americans are said to have changed in the last quarter-century, I discovered a consistency in the sense of excitement, the feeling of commitment, the elation of self-discovery, and the good-natured innocence that volunteers, and staff members no less, brought to their work. Even as I sat poring over documents at a desk in the National Archives, where many of the files are stored, the words conveyed to me the special electricity that has characterized the experience of the Peace Corps throughout its history.

In addition to those who wrote the essays for *Making a Difference*, I would like to acknowledge the invaluable help of Ailene Goodman, who did much of the initial research; James Mayer, who was patient and proficient as liaison to the Peace Corps headquarters, and his stalwart office associates Sharon Statham and Margaret Pollack; Audrey Wolf, who was indefatigable in organizing the project; Deedie Runkel and Tom Scanlon, who labored behind the scenes; Harris Wofford and Francis Luzzatto, who tendered not only essays but advice; Perdita Huston, who conducted the interviews with foreign officials; Kerry Pelzman and John Zimmerman, who shared their letters; and others too numerous to name, who searched files, offered suggestions, prepared papers, and translated documents. It was amazing to me to see what so many people were willing to do for the love of the Peace Corps.

Milton Viorst
February 1986

About the Editor

Milton Viorst has been a reporter at *The Washington Post* and *The New York Post,* and has written for *Esquire, The New York Times Magazine,* and other periodicals. His many books include *Hostile Allies: FDR and Charles de Gaulle; Fall from Grace: The Republican Party and the Puritan Ethic; Hustlers and Heroes: An American Political Panorama;* and *Fire in the Streets: America in the 1960s.* Mr. Viorst lives in Washington with his wife, Judith, who is also a writer, and their three sons.